Made in India

A Study of Emerging Competitiveness

Author's Profile

SUBIR ROY is currently Associate Editor (South) with *Business Standard*. He studied economics at Presidency College, Kolkata, and has spent the better part of three decades in journalism, with a stint in between at a bank. He is a foodie and a keen traveller, and was an eager photographer until modern automatic cameras made good photographers of almost everyone who could click a shutter. He lives in Bangalore with his wife Indrani and their two teenage children, son Satyaki and daughter Raikamal.

Made in India

A Study of Emerging Competitiveness

Subir Roy

Tata McGraw-Hill Publishing Company Limited
NEW DELHI

McGraw-Hill Offices
New Delhi New York St Louis San Francisco Auckland Bogotá Caracas
Kuala Lumpur Lisbon London Madrid Mexico City Milan Montreal
San Juan Santiago Singapore Sydney Tokyo Toronto

338.954
ROY

 Tata McGraw-Hill

© 2005, Tata McGraw-Hill Publishing Company Limited

Second reprint 2006
RAXCRRLKRZCBL

This edition can be exported from India only by the publishers,
Tata McGraw-Hill Publishing Company Limited

ISBN 0-07-048366-3

Published by Tata McGraw-Hill Publishing Company Limited,
7 West Patel Nagar, New Delhi 110 008, typeset in Garamond at
Le Studio Graphique, 12-C, Sector 14, Gurgaon, 122 001 and printed at
Adarsh Printers, C-51, Naveen Shahadra, Delhi

Cover: Kapil Gupta
Cover printer: Mudrak

To my mother,
Indrani, Satyaki, and Raikamal

Preface

This study has been fairly long (too long in fact) in the making. In 1999, the feeling grew that small parts of the Indian economy were becoming globally competitive and a study of this emerging competitiveness would be able to capture, in a unified logical manner, key aspects of the economy that mattered in going forward. Work eventually began in April 2001 when I went on a year's partial sabbatical. It was soon over but the project was not. The rest of the work had to be done while hanging onto a regular journalistic job to keep body and soul together for both self and family. A lot of what has emerged from this research is today commonplace knowledge, almost axiomatic. As I look back, I cannot help but wonder at how strong an intuitive insight I started out with.

Another downside of the time it took to complete this project is that many of the people referred to have moved on in life. This is typical of fast moving sectors which are at the cutting edge of technology or business practice. Reassuringly, what they had to say remains relevant despite the pace of change. Lastly, sections of Indian business which have become globally competitive in the last three years do not figure in the study. Were I to start afresh today, I would surely have included Bharat Forge and taken a more comprehensive look at the auto components industry. Maybe a second edition will address these shortcomings.

A total windfall gain from this project has been the chance to discover Bangalore where I have been relocated since 2002. It was in researching the most promising area of Indian competitiveness, software, that I came to Bangalore repeatedly. It is the charm of its forward looking professionals, as also the innate civility of the average Kannadiga, that made me stay.

This project would not have been possible without the help and cooperation of a large number of people. I would like to put on record my sense of gratitude towards a few key persons among them. The project was made possible because of a grant from Tata Steel and ICRA. For this I am grateful to Dr J J Irani and Mr D N Ghosh. Equally, without the sabbatical and a generous financial arrangement, the project would not have taken off. For this I am grateful to my editor at *Business Standard*, Mr T N Ninan. A lot of people have been very generous with their time and a source of personal inspiration. Among them I want to particularly mention Mr Srini Rajam, CEO of Ittiam, the software product startup. Lastly, and perhaps most importantly, such a project would not have been possible without the bulwark of a supportive family. To all these and to many more who must remain unnamed (the list would be too long and boring to those who don't know them), I say, thank you.

SUBIR ROY

Contents

Introduction and Overview

As trade barriers have gone down through the nineties, the idea of competitiveness has gained increasing importance. While firms and industries have sought to benchmark themselves against global best practices, nations have sought to adopt policies that can make them good hosts for competitive firms and industries. Also, through the nineties, annual competitiveness studies and league tables of the relative competitiveness of nations have been refined and made more and more elaborate. These have addressed two needs. With the freeing of capital movements, firms have looked for a guide to the best places from which to do business. Similarly, nations have looked for a guide to know where they stand vis-à-vis other nations in attracting global business. In India, reflecting this growing concern for competitiveness, the Confederation of Indian Industry made promoting competitiveness its prime focus for 2002–03.

India figures very poorly in the league tables of national competitiveness put out by agencies like the World Economic Forum. But lately the Indian economy has begun to sprout some competitive shoots. An emerging competitiveness has been perceived successively in the following sectors—software, pharmaceuticals, information technology enabled services, automobile components, and research and development. Our study, which was conceived in the late nineties and undertaken mostly during 2001–2002 validates this. It establishes that the aggregate competitiveness scores hide critical details and micro realities. These are vitally important in grasping the idea of competitiveness and devising a roadmap for becoming competitive. The inadequacies of Indian economic policies which were followed till the late eighties are well known. The policies adopted since the early nineties have sought to address those inadequacies. This study has avoided the well trodden path of diagnosing and analysing the malaise and instead focussed on Indian best practices to identify role models and determine what needs to be done to become competitive across various sectors.

In undertaking this study, we have had to overcome a methodological hurdle. A competitive firm will conform to global benchmarks in terms of cost, productivity and quality and earn a significant share of its revenue globally. But what if a firm in a particular industry has been unable to go global because of market barriers? In such cases, we have determined that conforming to global benchmarks alone will be taken to indicate competitiveness. We have also chosen the anecdotal or oral history route and not the quantitative route of enquiry. This study mainly seeks to capture how the main players see and remember competitiveness emerging, be it in their firms or industries.

Some important qualifications need to be made upfront. This is not a historical narrative but a historical analysis. It seeks to identify the issues and reasons why certain trends emerged and developments took place in Indian competitiveness. Hence the coverage of sectors is not very comprehensive. No attempt has been made to examine firms according to their size in their relevant sectors. A large player in a competitive industry may not have been mentioned, but hopefully no important or significant trend has been left out. Players who have been important witnesses to the unfolding of the competitiveness saga, have recalled and analysed how it all happened.

Going by the composite criteria outlined above, among sectors we have identified software, IT enabled services, pharmaceuticals, biotechnology, and dairying and milk processing as competitive and made them the subject of our study (dairying and milk processing are treated as one sector). Among individual firms which are globally competitive but whose sectors are not, we have identified and chosen for our study—Tata Steel, Reliance Industries, Larsen and Toubro, Bharat Heavy Electricals, Sundram Fasteners, Sundaram Brake Linings, TVS Motor, and General Electric.

In studying the competitiveness of sectors, to begin with, we have examined what were the initial attributes and historical circumstances that gave them a competitive advantage. Thereafter, how have they had to change the basis of their competitiveness as they have grown and matured? A sector or a company, usually, initially establishes a competitive bridgehead to the rest of the world as a new low cost producer. But it cannot continue to remain competitive purely on cost as sooner or later, newer, lower cost competitors emerge. So it has to go up the value chain, build brands, get out of the commodity end of the market by developing differentiated products and start earning a premium. Lastly, we have tried to end every study with a glimpse into the future by asking, what are the prospects of the sector or company and how is it likely to fare in the competitiveness stakes in the medium term?

A classical example of this process is the competitiveness story of Japanese companies after the second world war. They first arrived with their low cost imitation products which were often considered shoddy. If a consumer was looking for value, he would usually pay a premium to buy a German, or an American product. But, by the nineties, Japanese carmakers like Toyota and Honda were posing a serious competitive challenge to Mercedes and BMW at the quality end of the global car market. There are remarkable parallels between the Japanese manufacturing firms' pursuit of quality through the fifties and sixties and Indian software firms' pursuit of quality through the nineties and later.

After the second world war, the Japanese invited W. Edwards Deming, a professor at the University of Colorado, to act as a quality expert and in 1950, the Union of Japanese Scientists and Engineers instituted the Deming award. Its recipients have come to represent the highest standards of quality in manufacturing—a field in which Japanese companies have come to be acknowledged as world leaders. The zest with which Indian software firms have pursued various quality certifications and the large numbers of them that have secured the SEI CMM (the capability maturity model of the software engineering institute of the Carnegie Mellon University) Level 5 certificate, the highest available, underline the maturing and changing basis of competitiveness of Indian software. Just as Japanese manufacturing firms beat their initial negative image about quality and became global leaders in quality, Indian software firms are on their way to beating the negative quality image of Indian business to become global quality leaders in software. The same concern for quality marks the approach of the leading Indian pharmaceutical firms.

SOFTWARE

Indian software exports began to perceptibly grow in the late eighties—led by Tata Consultancy Services, Wipro and Infosys Technologies—on the basis of several initial advantages and a compulsion. The advantages were many—a knowledge of English, mathematical aptitude, a pool of scientific skills and low cost. The compulsion was to send engineers abroad for onsite work as the telecommunication facilities and low level of domestic computerisation did not permit offshore work. From the early nineties, when the software technology parks were set up, software exports grew much faster by following the offshore route. The peak came with the dotcom and the Y2K boom. The latter took Indian companies right inside major firms in the developed economies, giving the software companies a key customer intimacy, which would be built upon later. Then came the bursting of the dotcom bubble and a slowdown in global IT spending in 2001. The slowdown affected the entire global economy and a recession was actively feared in the wake of 9/11, affecting the IT sector even further.

In 2002, the growth rate of the Indian software sector decelerated but, simultaneously and in response to this challenge, it underwent a major change. There was a shakeout and reorganisation in which the generic part of the business went down but the leading players and those with specialisations sought to raise productivities, go up the value chain, acquire domain knowledge, offer business solutions, develop products and build brands. Along with this, Indian software companies with the right type of skills began to establish a presence in electronic and high end chip designing services. The result was that the sector continued to evolve, mature and remain competitive. As 2003 progressed, offshoring became mainstream and India emerged as its prime global destination.

IT ENABLED SERVICES

As software growth slowed down through 2001–02, a new fast growing sector emerged—IT enabled services. It showed the same 50 per cent plus growth that software had done earlier. IT enabled services first began as simple data processing operations, including medical transcription, and quickly expanded into call centre work. The role played by Texas Instruments in discovering India as a competitive location for software development was performed in the case of IT enabled services by American Express in the mid-nineties. It located a regional back office in India because it found that here the work could not only be done by more skilled persons than elsewhere but at a substantially lower cost. Moreover, the work, done at a lower cost, was soon being done better than elsewhere. American Express was quickly followed by British Airways and a major breakthrough took place with General Electric coming in to set up large call centres.

Into the new decade, the outsourcing stretched to the entire range of operations conducted in a business and the term 'Business Process Outsourcing' (BPO) began to gain currency. Indian firms like Daksh, Spectramind, Customer.Asset and 24/7Customer sprung up and grew very rapidly. Several specialised smaller firms led the journey up the value chain—from data entry and call handling, to rule based processing, discretionary processing, tele-marketing of complex products like insurance policies and technical support. The basis of competitiveness in this has been the same as in software—skilled people in sufficient numbers, low cost and quality assurance. As software services mature and their growth slows down, IT enabled services are expected to carry the can and deliver very high growth in the overall software and services sector.

PHARMACEUTICALS

The next sector studied is pharmaceuticals. Its journey down the road to global competitiveness began with the export of bulk drugs in the eighties. Contrary to software where a lot of the dynamism and success is attributed to the absence of government regulation and critical government help at the right time in the right area (setting up of software technology parks in 1991), the Indian attempt to acquire capabilities in pharma was kicked off with the government decision in 1970 to initiate the Indian Patent Act which recognised process patents and not product patents. The government took up two other policy measures, issuing the drug price control order and pressuring drug MNCs to take up local manufacturing. While the beneficial effect of the latter in terms of spreading the manufacturing ethos and quality standards is undisputed, that of the former (price control) is debated. One view is that price controls kept Indian costs in restraint and enabled the Indian industry to develop its low cost capabilities. The other view is that price controls were largely a nuisance and India emerged a low cost producer as a result of the competitive atmosphere created by the loose patent laws. The absence of product patents unleashed a ferment of activity in the area of process chemistry. Indian expertise in this area was soon established and pharma companies graduated from bulk drugs to formulations. Indian companies exported their bulk drugs and then formulations to first unregulated markets and then regulated markets once patents expired.

Today, India is a major player in the generic (off patent) sphere in regulated markets, most notably in the United States where a sizeable part of the pending applications for launch of generics on the expiry of patents is from Indian companies. Over the years, a dozen plants, belonging to the top outward looking Indian companies, have secured US regulatory (Food and Drug Administration) approval to achieve global standards and access the most lucrative pharma market in the world.

In the early nineties, another big change took place in the Indian pharmaceutical industry. The launch of the new economic policies soon made it clear that the Indian government would fall in line with global patent protection norms and protect product patents. Top Indian drug companies like Dr Reddy's Laboratories and Ranbaxy Laboratories took the decision to get into new drug discovery. A lead was taken in this respect by Anji Reddy, founder of Dr Reddy's Laboratories, who surprised everybody in 1993 by declaring that not only did Indian companies have the ability to discover new molecules, they in fact had a competitive advantage in doing so. His logic was based on the availability of adequate scientific manpower of acceptable quality at very competitive costs which could enable Indian firms to achieve very high productivity in research.

Dr Reddy's, Ranbaxy and a few other firms have made discovery of new molecules, non-infringing process and novel delivery systems a part of their business model.

CONTRACT RESEARCH AND BIOTECHNOLOGY

To top it all, specialised contract research organisations have started to custom synthesise molecules and undertake work in various parts of the drug development chain, giving the Indian pharma industry a capability in virtually every part of the research, development and manufacturing process. Indian pharma companies started out with the basic skills and a very low cost capability. Over time, the cost advantage has slowly reduced even as companies have concentrated on acquiring intellectual property and earning higher margins. The best Indian companies are now looking at the global market as the main engine of growth (drug prices are higher almost anywhere in the world than in India) and Ranbaxy has taken the lead in globalising its business. In the financial year 2001–02, its global (non-Indian) revenue exceeded its Indian revenue.

The expertise in pharmaceuticals and the adequate supply of scientific skills has aroused keen interest in India in biotechnology, the area that has received a tremendous boost after the decoding of the human genome. Here, also, the government has played an important part by setting up an elaborate network of public laboratories which have conducted steady research in the last fifteen years. The Indian biotechnology scene is currently marked by high tech startups, which are using the fruits of the basic research and thus seeking to establish pilot plant capability and waiting to see the larger established pharma companies take up the baton from there onwards.

Among the leaders in the field is Wockhardt which has now spent a decade in establishing a capability and is ready with a range of generic products that will step in once the first biotechnology patents expire. Biocon has acquired intellectual property and taken a lead in the area of fermentation and Shantha Biotechnics, another player which is seriously interested in research, has been the first to release its hepatitis-B vaccine in India. The intellectual challenge in biotechnology is far greater than it was in conventional chemistry. Hence, it is yet unclear, as to what success the fledgling Indian industry will be able to achieve. But the chances, of at least a couple of companies, which are successfully developing a handful of products for the global market in the medium term, are realistic. This puts the Indian industry right behind those of other emerging economies like South Korea and China which perceive a role for themselves in biotechnology.

DAIRYING AND DAIRY PRODUCTS

The last of the sectors that we will study is dairying and dairy products. India, from being deficit in milk in the fifties, is now the global leader in milk production. What is more, this has been achieved while keeping costs very low, just above the cost structure of New Zealand and Australia which are the global least cost producers through the factor advantage of having adequate rain and pastures. The success in dairying has been followed by low cost production of milk products like butter, milk powder and more recently ice cream and cheese. As with software and pharmaceuticals, milk and milk products have been able to maintain acceptable quality standards. Quite uniquely, the massive rise in low cost milk output has been achieved by a range of producers' cooperatives. The process began in Gujarat and now most Indian states have a vibrant structure of milk cooperatives, beginning with the village cooperatives at the grassroots level where milk is collected and going upto the state level cooperative milk marketing federations which run the large milk processing and milk products' plants.

A uniformity in business structure, quality and costs has been achieved by extensively replicating the first successful model that was developed by Verghese Kurien in Anand in Gujarat, so that all these orgainsations across the country with millions of farmer members are known by the common rubric 'Anand type' cooperatives. The cost competitiveness has been achieved by evolving a unique Indian model which has produced an ever increasing supply of cheap milk. The farmer with one to at the most five animals is able to produce cheap milk by feeding his cattle with waste byproducts of the agricultural process like straw. Unlike the scientific skills that have made the software services and pharmaceutical industries competitive, the competitiveness in dairying has been achieved through the execution of a grand countrywide marketing plan. As farmers have been able to supplement their income through dairying, they have had the incentive to produce more. On the base of the village cooperatives, have been built the district and state cooperative federations which have been provided with machinery, vaccines for animals and finally an aggressive marketing strategy by the promoter institution, the National Dairy Development Board, started and built by the same Verghese Kurien.

TATA STEEL

The first competitive Indian firm in a non-competitive sector studied is Tata Iron and Steel Company. It has emerged as one of the global least cost producers of first iron and then steel. Till the year 1991, Tata Steel was considered a blue chip among Indian steel companies but paid little heed to global competitiveness as it operated under cost and distribution controls and was insulated from foreign competition. But when price decontrol came in the year 1992 along with the clear warning that the domestic market would be opened up, the company embarked on a long process of change that in a decade totally transformed it, reducing its employee strength by nearly half and trebling its worker productivity. It first set up a management information system and cost centers. Then it determined how it stood vis-à-vis global benchmarks in terms of cost and productivity and thereafter embarked upon a programme to come upto global standards. It began with the factor advantage of having captive coal and iron ore mines but built on it by improving the efficiency of its mining operations. It undertook a rigorous programme of energy saving as steel making is a very energy intensive process. It also innovated substantially with its metallurgical processes so as to reduce costs by waste recovery. It made information technology a key driver in its business processes and also in customer relationship management. Most recently, it has taken steps up the value chain by adding a global class cold rolling mill to produce steel which can be used in consumer electronics and automotives.

Tata Steel has emerged globally competitive in costs but is able to earn a brand premium only on domestic sales and not on global sales. The basis of its competitiveness is low energy costs, low manpower costs and adequate managerial capabilities. By global standards, with a capacity of 4 million tonnes it is at best a medium sized producer. But it produces only mild steel and not special steels which are the basis of competitiveness of small niche players. As it is slowly able to supply high value items like steel for car body panels to the several global automobile firms which have started manufacturing in India in the last decade, it will be difficult for any global player to beat it on home turf. As future growth in global steel demand will be mainly concentrated in India and China, Tata Steel will be able to grow and progress in the medium term by concentrating on the domestic market and remaining a marginal exporter.

BHARAT HEAVY ELECTRICALS

Our next study of a competitive Indian company is Bharat Heavy Electricals Ltd, the major Indian manufacturer of power plant equipment which is one of the half a dozen global players in the field. BHEL, the acronym by which it is popularly known, lays its claim to competitiveness by being able to win over seventy per cent of the orders for power plant equipment placed in India through competitive bidding, mandatory for projects under multilateral funding. It is the only public sector organisation in our list of competitive companies and has held its own, despite a sea change in its market conditions. In the year 2002, it was voted one of the ten best companies in India to work for, despite its inability to match private sector salaries.

The company was set up in the high noon of economic planning, in order to deliver the goals of self-sufficiency in power generation and growth through capability in heavy machine building. Over the years, it has secured its technology through collaboration agreements with global leaders in power equipment like Siemens in steam turbines and GE in gas turbines. BHEL has remained competitive mainly because of cheap Indian skilled labour, an important cost element in work involving metal fabrication. Also, like Tata Steel and other robust Indian companies that have taken up the challenge of attaining global competitiveness as the economy has gradually opened up, it has through the nineties improved its productive efficiencies and sharply reduced its staff strength. It has also reduced the time it takes to build major equipment, thus further reducing costs.

As a major part of global demand for power plant equipment in the next few decades will be concentrated in India and China, BHEL appears capable of holding its own in getting a large chunk of such orders. But its main problem in future is likely to be sourcing of technology. Some of the major global players from whom BHEL has so far accessed technology appear unlikely to continue the arrangement as it is increasingly being perceived as a competitor. As the company has so far been content to absorb technology and adapt it to local needs without seeking to develop its own technology, a question mark hangs over the company's future beyond the medium term, when current technology agreements run out.

To counter this, it has entered into a technology transfer agreement with Max Industries of the US for control and instrumentation. It has adopted a new goal of developing its own technology in this area by the time the present agreement runs out in the year 2007. It has also entered into another collaboration for the manufacture of supercritical boilers. The company, in order to benchmark itself against the most competitive global companies, has planned to increase its exports to 20 per cent of turnover by the year 2005, building on the orders it has secured over the years in the Middle East and the Asean region. It is also developing its capabilities in the area of non-conventional energy, like solar and wind energy, which it expects will become critical in the medium to long term. Thus BHEL can be termed as a company that has the potential to become a global player and is focused towards achieving that goal.

LARSEN & TOUBRO

BHEL has mainly established its competitiveness in the domestic market under the emerging open trading conditions. In our next study of firms, we look at Larsen and Toubro which has adopted globalisation as a business model to overcome some of the non-competitive aspects of the Indian environment. It began with manufacturing machines and simultaneously built a construction business. From building machines it graduated to manufacturing entire plants and setting them up in India and overseas. In recent years, it has got better in doing this, by using information technology. It is seeking to carve out a globally competitive niche for itself, based on its traditional engineering skills, its practice of keeping abreast of technology and most recently by using e-engineering as a means of upgrading itself and also offering the same service to others as a new revenue-earning stream. To its traditional cost advantage in the field of fabrication, has been added the new cost advantage of being able to source very competitive IT skills. It is also one of the few engineering companies in the country with a stand alone software business which is highly profitable.

Its absolute core competency and the area in which it is globally competitive is manufacture and erection of high end heavy engineering equipment like high pressure reactors. It is also very competitive in handling entire projects on a turnkey basis—the engineering, procurement and construction work that goes into the setting up of a plant. But what is holding it back is the cost of capital in India and the absence of an adequate home market demand for setting up of new plant and machinery in the last couple of years. It has decided to divest its cement business which was a drag on its profits. To overcome some of its other handicaps, it has set its sights on becoming an increasingly global company as in many areas it finds overseas costs cheaper than Indian costs. Thus it represents two realities. It is one more company which is seeking to achieve global competitiveness and underlining the status of India as an emerging economy with limited but clear areas of competitiveness. It also highlights some of the non-competitive aspects of the Indian business environment.

RELIANCE INDUSTRIES

Reliance Industries is one of the youngest companies we have studied, beaten only by some of the software companies. A first generation company until the death of its founder Dhirubhai Ambani in the year 2002, it displays all the innovativeness and aggression of a startup. It is a remarkably integrated company with operations stretching from oil exploration to refining, petrochemicals, synthetic fibres and fabrics. But its key claim to being competitive, rests on its global sized plants and globally benchmarked conversion costs. Its most remarkable feat, in the latter nineties, was to set up one of the biggest greenfield refineries in the world, at a 20 per cent lower capital cost than the benchmark established till then. This has given its refining operations one of the lowest conversion costs in the world. From its beginnings in the brick and mortar industries, Reliance has adopted at the turn of the century a remarkable programme of diversification. It is seeking to set up an extensive broadband network in the country and it has also become overnight, a countrywide mobile telephone service provider. In telecom services also, it is seeking to set new benchmarks in software costs and affordable pricing which will vastly expand connectivity in the country. Its other areas of diversification are power generation and distribution and life sciences.

MEDIUM-SIZED COMPANIES

After examining a set of competitive large companies we look at a set of three medium-sized companies which are remarkable in being run independently but by members of the same family. Sundram Fasteners, Sundaram Brake Linings and TVS Motor form a unique cluster. They are all in automotives, all based in the state of Tamil Nadu, and all share the same ethos. First in this group is Sundram Fasteners which has achieved global distinction as a highly successful OEM supplier to General Motor. It has earned the distinction year after year, of being the number one zero defect supplier of GM in its area. This has led GM to entirely outsource its supply of the particular item, radiator caps. The second company is Sundaram Brake Linings which is a global cost and quality leader in its field.

The third is TVS Motor which has won a hard fought battle in establishing both its independence and its technological capabilities. Even as it ended its technological collaboration with Suzuki Motors, it stunned the Indian motorcycles market in 2001 by launching a winner entirely conceived and designed by itself. All the three companies share certain common family values—care for the worker, concern for the customer and an almost religious devotion to quality. Two of them, Sundaram Brake Linings and TVS Motor, have won the Deming prize and all three have gone through Japanese quality programmes. All three companies are outward looking. Sundram Fasteners and Sundaram Brake Linings export a significant part of their output and TVS Motor is firming up plans to establish manufacturing facilities for its motorcycles in the Asean region.

GENERAL ELECTRIC

The only multinational in our study is General Electric. It has been included to answer in the affirmative the question that if there are certain competitive advantages to be gained by operating out of India, multinationals should be basing such operations in the country. GE's operations in India cover diverse areas—medical electronics, motors, business process outsourcing and research and development. GE has made rapid progress in developing its Indian operations in these areas after the liberalisation policies were initiated in the year 1991. In medical electronics, first manufacturing facility was shifted to India, then vendor development took place rapidly and finally designing of new equipment took off very successfully. Today, some of the most sophisticated medical equipment like scanners and x-ray tubes, as also their components, are being designed and manufactured in India and then exported.

The fraction horsepower motor (used in refrigerators) is manufactured by GE in a taken over factory where processes have been redesigned by arriving at a careful balance between man and machine so as to achieve very low costs. Quality is achieved in the semi-automated processes through the use of Six Sigma discipline. The BPO operations began in the year 1997 and grew speedily because of success in not just performing the operations more cheaply and efficiently than elsewhere, but eventually changing the systems so as to achieve greater productivities. The processes handled in India have quickly become more and more complex, gaining in value. The most remarkable GE operation in India is the John F Welch Research Centre in Bangalore, the second most important R&D facility of the company in the world. It conducts research in fields stretching right across the range of businesses of GE like aero engines, advanced materials and electronic designing. GE, whose main aim was to sell its products in India, now sees greater promise in outsourcing to India.

JHUNJHUNWALA & CO

In the last of our case studies, we look at a fascinating technology cum business initiative which seeks to use Indian technological prowess to address its economic underdevelopment. In the early nineties Ashok Jhunjhunwala, professor of electrical engineering at the Indian Institute of Technology, Madras, and several fellow academics formed an informal group called TeNet. It set out to use Indian scientific and designing skills to rapidly bring connectivity and internet access to large numbers of Indians.

They realised that technology and costs for providing last mile access were not going forward as universal connectivity had already been achieved in the developed economies. Their telecommunication companies were concentrating on increasing bandwidth and providing value added services at lower costs. The TeNet professors joined up with engineers and floated several startups that were by early 2002, offering a highly affordable complete package for connectivity and access through the use of wireless in local loop technology. They went one step further, used successful models of grassroots Indian entrepreneurship like the telephone booths and cable TV operators to provide models for business delivery also.

By early 2003, the viability and commercial attractiveness of TeNet technologies was evident from both domestic and overseas orders received. Major Indian telecom service providers have placed substantial orders for the CorDECT technology, designed by a TeNet startup Midas Communications. Orders are also coming in from elsewhere in Asia, Africa and Latin America. The Indian rollout has been further accompanied by multilingual content creation and e-governance initiatives.

THE HYPOTHESIS

From these sector and firms studied, five major common points emerge. Firstly, simply from the small number of sectors and firms considered as globally competitive, it is clear that most of the Indian economy and the firms in it are not globally competitive. Only a few are. What is more, this small group is only at the end of the first stage of the journey to becoming globally competitive. Some of them have only just ceased to be low cost producers of generic products and are seeking to go up the value chain by attempting product differentiation to earn a premium. But considering the competitive conditions within the Indian market and the corporate capabilities residing within these dynamic sectors and companies, there is every likelihood that they will improve and not slide back in the competitiveness stakes. They all have an active globalising mindset and a firm agenda for it.

Secondly, India seems to have a competitive advantage in anything knowledge based. Indian companies are able to access higher skills very cost effectively. A person with a PhD degree in India costs one tenth of what she does in the US and her productivity is far above that ratio. This has been aided by a partial reversal of the brain drain made possible by increasing opportunities for higher end work in India. The liberalisation initiated by the new economic policies from the year 1991 sharply hiked the stakes of Indian companies in acquiring and retaining competitive advantages. This has put a premium on cost-cutting and technological upgrading. Corporate support for research has increased and there have been a range of high-tech startups in software, biotechnology and contract research. So the knowledge advantage is being leveraged.

Thirdly, fortunately for India, its emerging capability in software and virtually anything knowledge based has coincided with a historical evolutionary process. Since the industrial revolution competitive leadership among nations has been largely determined by manufacturing prowess. The baton for the manufacturing relay race has been successively picked up by Britain, Germany, United States, Japan and China. Today as the power of competitive advantage in manufacturing is overtaken by the competitive advantage in knowledge based activities (the designers and conceptualisers create far higher value than the manufacturers), India finds itself abundantly endowed with cheap knowledge skills. The need to design virtually all manufactured items on computers, the growing use of embedded software in items from the simplest manufactures to the most complex, and the increasing importance of system on chips in devices like the mobile phone have coincided with India's growing expertise in software.

Fourthly, a low cost ethos has marked the Indian competitive effort. Software services and IT enabled services have begun their global journey riding on the back of the low cost advantage gained from the availability of cheap skills. The low purchasing power of the Indian consumer and the vastness of the Indian market have forced Indian business to evolve a low cost high volume model in diverse sectors such as pharmaceuticals, milk, dairy products and fabrications. Individual firms in steel, chemicals and automotives attempting to become competitive by globally benchmarking themselves have also achieved a low cost capability. Thus, there is now a strong low cost ethos in the best of Indian businesses. There is a parallel in this with the way the global competitiveness of Japanese companies emerged from the intense domestic price competition, termed in management literature as "price destruction".

Fifthly, a strong quality consciousness has driven all the progressive sectors and firms of the Indian economy that have sought to become globally competitive. Thus, the emerging structure of Indian competitiveness that we have before us is made up of the following elements—a knowledge base, low cost and high quality.

How can this hypothesis be tested? If India is emerging with certain competitive advantages, then parts of global business should be seeking to relocate to India. This has begun in a small way. There is hardly an important IT company in the world which has not set up a software development center in India. Since the year 2000, outsourcing of business processes has galloped ahead. Increasingly, IT products are being extensively developed in India and marketed worldwide by the associates of the Indian operations. Further, electronics products like chips, system on chips and embedded software are being increasingly designed in India. In fact, prowess in software services is aiding almost any kind of designing activity in India. It is also acquiring a growing business in drug research and development and clinical research through a crop of contract research organisations. After software and business processes, there has been a growing trend since 2003 of outsourcing automotive component manufacturing and R&D work to India.

Does any of this show up in quantitative studies of Indian competitiveness? Mostly not. India continues to figure very low in the annual global competitiveness rankings put out by the World Economic Forum and others.

Suresh D Tendulkar's (2000) study of India's share of the growth in global exports shows an Indian presence in only a few areas. It is significant mainly in labour intensive areas like textiles, cotton fabrics, clothing and floor covering; a few scale intensive areas like synthetic dyes, pearls, semi-precious stones, gold and silverware jewellery; and only one scientific based area, medicinal products. The last is the only overlap with our study. Vivek Srivastava's* study of the impact of reforms on industrial productivity, efficiency and competitiveness says that the "key, and seemingly most disturbing, finding of this study is that productivity and efficiency of Indian industry in the nineties is worse than during the eighties." Clearly, an enormous policy challenge lies ahead in turning the narrow sectoral advantages and the few success stories that we have identified, into at least a modest level of competitiveness for the overall economy.

ROLE OF POLICY

To understand the inadequacy of the policy regime, we have studied why in tremendous contrast to the success in software, Indian IT hardware failed to take off despite an early start from the eighties. We then, look at the policy options emerging from the sectors and companies that we have studied. These do not add up to a comprehensive policy prescription but what they do point to, is the importance of policy in creating a framework for the pursuit of competitiveness.

A comprehensive view of the regulatory changes needed are available in two recent studies, by the consultancy McKinsey (2001) and CII–World Bank (2002). The conclusion of these two diagnoses differ somewhat. The former lays emphasis on product market restrictions and rules and policies covering different sectors which restrict GDP and productivity growth. It downplays the importance of inflexible labour laws and poor transport infrastructure. The latter study, on the other hand, highlights the cost disadvantages that Indian business suffer from power costs, interest rates (described as 'major' and 'crippling'), delay in customs houses, infrastructure bottlenecks and, 'to a lesser extent', regulatory hassles.

CONCLUSION

Our final conclusions are three-fold. Firstly, the policy initiatives represented by the new post-1991 economic policies need to be taken forward to prepare

---

* The Impact of India's Economic Reforms on Industrial Productivity, Efficiency and Competitiveness (NCAER, 2001).

the ground on which globally competitive companies can grow. In the continuing public debate and advocacy in India over the dismantling of the public sector and the removal of the remaining government controls, the necessary role of government or the right kind of regulation has been somewhat overshadowed. But this is not our most significant conclusion. The successes of companies like Tata Steel, Reliance Industries and Sundram Fasteners point to what the McKinsey study calls "organisation of functions and tasks" or plain old management.

Our second and most significant conclusion is, that with the right type of entrepreneurial leadership and management practices, it is possible to grow globally competitive companies in almost any sector in India. What is therefore, critically important, is a firm's response to emerging competitive challenges. Thirdly, there is a future for India to become a research platform for the world to capitalise on its low cost scientific skills.

So India is emerging as a low cost competitive player in anything knowledge based. Individual manufacturing companies with the right approach to cost, quality and achieving competitiveness are becoming globally competitive. For the entire economy to become so it is necessary for the government to adopt the right policy and regulatory approach.

2

The Software Advantage

In the slowdown of the year 2001, which ended the longest boom the US economy has ever known, expenditure on information technology fell marginally. Yet India's software exports, 60 per cent of which went to the US market, grew by 23 per cent during 2001–02 to touch $7.6 billion. In the same year, India's total exports barely moved, thus dramatically raising IT's share of total exports and providing further evidence that software remained the most competitive sector of the Indian economy, way ahead of any other sector. There can be no better way of understanding what drives Indian competitiveness and what doesn't, than by looking at the rise and tenacious progress of its software sector.

In India, it all began in the late sixties when the Tatas thought they ought to do something about this new animal called automation which involved EDP (electronic data processing) and computers. So they set up Tata Consultancy Services in the year 1968, not even as a separate company but as part of Tata Sons, the group holding company. The only computer available in those days was the IBM1401 which used punch cards, and TCS started working with it like preparing payrolls for Tata Steel, mainly to get familiar with EDP processes.

But very quickly it became clear that the world was fast moving ahead and TCS needed proper direction and leadership. Thus F C Kohli joined TCS in 1971, to eventually lead it for nearly three decades, during which period it remained consistently at the top of the software heap in terms of both topline and bottomline. Kohli came from Tata Electric where he was a frontline engineer seeking to improve load despatch which lent itself easily to automation. He and his colleagues quickly realised that the 1401 computer could not last for ever and they had to look beyond India's shores for newer and faster machines. So discussion soon started with the US company Burroughs (now Unisys), then the second biggest computer company in the world, for work in automation and computing. The possibility of importing computers came up and some people from TCS went over to Burroughs for training.

But the problem was that it took 3–5 years for the government of India to clear an application for importing a computer, by which time what you had set out to import had become dated. So it became obvious that getting technology quickly into the country would be difficult. But an alternative line of work emerged. Burroughs could not only train TCS people, some of them could even be deputed to work abroad for Burroughs and thus yield a revenue stream for TCS. The more difficult task of importing computing technology into India was separately pursued. Thus as India stepped into the seventies, TCS supplied its first batches of software professionals to work onsite for western computer companies and with their customers, earning export dollars for the company and the country. And so began India's software story—through what was later somewhat disparagingly called body shopping.

Software exports remained 100 per cent on site through the seventies and around 95 per cent on site till the late eighties. Recalls N R Narayana Murthy, chairman and one of the founders of Infosys Technologies, "In 1981, when we started, we were forced to look outside because there was no domestic market. There were very few computers in India, importing computers was very difficult, data communications were not available. There was enormous friction to business; in fact, it took a year to get a telephone connection in Bangalore. The cost of a 64 kbps line at that time was $300,000 a year, as against $20,000 today (2002)." The little bit of offshore development that took place in the early days came from physically shipping tapes to customers after completing the work. As an industry veteran recalls, "Till the late eighties the Indian part of the industry was not really an industry, but a bunch of programmers working under different company letterheads, big or small, which were effectively contracting houses".

INITIAL ADVANTAGES: SCIENTIFIC SKILLS; SOFTWARE NATURALS

How could India produce an expanding stream of software professionals, initially equipped with very basic skills of course, who were found acceptable by western information technology (IT) vendors? The answer to this question provides the most fundamental explanation for the competitiveness of Indian software. Through the seventies and the eighties, India was laying the foundations for a capability in electronics and computer science that turned out to be its first strength. This potential was developing in some of the country's leading educational institutions, foremost being the Indian Institute of Science in Bangalore and the various IITs (Indian Institute of Technology). The very first personal computer designed by Wipro was in collaboration with IISc and the very first IT professionals the company recruited were from the Bangalore institution. There were also a number of government owned research institutions in the fields of defence, aeronautics and electronics centred around Bangalore. Thus even as India was developing a science capability, this capability was getting clustered around Bangalore.

"The initial investment in terms of educational and scientific institutions was something India did very well to position itself for a market and an opportunity that was not probably known at that time," says Srini Rajam who left Texas Instruments in 2000 after working in it for 17 years to join his own startup. Texas Instruments was the pioneer in setting up its own software development centre in 1984 in Bangalore and is partially credited with discovering India as a place for developing software, the off shore part of the business whose on site bit was pioneered by TCS. It was preceded by a whisker's breadth by Citibank Overseas Software Ltd, which decided to source software services directly from India rather than get it through companies like TCS and Infosys. The difference between Texas Instruments and Citibank was that whereas the former set out to source technology, the latter was in the business of maintenance services.

How did Citibank and Texas Instruments find out what was possible in India? In the seventies and eighties there were a lot of Indian scientific professionals in the US who had gone there to do their masters and stayed back to work in the research and development areas of companies like Texas Instruments, GE and Nortel. They, perhaps unconsciously, worked as a bridge. Says an expert who was right there in such an institution, "If I work in an IT company that is looking for more quality people and see these smart guys from India working for us, then I say, what's there in that country? Can we go and get some more good people? They first started looking at people from IISc, the IITs and other engineering colleges and probably realised they were getting a better quality and deal out of them than their American counterparts. Those were the days when everyone spoke of the brain drain from India. And these people were costing them less! They actually stretched, gave their employers great value for money. They worked 12–14 hours a day without saying, I have been hired to work only eight hours a day, as typically their American counterparts would".

T G Ramesh, CEO of Bangalore Labs, another high end startup, has an explanation for the quality of education in the better science colleges in India: "The Indian educational system is one of the best in the world when it comes to the bachelor's programme. The freedom to do what you want has robbed the American undergraduate system of its focus. The Indian school system requires you to pass an exam every year. With that kind of a foundation you go and do a very structured eight or ten semester engineering course in India where again you are tracked on a half yearly or quarterly basis. It is like going through a military training. But the whole scenario changes at the master's level. That's where the Indian system slips and the US system works. In India at the post-graduate level you are still putting people through a regimen. That is the stage where you really want to unleash people, see what they can contribute from what they have learnt in the past 16 years by thinking differently, on how knowledge can be useful in real life in firms and industries".

The difference in the quality of post-graduate studies between the US and India is explained by the degree of involvement of industry in post-graduate studies. Adds Ramesh, "Our industry participation in post-graduate education is negligible, pathetic. On the other hand, most of the post-graduate courses in the US are related to projects, industry centric work sponsored by industries and government agencies with research grants".

When Texas Instruments looked around the world for a place to set up an R&D centre of global proportions, it was not looking for a local partner or at one particular segment. It wanted to do market development and R&D for a global market. It surveyed the world and looked specifically at the Asia Pacific region because it lacked in R&D, having primarily manufacturing capabilities. "India came out on top," recalls Rajam, "because of the investment made in its educational institutions. If you looked at the Asia Pacific countries which were at that time considered very competitive, the Indian professionals' ability to communicate and coexist with peer groups around the world played a very important role. When an Indian engineer received information from an American engineer he felt at home. At that time no other country could have matched it except maybe Singapore." The scientific capability was thus made more useful by an accompanying second skill—ability to communicate in English, the preferred global language for software.

Some offer a slightly varied explanation as to why Indian scientific skills are peculiarly suited to software development. Says Sanjay Chakraborty, CEO of MobiApps, a Bangalore based telecommunications startup promoted by the consultancy Arthur D Little, "Competitive edge in software is contributed by analytical skills. As a nation, historically, our analytical and mathematical skills have been inbred. The word 'algorithm' comes from an Arabic translation of an Indian concept. That analytical skill has been coupled with the fact that the competitive basis for this industry is not capital or manufacturing intensive, but primarily innovation intensive. In the late seventies, or earlier there was no Indian software industry but Indians in the software industry. Indians were already very successful the world over in higher education. Earlier such educationally oriented people did not find a direct application in industry for their work. Computer science and the software industry provided a direct application of that skill set and capability to entrepreneurial ventures."

Rajam puts across similar ideas a little differently, "There is what I call the adaptive skill of an Indian professional. This is a very interesting theory though I don't think there is any study validating it. If you look at other cultures in Asia, some of them are fine tuned or oriented to excel in a very predictable environment which is typically the manufacturing one. Indian culture, I would say, is oriented to excel in a relatively unpredictable or chaotic environment. Which is to say that the typical engineering mind here would get very bored if you have to repeat the same set of steps every day but do it better by getting more efficient. I don't think we can produce very predictable results.

We don't seem to excel in a manufacturing process oriented setup. But we do in a setup where on a daily basis we have to think, innovate, adapt, change and finally achieve the goal. If you look at product development and R&D for which India is recognised today, it is exactly the second type of environment. Because the specs are rarely frozen in software development. They keep on changing to the extent that the final specs or product might not even be close to the original specs. You have to evolve it, based on the market, and you have to do that in collaboration with other teams around the world, which may be doing parts of the same product. We have inherent strengths in this type of environment, because that is what we like to do. Our adaptive engineering skills are even today perhaps among the best."

HAPPENSTANCE AND COSTS

A third reason is pure happenstance. Indian software became globally competitive because the first software companies, as Narayana Murthy has explained, had no opportunity in India. Forced to operate globally, they learned to survive without domestic props. Ashok Soota, CEO of MindTree and one of India's IT veterans, feels that the R&D part of software actually benefited from the closed environment. Indian engineers were forced to design a good part of hardware and thereby "created a huge design capability in the country. When the market opened up (from mid-eighties onwards) we had this very large number of people who were exceedingly good designers. That skill we were able to convert into one which the rest of the world needed. Historically, it was a great thing for this country that IBM actually went out (in 1977). That created a vacuum into which came in many small companies which later on became large companies. In IBM's presence maybe they would not have been able to grow."

A fourth reason why Indian software capabilities were initially recognised and rapidly patronised was cost. Various industry experts have their own recollection of cost benchmarks over the years. Parthasarathy S, CEO of Aztec, recalls that initially, in the early eighties, the cost advantage to an American developer between hiring in the US and sourcing from India was ten to one—you could get it from India at 10 per cent of the US cost. That is when the first set of Indian companies dedicated to offshore development like Infosys came up. By the early nineties this had become 7–8 to one and in 2000 it was 2–5 to one, reflecting the rapid growth and heightening visibility of Indian software in the late nineties when the Y2K boom was in full swing. Phiroz Vandrevala, executive vice-president of TCS, recalls that, in the early nineties the on site rates were benchmarked at around $24–25 an hour. This had turned to $30–32 an hour by the mid-nineties and risen to $40–60 an hour in 2000. Underlining the sharp rise in revenue in recent years, Nandan Nilekani, managing director of Infosys, recalls that as late as March 1997, Infosys' billed revenue per employee was $42,000 per man year. By March 2001, this had gone up to $90,000 per man year. Ranjan Chak, vice president and executive director of Oracle's India Development Centre, provides another benchmark. "In a professionally run outfit in India an engineer could cost $35–50,000 a year (2001). This is for work done here, including costs, as opposed to what is billed. We are still 30–50 per cent of US costs but you can't climb much higher than that."

Narayana Murthy acknowledges that during the 81–91 period, when Indian software was hemmed in by constraints, it had to rely on "cost as the initial competitive advantage." But if the cost advantage has slowly been whittled down, what has been the continuing basis of success? Explains Rajam, "R&D centres had been set up in other places also, in Europe and to some extent Taiwan and Korea. But one of the key strengths India had was that success started showing from day one. There was a *huge* positive snowballing effect. If Texas Instruments comes in and makes a new product very successfully and says we are very happy with our India centre, then IBM comes, HP comes, Motorola comes. It almost becomes a situation that whoever is coming in is making a big success and communicating very positively. It is very rare to have every consumer of a product endorsing it in a very voluntary way. I think this kind of advertising, resulting from natural, voluntary endorsement, is very rare in history."

GOVERNMENT AS FRIEND AND FOE

Software exports became discernable from the late eighties and by 1990 began to attract official attention. N Vittal, electronics secretary to the Government of India, told a gathering in 1990, "Software is emerging as a potential star performer. Barely Rs 34 crore three years ago, today our software exports are of the order of Rs 150 crore. We are talking in terms of reaching a figure like

Rs 2,000 crore by the year 1994–95." This success began to attract international developmental attention. The World Bank sponsored a study for the department of electronics which in 1992 set out the strategic goal of achieving $1 billion of software exports by 1996. And the now famous McKinsey study of 2000, commissioned by the National Association of Software and Service Companies (Nasscom) has set the new strategic goal of software and services export of $50 billion by 2008 (Chart 2.1).

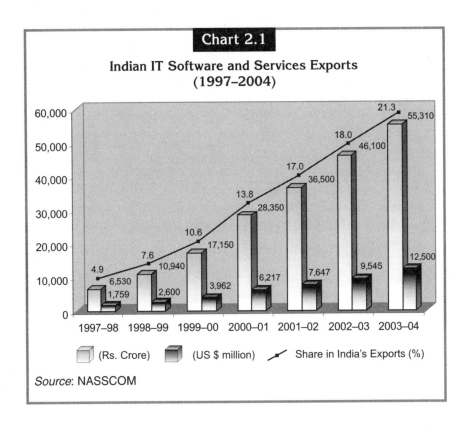

Chart 2.1

Indian IT Software and Services Exports (1997–2004)

Source: NASSCOM

The initial capabilities that enabled India to make a good start as a global supplier of on shore software services and made it an attractive centre for off shore software development, beginning with the setting up of the first such centre by a multinational Texas Instruments, have been discussed. The quick growth of exports in the late eighties was also aided by regulatory help. Rajiv Gandhi announced his electronics policy and the telecommunications infrastructure began to change, albeit slowly. With the movement of people becoming an issue, focus began to shift to off shore exports. TCS, which was in 1988 a Rs 14 crore company and accounted for over half the country's software exports, decided to undertake a single capital expenditure, import an

IBM 3090 mainframe, costing Rs 10 crore. This was prompted by the realisation that to go to the next generation, the transition had to be made to off shore development. The computer was set up in Chennai, then Madras, and was the biggest Indian project to export software through the wires.

But those sections of the government seeking to help the software sector had to fight an uphill task. Vittal remained the electronics secretary almost continuously for six years from mid-1990 under three governments and attributes the growth in software to the "strategic alliance between the DoE and the industry." This is how he recalls the unique cooperation which meant sometimes taking on other branches of the government, "Within a week of my becoming electronics secretary I met the industry and asked them what it is that comes in the way of your progress. (In two months) I took a paper to the committee of secretaries and the concessions slowly came one by one. Manmohan Singh, in his first budget, granted the important tax concession under section 80HHE which exempted software export earnings from income tax.

But the experience on high speed data communication, which the department of telecommunications is supposed to provide, was different. I requested the chairman of the Telecom Commission whether he could provide it. He said no, our priority is rural telephones. If industry wants it let them pay upfront and we can provide it within 18 months. At that time there was only one earth station, software technology park, that of Texas Instruments. They brought the earth station and it was to be given to the department of telecom, and the department was charging them a huge amount for that! So I informed the government that we could divert the funds that we had for the Semiconductor complex which was under construction. This was done, and six earth stations were set up at Bangalore, Hyderabad, Thiruvananthapuram, Noida, Chandigarh and Bhubaneshwar. DoT and VSNL at times adopted the attitude of a dog in the manger. They themselves will not provide the facilities and at the same time raise questions on whether we could do it. Once these earth stations were set up, software exports took off."

NINETIES: DECADE OF INDIAN SOFTWARE

The global telecom revolution made the offshoring of software development possible. But India had to wait till the new economic policies which began unfolding from 1991, to get onto the off shore bus. Narayana Murthy recalls the other changes that made up the difference: current account convertibility, easing of foreign travel, ability to bring in quality consultants from outside. The off shore model was good for both customer and vendor. It reduced costs for the customer. For its part the Indian vendor, because of reduced costs, could put in larger teams. This led to compression of cycle time, better turnaround and response time per customer, better quality (lower rework) and overall better productivity. "This went on till 1995 when Indian companies started looking at advanced software quality models, like the capability maturity model. Then we also started creating customer specific off shore software development models, development centres. We replicated the customer's technology, process, tools, etc. In other words we started a virtual software R&D development facility for a customer."

The industry made tremendous progress during the nineties, from $50 million exports in 1990–91 to $6 billion in 2000–01, from a few large companies to hundreds of companies, small, medium and large which entered into every segment of the market. Indian entrepreneurs could see that this business model could be very successfully replicated and even expanded. Thence emerged the success stories like Wipro and Infosys, in tandem with TCS (Chart 2.2). Analysts see Infosys essentially as a business model, like Texas Instruments, for multiple customers. Thus this wave of growth was driven by entrepreneurs providing services to the global companies instead of those companies having their in house setups for various reasons like flexibility and logistics. In the past you had a software development project which you passed on to a vendor to execute. But this began to change from the mid nineties and this change is still paying dividends. On the basis of a strategic relationship, client organisations were ready to downsize their own activity in a critical

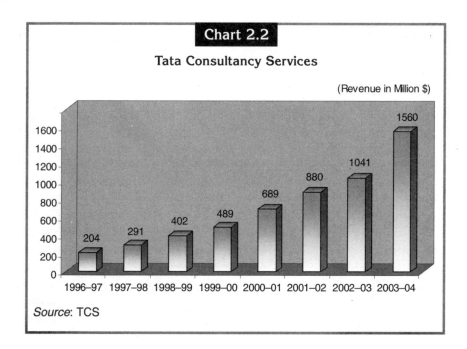

Chart 2.2

Tata Consultancy Services

(Revenue in Million $)

Source: TCS

business area and leave it to someone to maintain, enhance and continue to provide production support. This meant that a core business was no longer with you in house. Where you had a hundred people in your IT department, now you have zero. But it is a critical part of the business. So, what began as a client–vendor relationship turned into a partnership.

THE EFFICIENT REPLICATORS

Wherein lies the success of the Indian software business model? Analyses Chakraborty, "If I were to do a value chain analysis then I would suggest that the competitive basis of the software industry has been the background, analytics and exposure for a selected group of people, who realise what world class means and the ability to replicate work in large numbers rather than pure innovation. In this replication the rest of the world does not have a competitive advantage but India does. In the whole business a huge amount of time is spent in replicating. And the core competence of the Indian software industry that evolved was and is the fact that they can take something that is repetitive, to a certain extent apply their analytics and replicate in large numbers. This basis of competitive advantage can still be used by a few large players. You can't replicate an Infosys today. Mass replication will constitute an advantage at a certain scale because then the barrier to entry becomes huge."

The first half of the nineties marked a steady progress—from pure body shopping to more organised body shopping, to time and material jobs, to taking on complete jobs, whose scope was clearly defined and price fixed. The work first involved maintenance of existing applications and business systems, testing and writing codes, and then went on to handling projects. Soon, jobs to develop parts of new business applications and new technology designs which had a high software content, started coming in. And after that came tasks to develop and manage end to end systems which required domain skills, that is knowledge of the area of business that the client operated in.

And then around 1998 came the Y2K panic, boom and bonanza, recalls Chakraborty. As the turn of the century approached, those with legacy systems whose software had not looked ahead to the year 2001 needed to get their systems 2001 compatible by the time the year came around. It was boring, manual work that nevertheless brought big money. But more than that, what it did was to give the more capable and established Indian software companies entry into the big enterprises of the west. It was a trial Indian companies faced and came up right on top. Not a single system that the Indian industry touched as far as Y2K was concerned failed. "Y2K gave us assured opportunity, at a good margin. It gave a big fillip to Indian industry in terms of strengthening their balance sheets. This meant that almost 50 per cent of Fortune 500 companies started their contact with Indian software companies. Though Y2K was the initial opportunity, it opened up other opportunities for Indian companies."

Around 1998 also came the e-commerce opportunity which Indian companies seized upon. There was nothing like past experience for anybody anywhere in the world in it. All were starting to learn at the same time. Recalls N Lakshmi Narayanan, president and COO of Cognizant, "The rapidity with which people in India learnt was much greater compared to the vast majority of the people in the US and such places. Suddenly the new industry provided the Indian industry with a very level playing field. That's where we have been able to establish our supremacy, primarily because we showed we were just as strong as anyone in the world in creating new applications. That's where Indian promoted companies and dotcoms were successful." Indian companies, particularly in the US, started to enter the internet or the e-business area, through e-enabling orgnisations. Silicon Valley saw a bigger and bigger Indian presence, aided by the successes of those who had earlier dug roots there like Kanwal Rekhi who helped set up The Indus Entrepreneurs to be venture capitalist and angel to the most aggressive of Indian professionals with entrepreneurial ambitions.*

THE TRAVERSE

Like all new entrants in any sector on the global scene, Indian software entered at the cost end. Indian costs were a big attraction to everybody initially (pages 21–22). But even at that time everybody knew that without credibility and quality, cost by itself would not do. No company will risk its next R&D plan in the hands of a new developer whose quality assurance was not established. More than gaining a foothold, what kept Indian software up and running was the ability to keep on upgrading quality even as more and more complex jobs were taken on. "By the end of the century we were confident, having gone up the value chain and created huge software factories. We had good training facilities, processes, methodology and started attracting better talent like PhDs," says Narayana Murthy. Agrees Chak, "there was a lot of entrepreneurial investment in technology, people started their own companies and high tech services, going up the value chain. This contributed to the change in quality and quality consciousness. Quality was maintained."

Adds Rajam, "We can explain the achievement of quality by the same adaptive skills of Indians I have referred to earlier. Software by definition is a

---

* For details of people of Indian origin scoring successes in Silicon Valley, see *The Horse That Flew*, Chidanand Rajghatta (Harper Collins, 2001).

very creative process and achieving higher and higher levels of quality means you are still working in an environment where the product definition markers are changing. In my view, there are enough challenges for an Indian software engineer to achieve high levels of quality as against the manufacturing environment where it is just process orientation."

We have described the initial advantages and how Indian software companies were able to make the traverse by upscaling. The key competency was to simultaneously maintain quality. If Indian manufactures are notorious for their lack of quality, how did Indian software companies manage to ensure the highest quality? We have referred to the inherent Indian adaptive skills but there is more to it and the story is best told by Arun Jain, chairman of Polaris. The primary benchmark is "quality of delivery because the customer will pay for what you deliver at the end of the day. In software we delivered to international customers to their expectations. At least 80 per cent of Indian software projects have delivered very well."

In the early nineties the software industry worldwide was so unstructured that there was no process management in it. Being knowledge based, it was seen more as an art than a science. Adds Jain, "We started in 1993 and picked up TQM because that was the only benchmark for us to see whether quality can be related to the service industry and benchmarks applied. Then we picked up ISO. Then in late 1994 Software Engineering Institute from Carnegie Mellon published their process manuals. Polaris was one of the first companies to get itself rated and its process assessed under it along with its customer Citibank in January 1995. There are five levels in their process or capability maturity index—SEICMM. It was amazing as we got assessed at level three as that put us among the top eight per cent of companies in the world. It is this kind of thinking process that has helped build on previous achievements and created a positive spiral."

Jain says there is an advantage in being a newcomer. Everyone shares his knowledge and practices with you as you are not seen as a threat. This was the case when GM and Ford first designed cars for Toyota and Honda. Once process know-how is shared you can improve on it. From 1997 onwards, Indian software companies had access to the best global processes. Delivering to a German customer teaches you what attention to detail is. Delivering to an American customer teaches project management. Delivering to a Japanese customer teaches how you can track a project on a day-to-day basis for defects and productivity. "When we got rated at CMM level 5, we were the first customer in the world to do so. The assessor who came here said the matrix we had created was one of the best in the world as those quality matrices have not been created anywhere else. We put together all the best practices and created our own quality management system which remains unique till today (2001)."

This going up the value chain, winning the confidence of large Fortune 500 customers with quality and delivery has led to the leading Indian companies seeking to establish themselves as global brands by getting listed in the US. First Satyam Computers through its subsidiary Satyam Infoway, then Infosys Technologies, and thereafter Wipro have all secured listings in the US. Says Nilekani of Infosys, "We have understood the value of branding. When you look at global companies, a lot of the value they command is from the brand. In the last three years we have made a significant effort to build a global brand. Our being the first Indian company to list on Nasdaq gave us a huge momentum in building a global brand. It also enabled us to go to the global capital market and meet the demands of investors in them. This makes you understand how they want you to position yourself and strategise. Since 98 per cent of our revenue is from the global market and we mostly compete with global players we need a much better understanding of international customers. The market in which you compete helps you to shape as a supplier. This kind of customers and competition creates a climate of continuous improvement and productivity gains."

3

Software:
Maturing Under Setbacks

As the old century bowed out, the dotcom bubble burst and the technology stocks on the Nasdaq went through a severe correction. In the financial year 2001–02 technology budgets of most companies in the US and Europe were severely curtailed. Indian software therefore faced its first major challenge. Through the nineties the industry had grown under conditions of a shortage in what it had to sell. Its main asset was its scalability and the ability to meet this demand. Price pressure was the last thing it faced.

How will it be able to cope with the new challenges and the pressure on its rates? Will it be able to formulate a new business strategy, find a new competency? Or, will its growth phase never return, thus proving right the doomsayers who had all along predicted an end of rapid growth once its string of unusual good luck ended? Will the Y2K bonanza be its last hurrah?

In this chapter, we will look at three areas of weaknesses that the industry has discovered under the scrutiny of its own introspection during hard times. These are:

- backwardness in product development,
- domain knowledge, and
- marketing.

But we will also argue that the slowdown is not the end of the road for the sector. It is acquiring what it lacked during its earlier generic phase of growth. It is developing new competencies higher up the value chain. In particular, Indian expertise in electronic product designing is in the process of establishing itself, thus indicating that it retains its edge in the knowledge sphere, the key resource in this sector.

As the global marketplace changed, the window of opportunity that was earlier so effectively exploited, had to close. In trying to cope with shortages, the industry had so over built up capacities that now there was an excess of it. Hence through financial 2001–02 a process of shakeout was on. It took the form of a bifurcation. The strong began to get stronger, the specialists dug into their niches; and those with merely generic skills found the going increasingly tough. Niche players with less than a hundred employees and biggies with over a thousand employees survived the storm. But redundancies and pink slips came to the industry for the first time and a few closures also took place, kept to the minimum by the Indian ethos of not closing down a business until it became absolutely imperative. Hence the number of those on the bench rose sharply, the induction of new recruits was delayed and in some cases confirmations not handed down. The financial year 2002–03 was the most trying for the industry which came under severe pricing pressure and faced declining margins. The gloom was accentuated by the disappearance of wealth as IT stocks declined and the value of stock options dwindled. Many millionaires were made and unmade in the space of a couple of years.

But there were plenty of people willing to take a positive view of the slowdown. Through the period of heady growth, not much attention had been paid to productivity. Now with stiff competition and price discounting, attention was paid to improving value propositions. People were definitely looking at doing more with less. "This is a defining moment, this is the time which will separate the men from the boys. Companies which have stronger brands, financial skills, people skills will win," said Nandan Nilekani.

The slowdown brought new business opportunities, too. To counter the slowdown, western companies looked again at another round of cost cutting in which attention focused on IT led productivity improvements. This time around it was the medium and small companies that looked to India to outsource. The last recession produced the first outsourcing wave in the early nineties. Another such wave was on early in the next decade. Software companies which redo their business plans under these new market conditions will do even better when growth returns again. Said Rajam in late 2002, "After the slowdown, India as a brand will be better off compared to others because more people will be realising the opportunity in India. And if we can keep up our delivery, quality and performance we will be an even more credible alternative. India is one of the very few IT industries around the world which is still growing. Positive growth, though slower, at a time when many are registering negative growth will itself make you a quality brand as you cannot do this without strong fundamentals."

In the slowdown, there have been at least two fortuitous developments for the larger Indian companies. Explains Narayana Murthy, when spending had to be tightened, companies didn't want to experiment. They started looking for better value, saying, we will deal with companies we can trust. This is not the time to experiment with newcomers, let us go with the time tested financially sound companies. We will go with those who can provide end-to-end solutions rather than engage both high end consultants and executors who will carry out the jobs according to the consultants' specifications. "In the last six months (early 2002) we find that we have to do much more higher end work, provide a 'concept to execution' service."

Arun Jain of Polaris has another positive scenario to offer. American and European companies have been much harder hit than Indian companies. In America, where cost structures are high, companies operate on 8–9 per cent margins, whereas Indian companies do 30 per cent. "For Indian companies growth has flattened but still there is a profit. In America, companies have bled so much in the past year that every month you see 10–12 bankruptcies, filing for Chapter 11 of US bankruptcy law. American companies that are surviving are either below 100 people or over 50,000, like KPMG, Accenture, EDS, CSC. The same trend is visible in India. Companies in the 200–300 range are in trouble. When someone has to outsource, he looks for some critical size, some infrastructure, some processes."

There is also a technological silver lining to the downturn. Prior to it, e-business and the net provided a great opportunity for the better Indian software companies which were rapidly proving themselves. In 2000, the e-business share of revenue of the big Indian companies was 30–40 per cent. In 2001 it was down to 20–25 per cent. There is no question that the internet holds the key to the future. Companies all over the world will eventually adopt the net as the communication medium for doing business, as soon as it gets more rugged and reliable. The net, within 15 years of its arrival, will mature the way the plain old telephone has matured in a 100 years. Nobody now thinks of an indonet type of network. The internet is there and products are coming out by the day making the net secure for the most confidential networking. And Indian companies, too, are beginning to come out with their products. The opportunity that the internet represents and Indian software companies' strong presence in it, affirms a robust life after the slowdown.

FROM SERVICES TO PRODUCTS

Indian software companies, mostly promoted by engineers and technical people who are first generation entrepreneurs, had so far concentrated on providing technical services and solutions. In product development, developing the product is the lesser part of the business. Core competency for product development is only tangentially linked with technology development. The competitive basis for product development is risk taking, customer intimacy and market knowledge. It is also very capital intensive. It is as much or more of a business proposition than a technological challenge. An entire team can work for a year on a product and the venture can thereafter have to be abandoned. Selling a product is 90 per cent of the work and takes care of a good part of the funding. To take a product to the market, the marketing investment might be an order of magnitude higher than in development. This will be a very unfamiliar situation for Indian software developers. Till now, most of the budget was set aside for things like building, people and technology costs. But getting ready to spend three times that on a product implies a total reorientation.

There is also the call to be made as to at which stage of development a product is licensed. To make a cutting edge technology product you may have to spend two years. On the sixth month, a company may come and offer you a handsome compensation for licensing the development that you have made so far—say, $5 million for a technology for which you have spent $1 million. For an entrepreneur this is very tempting but a suboptimal position to take. If he wants to be more ambitious he can decide to develop the product completely for two more years and capture an across the board market. Then the returns can probably be $50–100 million. But at the end of it all there may be nothing—the product may not eventually yield its full potential or may be overtaken by another product. This is how investors in the satellite project Iridium lost their money because of the rapid progress made by cellular phone technology.

A new kind of Indian product company is emerging. Says Srini Rajam, CEO of Ittiam, "We had the capability but invariably it was tapped by people who had the marketing strength. Today we do see a momentum picking up among small companies in getting into products. When they get bigger you will see a significant proportion of exports coming out of products. Today (end-2001) it is probably five per cent, but it will be 10–20 per cent by 2004. Remember the service part of the industry is still growing at 30–40 per cent. The difference between services and products is between having the space capability and being able to deliver space products. The difference between a product company and a service company is marketing. In a service company you don't decide exactly what products to make and what has market potential. You have to make the call if you have to be a product company and there is an inherent risk. Ittiam (Rajam's startup) is based on moving to the next level of product and technology, and of course risk. We want to take control of what we do in terms of product development, the risk that it might not be successful and try to make a hit at the global marketplace through a technology and product that Indian entrepreneurs will evolve."

In Rajam's view, "the biggest gap is still marketing, not only in the sense of promoting a product but more in the sense of understanding the market dynamics and determining what could be the right product to invest in and having invested, creating the marketing channels to take it to the customer. It is understanding where the market is going because once you develop a product it has to come to the market. You may have the ability to assemble a car but can you decide what are going to be the features of the next generation car? Companies in India have the ability to design a cellphone today but do we know what kind of a phone will win in the marketplace two years from now? This (marketing) gap will be closed slowly with people taking the initiative. I feel there is an awareness among the leaders of the industry that this is the next step but I can't call it widespread or a widely accepted notion. The cost advantage is reducing but not going away. I think we still have a very good window for companies that can manage their efficiencies, at least a five year window. But it is definitely reducing. Hence you want to offer more value in terms of deep technical competencies, project management abilities and quality so that price performance is falling but is still there.

"In our company we are starting with a very clear focus. We are a hundred per cent digital signals processing (DSP) company. We are starting with the vision to be the world's best DSP software systems company. We know this will not to be achieved in a short time frame. Hence we are committed to pursuing this goal in the next ten years. DSP is the core technology driving communications. We are trying to create a lot of intellectual property and products which will start paying into our revenue stream at a future date. We are looking at a lot of collaborative R&D that we want to do with our customers around the world. We believe we can offer very attractive products which our customers can straightaway integrate with their systems solutions in order to cut down the demand on their time and innovation. We can also provide them custom product development capability, an additional R&D bandwidth. We are very happy to report that Ittiam has come up with several products in terms of signal processing applications—audio, speech, video and communications. We are achieving design wins. Our products are being used by our customers in Asia, US, Europe both in communications and multi-media. We are a very ambitious, focused company and so have to invest a lot in design and marketing. That is why we are starting by basing our business development VP in the US."

Realising the marketing deficit and in view of the fact that the major market is in the US, software companies are increasingly concentrating their top marketing muscle in the US. The logic of the process has in some cases gone one step further. Not just marketing but the corporate functions of many software companies have shifted to the US and what is left in India is really the development centre. Vivek Paul, president of Wipro Technologies, the global software services arm of Wipro, operates out of the US, In fact, a highly successful hybrid Indo-US business model is emerging—corporate office and marketing in the US, development in India. The services company Cognizant and the product company Talisma are examples.

Ranjan Chak says, "Today you can talk to Indian companies equally about product design and product management issues, revenue models and just in time materials. You couldn't do that four years ago. Today you have companies out there whose revenue models are based on product sharing and licensing revenues, rather than pure man hours. Today there is a much greater percentage of product development for others in India but it is not owned by the Indian company in most cases. In products, things have changed drastically because of multinationals like us (Oracle). We are a technology company and have been focused on products and technology development. If Ford comes in here and designs an engine for its worldwide market then that would be the equivalent of Oracle coming in and designing software. When we came in 1994 we were confident that software development could be undertaken and managed in India. Taking the risk and saying that products, which are like our crown jewels, can be developed and designed here was a big leap of faith. Today there are many big companies, doing more than 70 per cent of their software work in India. Today, there are quite a few products that have been announced in the world media which have originated from India and have been designed and developed here, like Oracle 8i and 9i."

DOMAIN KNOWLEDGE, VERTICAL SPECIALISATION AND MARKETING

To get into products you have to understand the market—what the customer wants. The market is divided into vertical domains or business areas like banking, retailing or insurance. Business knowledge of a vertical is usually the speciality of management consultancies. Along with the journey from being service providers to product developers, is the journey to acquire domain knowledge and vertical specialisation. This is needed to earn higher value for providing services.

Domain knowledge comes in two ways. First let us take the organic route. As a customer outsources more and more of his work to you you get to know him better, there is greater customer intimacy. Thus, at one stage while executing a technology solution you propose also a wider business solution as while getting to know the customer better you have also acquired a consultancy capability, set up a consultancy group. The big Indian software companies are following this route. Says Narayana Murthy, "We have a small consultancy group located in Dallas, we have a domain competency group here. We have created domain expertise in telecom, banking, insurance and retail, the main areas. More and more people are going into the domain competency and consultancy group."

But journey down this route is predicated on getting more and more of a customer's work outsourced to you. Arun Jain sees a lot of this happening soon and foresees a bright future for Indian software companies after the slowdown is over. Much of the competition among the western software companies has been eliminated and the pressure to outsource to cut costs on western companies is massive. Jain sees the top 20 global financial companies with an annual IT spending of $40 billion ($2 billion each) seeking to save ten per cent, that is $4 billion and thus having to outsource $8 billion. This is on the assumption that Indian companies will be able to do a 50 per cent cost saving. This quantum of business will be significantly larger than earlier (Chart 3.1) and gain a deeper entry into the customers' organisations.

Chart 3.1

TOP 20 IT Software and Services Exporters from India (2002–03)

Rank	Company	Rs Crore	US $ million
1.	Tata Consultancy Services	4545.3	963.0
2.	Infosys Technologies Ltd	3543.5	750.7
3.	Wipro Technologies Ltd	2787.4	590.5
4.	Satyam Computer Services Ltd	2003.3	424.4
5.	HCL Technologies Ltd	1530.5	324.3
6.	Patni Computer Systems Ltd	914.0	193.6
7.	Mahindra British Telecom Ltd	634.7	134.5
8.	iFlex Solutions	593.3	125.7
9.	HCL Perot Systems Ltd	449.0	95.1
10.	NIIT Ltd	426.3	90.3
11.	Mascot Systems Ltd	421.0	89.2
12.	Digital Globalsoft Ltd	415.3	88.0
13.	Mastek Ltd	374.4	79.3
14.	Polaris Software Lab Ltd	367.2	77.8
15.	Birlasoft Ltd	346.4	73.4
16.	Mphasis BFL Ltd	335.6	71.1
17.	Pentasoft Technologies Ltd	296.5	62.8
18.	Hexaware Technologies Ltd	257.9	54.6
19.	Tata Infotech Ltd	256.0	54.2
20.	Infinite Computer Solutions India Pvt Ltd	249.1	52.8

Note: Companies such as C Technology Solutions, Syntel, among others that are registered in the US but offer India-based services delivery have not been included in the ranking.

The global revenue for Cognizant Technology Solutions and Syntel for the year 2002–03, registered with NASSCOM, are Rs. 1236.53 crore and Rs. 799.10 crore, respectively.

Source: NASSCOM

Jain also sees the nature of outsourcing changing. Through the nineties, most of the savings has been done by operational managers, not strategic managers. "But in the last six months we are observing that outsourcing decisions are being taken by the board." It is commiting a senior member full time for it. Earlier outsourcing was mostly done by the contracting manager who had a commodity buying and selling approach. "In the last six months (second half of 2001) we have had personal meetings with four CIOs of very large banks. Earlier we would never get such appointments; they would never respond to our letters. Now they are saying, make a presentation, give us a proposal on how you will do the saving, what differentiators do you have. Polaris has been able to take advantage of this development as we have chosen a particular domain. We have a lot of domain experts, we call them business solution experts. We have hired them from banks—Citibank, BoA, ICICI— to become front end solution providers."

The customer intimacy which Polaris is cashing in on has worked in another way also. "Now we are dictating our process to some of our customers. Some of the US and Canadian companies which are choosing us are saying, we would like to work with you not because of money saving but your processes of delivery. I think by 2005 the country will make a leap in the product business. The products will be sold on efficiency basis. The same products that Americans are selling at $1 million we will be selling at half million or less." This is like the price advantage Japanese cars have over American cars, without sacrificing on quality. Jain is nothing if not a dreamer and an outrageous optimist. By 2010 he sees Indian companies delivering premium products!

Not everybody is so unreservedly optimistic. MindTree Consulting, founded by Ashok Soota, as its name suggests, has structured itself around the business of consulting itself. Soota feels that the biggest handicap for the Indian software sector has been lack of domain knowledge, that is inability to offer consultancy in a chosen area of business. MindTree has chosen a particular business model to deliver the goods. It has brought in American employees with consultancy backgrounds who provide the knowledge of the customer's needs. MindTree also brings in people from India in a distributed development setup. This is the beginning. After that there is a process of osmosis by which knowledge once acquired is used to train people in India. "Today when we do a state of the art project for a customer in India we are doing what is available to anybody on a worldwide basis. We did a set for stores for Fabmart. The work we have done for Prudential has led to work for them in Singapore and Japan. One thing leads to another. Domain knowledge can only come from being able to develop state of the art solutions. Where will you get that experience? Either an Indian company will acquire an American company or do what we did, hire a lot of seasoned professionals."

The single biggest issue today before the most aggressive Indian companies is how to get into a customer's company at the highest level. That is the key to realising higher value, keep going up the value chain. It means taking more of the customer's responsibilities and providing higher value added solutions. Indian software companies have so far mostly implemented solutions that have already been defined—first onsite, then offshore and then off and on shore. Going up the value chain means defining the solution, defining the technology to be used in implementing the solution, maybe even identifying the problem. For that to happen you need to know the market, the industry, the vertical. And this knowledge is unique to a consultancy. Says Lakshmi Narayanan of Cognizant, "Currently the single biggest imperative is acquiring consulting capability and domain knowledge, and more than that the positioning you want to achieve. So you have to make a very gradual transition, lean on or partner with some of these people."

One way of partnering with someone is to make joint bids. In that case the total responsibility is taken by one or the other. But Infosys doesn't like being a sub-contractor. "In the last 16 years we have not been subcontractors and I don't think we want to be," declares Narayana Murthy categorically. So the third option for Infosys is to acquire a management consultancy. It has a war chest and has also approached the government for a large standby facility. For a long time the guessing game was on as to which well known western consultancy Infosys would set its sights on. On the other hand Wipro has made small acquisitions to bolster its consulting capabilities.

DESIGNING PRODUCTS

Till now, while discussing products we have concentrated on software products. But hardware products are increasingly emerging within the vision of Indian companies. How is this as Indian capabilities in hardware manufacture remain infant by global standards? The reason is that actual manufacturing has by now become a very commoditised high volume low margin business which is largely concentrated in places like China and Taiwan. The high value realisation lies in designing a product which can then be manufactured by someone else. The Indian journey up the value chain is, other than moving towards consulting, increasingly turning to electronic product designing. It could be software or hardware. A disaggregation is taking place in product development—the entire designing can be outsourced. The manufacturing of the hardware, as in the case of a microprocessor or chip, would then be the job of a fabricator. The designing of hardware and software are both intensively knowledge based activities and addressed by the same IT companies or technology firms.

Indian designing experience in fact predates its emergence as a software vendor. In the eighties companies like Wipro and HCL had full fledged R&D capability which was mainly devoted to designing systems. The system houses outside India earlier thought electronic designing was proprietary. Nobody believed electronic design could be outsourced. India had the system level design expertise but not the others like simulation, synthesis and domain expertise. In the initial years after liberalisation in 1991, Indian companies with design expertise used the time to bridge the gap. Then came the first design centres led by Texas Instruments.

Indian designing is now becoming fairly advanced in terms of methodology and expertise and in the last five years things have changed considerably. VLSI (very large scale integration, the more advanced chips available today) design has come of age in India since the early 2000s. And the new design centres have started driving projects. It is TI Bangalore, not TI Dallas that drives its Ankur project. One of Analog Devices major processes, short process, has come out of their India centre. As expertise has built up at these design centres, the major barriers to entry, expertise and knowledge, have come down and designing startups have proliferated in India. And with it has come an understanding of the importance of intellectual property in designing and its pursuit.

Designing by these startups was initially confined to front end designing of a chip, the logical simulation. The back end, which was the silicon part, was done at the customer's end. But that is also being done in India now. For this, it is necessary to interact with the fabricator and that service has also started to come up in the country. So now VLSI service providers have come up who not only design and prototype the chip, but get it tested and then ship it out to the fabricator. There is very high value in being able to function like such a one stop shop and Wipro, Infosys Technologies, Sasken and MindTree are among the more prominent VLSI service providers. Wipro is in fact one of the top VLSI service providers in the world, employing 400 professionals in this facility of theirs. This is very high end profitable work, earning anything in the range of $65–250 per hour, depending on what domain expertise you bring to bear on the designing (Chart 3.2).

There is considerable activity in developing intellectual property in areas like Bluetooth, wireless LAN, networking and communications. Once having acquired that intellectual property, firms use it as a certificate to get service projects, product design jobs. In the last couple of years many product design companies have come up. Prominent among them is the internet music and audio download solutions provider PortalPlayer. Its development centre in Hyderabad has come out with a multimedia chip which has been entirely designed by them and will be globally marketed by PortalPlayer, USA.

Ramco has developed a database product which has been acquired by Microsoft and integrated into its product. Tejas Networks has started to design fibre optics telecommunication products for which a large market is opening up with the arrival of private telecom service providers in India. Also active is MosChip, a chip designer.

Chart 3.2

Top 20 Software Exporters (MNCs) 2001–02

Rank	Company	(No. of employees)
1.	IBM Global Services India Ltd	3,100
2.	Cognizant Technology Solutions	2,712
3.	Oracle India Pvt Ltd	2,000
4.	Hughes Software Systems Ltd	1,500
5.	Hewlett-Packard (I) Software Operations Ltd	1,489
6.	Digital Globalsoft	1,480
7.	Syntel	1,464
8.	Covansys (I) Ltd	1,449
9.	PwC	1,200
10.	OrbiTech Solutions	1,191
11.	Siemens Information Systems Ltd	1,187
12.	Xansa (India) Ltd	892
13.	Motorola	800
14.	ST Microelectronics	800
15.	Texas Instruments India Pvt Ltd	741
16.	Intel Tech India Pvt Ltd	700
17.	i2 Technologies	700
18.	Cisco	670
19.	Robert Bosch	629
20.	Huawei	500

(No. of employees as of March 2002)

Source: NASSCOM

One indication that electronic product designing is making rapid progress in India is the rising fortunes of Cadence, a leading global supplier of designing tools. In the last four years (1998–2002) its customer base has gone up from 15 to over 80 and it affirms that there is tremendous growth in this market space. Says Himangshu Singh, who leads its Indian operations, "This is very encouraging for us. Most of the semiconductor companies in the world are present here for development work. And a few like Texas Instruments is outsourcing a part of that work to Indian companies. Design houses for product companies have started mushrooming. Electronic design all over the world is shifting to what is called 'system on chip' which is creating a great demand for readymade 'components'. Chip designers will be able to pick these up and integrate them into chips. So India can play a role in becoming a world leader in SOC (system on chip) components."

It is important for the electronic design industry to grow in India as that will enable it to move up the value chain in software services, create a knowledge base and domain competency in areas like communications, networking and multimedia.

If financial year 2002–03 was a highly testing period for Indian software, financial year 2003–04 was the year of transition. Pricing pressure persisted through a good part of the year. The year eventually turned out to be one of recovery when the growth rate for software exports picked up to 24 per cent from 16 per cent in the previous year. This recovery came about mainly through the industry's ability to pursue volumes and upscale. The volumes came from the need for companies in mature economies to outsource more and more to cut costs. In terms of capabilities, the recovery in growth despite a much greater customer concern for return on investment signified improving control over process and quality while executing increasingly complex jobs. Srini Rajam had foreseen correctly—when an industry recovery came, Indian software would emerge stronger. This is because it successfully addressed its weaknesses in all the three areas mentioned earlier in the chapter—domain knowledge, consulting skills and product development.

4

BPO Destination

The same factors that have given India a global competitiveness in software and services are doing so in information technology enabled services (ITES). But the emerging difference is that the opportunity in ITES or business process outsourcing (BPO), as it is increasingly being called, is rising rapidly, whereas software is maturing and recovering from a slowdown. In 1999, McKinsey, in its study for Nasscom, had estimated that the global market for IT enabled services would be $142 billion by 2008 and could account for $17 billion of the goal of $50 billion software and services exports set for the country by it. But after the 'explosive' growth of 2000–02, the Nasscom McKinsey study of 2002 had upped the targeted ITES exports for 2008 to $21–24 billion (Chart 4.1).

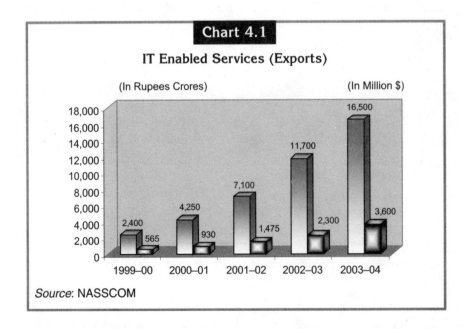

Chart 4.1

IT Enabled Services (Exports)

(In Rupees Crores)   (In Million $)

Year	In Rupees Crores	In Million $
1999–00	2,400	565
2000–01	4,250	930
2001–02	7,100	1,475
2002–03	11,700	2,300
2003–04	16,500	3,600

Source: NASSCOM

Globally, two processes are taking place simultaneously. The virtual corporation is becoming a greater reality every day with more and more of core activities, hitherto considered indispensible inhouse functions, being outsourced. This pool of outsourcing opportunities consists of both manufacturing and services. But over time, the proportion of services in overall value creation is rising. Thus the scope for outsourcing services is growing faster than the scope for outsourcing per se. As India's ITES opportunity has grown out of its software opportunity, the scope for the two activities are regularly compared. Raman Roy, CEO of Spectramind, one of the largest independent BPO operations until its acquisition by Wipro in 2002 and an acknowledged pioneer in the industry, points out that whereas software accounts for no more than 2–3 per cent of a company's spending, back office and customer interaction can account for anything upto a third or more. Says Arun Seth, CEO of BT operations in India and another industry veteran, "If the IT market is x, the IT enabled market is 10x."

Aside of the size of the ITES market, it has another fundamental impact on the Indian economy. By doing more and more back office work for global companies, Indian skills and productivity of its economy are correspondingly upgraded faster. All this makes the Indian stake in BPO rival the stake in software, despite the wage rates for software services being much higher than those for ITES. Thus the impact of ITES on the Indian economy and the Indian way of doing business can turn out to be significantly more than earlier expected. All this is enabling ITES to capture the popular imagination more and more.

WHAT'S IN A NAME

Before we go any further, it is necessary to explain the difference between what is meant by 'IT enabled services' (ITES) and 'business process outsourcing' (BPO). ITES is any service that can be provided remotely through the wires, whereas BPO is also delivered over the wires but involves entire business processes in a company. Indian players in the field like Raman Roy say that ITES is a misnomer and the nomenclature was adopted in order to ride piggy back on the tax benefits that were available to IT companies. He prefers something like remote servicing. With time the nomenclature 'business process outsourcing' (BPO) is gaining greater currency and we will use it for the rest of this chapter as it tends to describe better the wide nature of activities that come under the rubric.

Outsourcing, the death of distance or when "geography became history", in the words of Raman Roy, has a particular geneology and economic compulsion to it. Multinationals came into their own in the sixties by setting up branches and subsidiaries all over the world. This amounted to a replication through a sort of binary division of the parent. Then, in the aftermath of the seventies slowdown, it was realised that such dispersal carried with it diseconomies of scale. This led to a huge move towards centralisation about two decades ago, yielding firms many economies of scale. Companies took their centralised units to places like Phoenix, Arizona, Brighton, UK, where average cost per employee was low. But infrastructure cost was high. This began to change when infrastructure costs in newly emerging economies fell. Manufacturing work began to migrate to Taiwan and made distribution critical. Blue collar jobs eliminated, white collar jobs stood out as a big cost liability. This led to first back office and then front office outsourcing. Business process outsourcing or locating services at remote centres came about because of the 50–60 per cent cost cuts that were obtainable. But there was a further gain. Those delivering the outsourced services did them better by specialising in them and gave better value, even at those reduced costs. The locating of BPO services in India came by a somewhat roundabout route. It first went to Ireland, then to Australia, thereafter to Singapore and finally to India.

India closed 2003–04 with BPO exports of $3.6 billion. (Domestic revenue was minimal.) This was a minuscule less-than-half per cent of global BPO business and well behind the Indian share of over one per cent of global software business. But whereas the software business is maturing, the BPO business for India is only just beginning. The more established players see annual topline growth of 100 per cent or more for several years to come until individual companies achieve a revenue of $50–100 million. Data capturing and processing, documentation, accounting, payroll processing, human resources, selling, customer interaction and technical support are the business processes that are being outsourced today by companies, manufacturing and non-manufacturing alike. The scope for outsourcing for transaction based service companies dealing with large numbers of customers in the English speaking world to Indian BPO companies is huge, says K Ganesh, CEO of Customer.Asset. Organisations like banks, credit cards, media, insurance, travel and utilities which deal with large numbers of individual customers represent a major opportunity for India. This is not counting the niche players at the higher end of the business who undertake activities like website hosting, remote network maintenance, CAD/CAM, geographical information systems and animation.

Prakash Gurbaxani, CEO of 24/7Customer clearly foresees a $8–10 billion BPO industry in India in four to five years' time. This is because India as a source for BPO servicing has already arrived. Says Raman Roy, "Three years ago it was more a case of establishing proof of concept, whether it could be done out of India. Now nobody questions that. In my younger days I had to first sell the idea that it could be done remotely. Today we are at Rostow's takeoff stage. We have to scale up and have to take out the constraints that inhibit that scaling up."

HOW IT BEGAN

How did it begin? Raman Roy recalls, "About ten years ago, large multinationals in India, based purely on the success of their Indian business, noted that cost here per transaction was dramatically lower and the quality of output much higher. I have worked for some of these companies and have heard them say, 'are you sure you have not made a mistake? You mean it costs you only so much to process an application, or issue a credit card, or open a bank account or pay an invoice'. To us it was quite a lot but it was minuscule when converted to dollars and compared to what they paid in their parent countries. That is when some of their forward thinkers saw the opportunity. I rate a guy called John McDonald, controller of Amex and CFO of the Amex TRS company, as a true visionary. He came down to India and saw for himself that these lower costs were real. He said 'I don't get this quality of people to do things like vendors payable and processing applications. Given the fact that I have centralised in America, why can't I centralise in India?'"

It was not Amex but British Airways which was really the first to start back office operations in India. In the early nineties, they began with data entry and others built on their success. Showcasing what BA was doing played a critical part in Amex's decision making. The Amex originality was to decide on India in something that was very important to itself. They had already decided to centralise their American back office operations in Phoenix and their European operations in Brighton, UK. They looked for a centre for their Asia-Pacific operations and chose India over Australia and Singapore. "They now have over a thousand people in this operation in India and the value addition done by them is the highest among such operations. This is because of the vision of McDonald who said you can do high value added job here because of the quality of manpower available. Amex and BA really ironed out the wrinkles, the initial hurdles in the way of doing business in India. They did for remote servicing in India what Texas Instruments did for software development," Roy asserts.

Following close on the heels of BA and Amex, TCS helped Swiss Air set up their back office operations in India. And thereafter came the most spectacular outsourcing operations out of India, by GE, which was also set up by Raman Roy. The operations, which in late 2003 employed nearly 12,000 people, brought in scale and gave stability to the industry. The GE venture did more. "What we were able to demonstrate in GE was that it was not just back office but front office jobs, direct customer contacts, that also could be done out of India. In the process we pioneered voice, the call centre. This was penetrating into the mass area. There are millions and millions of requirements on voice and that is what allowed it to grow dramatically. In GE we simultaneously tested out some very high end services. To my mind this was incredibly successful."

VALUE CHAIN

Arun Seth of BT recalls how things began with the simplest processes, data entry, which was also what medical transcription was when the processing and analysis used to be done elsewhere. Then came rule based processing which involved the application of very simple rules. The next process was direct customer service where a customer calls in with a problem, for example when your computer breaks down. There can be a first level or a second level problem and the interaction can also be through the chat mode on the computer. In this there is a process but no rules. The next step was a little more complex decision making, risk analysis. It can have to do with insurance, debt management, credit card. And finally, at the highest level, to do a full sales process, you need very highly trained skills in specific domains.

The benefit of going up the value chain is not, however, an unambiguous one. Processes higher up the value chain earn higher revenue rates but do not necessarily yield higher revenues overall because of paucity of volume. Hence it is the conscious decision of many players aspiring to become big time to concentrate on high volume low unit value realisation work. Says Ganesh, "We focus on customer impacting processes. At one end of the value chain is data entry, back office processes. At the other end is telemarketing, tele sales, cross selling. We do multiple processes. Not everyone is at the high end of the value chain as that requires more investment in capabilities and infrastructure. The three main segments are back office processing work, passive customer support and customer impacting. We play across all the three segments. The lower end helps us utilise capacity. But typically 60–70 per cent of our business comes from high end work. Lower end work is not to be frowned upon. It depends on your focus, how profitable your operations are. For example, there are companies in Ireland that simply put letters in envelopes and post them and they do that very well. It is extremely profitable for them. You need to choose your segment. People are going up the value chain but there are clear cut good business models available even at the lower end of the value chain as long as you can handle the work consistently."

So the greatest priority, even beyond going up the value chain, is to master the complexities of upscaling. BPO is for the most part a volume game and success lies in being able to upscale while retaining quality. Says Ganesh, "BPO is a very manpower-intensive work. Software is project based, this is transaction processing—10,000 people receiving a million calls a month. It is huge. Handling this scale is the biggest challenge." BPO agents, those that man a position, in India have to work on US and UK processes. Most have never travelled to those countries, the culture is alien and they cannot understand the slang and jargon. At the corporate level, there is a need to understand the quality processes prevalent in the customer companies. "The contradiction is that they don't have our people quality and we don't have their process quality. The challenge before Indian BPO companies is to adopt the meticulousness in systems and processes of their customer companies."

The cardinal need to ensure quality has led the way to certain innovations. Nasscom is working with industry leaders to evolve quality parameters as these do not exist for some BPO operations (call centre work is however well established) which are still evolving globally. The emphasis on quality stems from the fact that in the absence of guaranteed quality standards, the only selling point will be price and premiums will never be earned. Nasscom's emphasis on quality is the result of lessons learnt from software. More than 50 per cent of the software companies that have achieved the highest quality standards, SEI CMM level 4 or 5, are Indian. Says Seth, "At the end of the day people should feel comfortable giving their work to you at long distance. In Nasscom we are evaluating all the standards available and are pushing three or four standards—COPC, Carnegie Mellon, ISO—and telling all our constituents, for heaven's sake pick up a standard or two and implement them. That is the only thing which will prevent what you are offering from becoming a commodity."

STRENGTHS AND CHALLENGES

In fact, what can emerge in BPO, is similar to what has happened in software. In software, the most successful companies are large, handle not very exalted work in large volumes, while ensuring quality. This combination of scalability and quality is what creates entry barriers for challengers and gives entrenched firms the competitive advantage. To begin with, there have to be some initial competencies and facilitating factors. The initial competencies for India are the same as those that have aided its success in software—cheap skills and knowledge of English. But there is an additionality that makes for particular success in BPO which Ganesh attributes to certain cultural factors. "Our education system and emphasis on education gears us for office, rather than manufacturing jobs. I am addressing the mindset of our people which enables us to score in this field. Culturally, we feel that the best job is in an airconditioned office in front of a computer. It is this mindset that makes a BPO job a career of choice and brings to it people with better skills. In contrast, in the US a BPO job is a temporary one, in between other preoccupations and one of the last options."

However, along with these advantages, certain critical factors and facilitators are needed. Gurbaxani outlines the following. First is infrastructure, key utilities like power and bandwidth. Both are available but not reliable. Building in redundancies to improve reliability adds to costs, which competitors from other countries may not have to worry about. Second is technology. It is critical but fortunately, with global vendors selling it to everyone, it is taken care of. Ten years ago, buying the latest hardware and software in India would have been difficult and probably prohibitively costly. Third is some level of domain expertise. And fourth is the ability to deliver quality on a consistent basis.

AN INITIAL FAILURE

To get a measure of how Indian BPO firms are faring, giving their initial advantages and the enabling factors needed for them to succeed, let us first look at an initial failure and then a few successes. The most spectacular setback has been in the field of medical transcription. Arun Seth sees it as the failure to avoid the pitfall of becoming commoditised. Too many units mushroomed, all competing on price. Their sheer numbers prevented operations of scale, without which standards could not be delivered.

A first hand victim of both success and failure was Veer Sagar. He recalls how there was a wave in 1997 with any number of people getting into medical transcription. "Overnight a new industry was born and everybody made the same mistake as we were all clones of each other." He recalls ruefully how he was initially paying students to teach them the job and his first contract with a US hospital offered him 50 per cent of the first year's revenue as an advance. The division of labour was—the US company would look after marketing and customer support and Sagar's Indian operations would take care of production, quality and training. Then, after one year, when Sagar had built up an international delivery capability, they parted company and from doing one million lines a month it came down to zero. The absence of marketing capability did his business in. Same was the case with others who suffered a similar fate. He is back in business for the second time and again breaking even, with the same marketing deficiency but not dependent on any one client.

This is a cautionary tale—pointing out the inherent dangers and not the entire picture. As we have narrated earlier, the captive BPO operations of global companies in India stretch back a decade and the most high profile company to join the band in 2001 was Dell. A new group of companies setting up BPO operations in India are well established BPO companies in the mature economies. Convergys, one such company, has announced plans for India operations. But the most important group of companies from the point of view of the Indian economy, since they will retain the maximum value in India, are the mushrooming Indian BPO firms (Chart 4.2). Some of the over half a dozen serious players among them have already been referred to earlier. Spectramind, set up by Raman Roy who helped set up the Amex and GE operations, is among the front runners. It first secured a key investment from software front runner Wipro and was thereafter acquired by it. Customer.Asset, promoted by Ganesh, was subsequently taken over by ICICI OneSource. 24/7Customer.com has sound business plans which place adequate emphasis on upscaling and quality. Daksh, headed by Sanjeev Agarwal, also lays store by large volume customer centric work. It is from among these and a few others that winners like TCS, Infosys and Wipro will emerge in BPO services.

Chart 4.2

Ranking of Third Party (Call Center and BPO) Players (2002–03)

Rank	Company
1.	Wipro Spectramind
2.	WNS Group
3.	Daksh e-Services Pvt Ltd
4.	ExlService (I) PVT Ltd
5.	HCL Technologies BPO Services Ltd
6.	Convergys India Services Pvt Ltd
7.	GTL Ltd
8.	MsourcE India Pvt Ltd
9.	Hinduja TMT Ltd
10.	ICICI OneSource Limited
11.	Sutherland Technologies Pvt Ltd
12.	Epicenter Technologies Pvt Ltd
13.	Zenta Technologies
14.	24/7 Customer
15.	Datamatics Technologies Ltd

Source: NASSCOM

One reason why the first decade of this century may turn out for India to be the decade of BPO, in the way the nineties was the decade of software, is the progress that had already been made by 2001. *Businessworld*, which tracks emerging industries, plots a part of what is happening in the area. There seems to be an equal mix of both high end and volume end work. This means that first, enough volume is being generated to give the sector size and importance. Second, the high end work being done by BPO operations in India indicates that the industry has the ability to undertake more and sophisticated work and has the ability to keep growing and improving margins. EXL Service in Noida handles insurance claims processing for its parent Conesco, a US insurance major. This is as complex and sophisticated as you can get in the business. Conesco eventually plans to shift 3,000 jobs from Indiana to India. eServe International, which is partly owned by Citibank, by end-2001 had 2,700 employees in nine cities serving Citibank operations in 23 countries, processing 70 million transactions and 20 million customer interactions a year. IndiaLife Hewitt manages payrolls for 270 companies and in 2002 will handle the payrolls of an MNC which operates out of ten countries in the Asia-Pacific region. eFunds serves several clients in financial services, including Deluxe, the largest cheque book printer in the US. Importantly, most of the leading big four among global consultancy firms are seriously into BPO work in India. PricewaterhouseCoopers, now part of IBM, employs dozens of consultants advising MNCs in a range of industries on BPO from India. Accenture, the consulting arm of the former conglomerate Arthur Andersen, has a full fledged BPO team in place in India. Ernst and Young has a medium size operation processing the filing of tax returns.

Till 2001 there was a preponderance of MNCs and those in partnership with them in BPO operations in India. This is natural as outsourcing of entire areas of operations of companies—a company, in effect, franchises out a part of itself, putting in play its own name—is a decision of major consequence to any company. Employees of another company will be fronting for a company whose customers and associates will not even know that they are dealing with a third party. It puts the highest premium on standardisation of operations and confidentiality. This is why the migration operation which gets a BPO process going, can take upto a year and explains why purely Indian firms working for overseas customers are slower off the block.

The key ingredients for success are command over the language (in India's case English), basic technical knowledge and capability over your customer's business area. Raman Roy terms them as "trainable constraints" as the raw material, learning skills available in India, are "trainable". Once these are delivered, the confidentiality that any corporate player will insist upon, is not a constraint. There are massive outsourcing organisations in the US and "confidentiality concerns are the same with us as with them." What is critical to him is the trainers. The amount you need to invest in training determines your costs and competitiveness. "If we retooled as an industry and a country, that will minimise my investment and make me more competitive." To that is linked the main challenge, the ability to deliver. "This is where the captive units of MNCs have demonstrated something and we have to take it from there."

Just as there was a herd mentality to get into software in the last decade, the same has happened in the present one over BPO. Just as there has been a shakeout now in software, a shakeout and consolidation have also begun in BPO services. This is happening as the sector realises that it is for the most part a volume business in which size matters. Long-term goals for BPO are no different from those in software—vertical specialisation based on domain knowledge and ultimately successful brands. By end-2001, some *Fortune 500* companies had begun looking at India for BPO possibilities and it is *Fortune 500* companies that can give business volumes which can enable the industry to arrive. *Fortune 500* companies with their Y2K programmes played a key role in the successful progress of Indian software. By end-2003, barely a day passed without one global company or another announcing its decision to outsource to India.

By 2003–04 around 245,000 people were working in India at the volume end of the business, compared to 4 million in the US. A million workforce by 2008, at 75 per cent utilisation and billed at $20,000 per head per year works out to $20 billion revenue for the industry. Important as this is in itself, it has two catalytic effects. One, every direct job creates three indirect ones which have a direct employment impact and a multiplier effect on incomes in general. The BPO sector has given a tremendous boost to the real estate, catering and transport sectors in cities like Delhi and Bangalore. What is more, the international skills generated by BPO raise the skill level in the entire economy which eventually leads to better skills and processes in domestic business as a whole. By being the back and front office for the most competitive companies in the world, the businesses whose corporate offices are in India, that is Indian businesses, get to have better back and front offices. This is plausible, because BPO work involves very large numbers.

Thus, to sum up, the same skills that gave the software advantage have also given the BPO advantage, but success in BPO can transform and modernise the entire Indian economy by giving it a range of international best practices.

Global Chemist

5

India's pharmaceutical sector is the next most globally competitive, after its software and services sector. Indian pharmaceutical exports account for over one per cent of global pharmaceutical exports, compared to overall exports accounting for less than one per cent of global exports. By exporting a third of its output, the pharmaceutical sector scores better than most others, but naturally remains behind software in which 80 per cent of the output is exported. In keeping with the pattern in any globally successful sector, its leading players export a substantial portion of their output. And the lead is taken by Ranbaxy Laboratories whose non-Indian sales exceed its Indian sales.

Indian pharmaceutical companies first made their mark internationally by being able to produce bulk drugs cheaply and of acceptable quality. Then they moved into formulations. Thereafter they sought to create some intellectual property by chalking out a few successes in the fields of novel drug delivery and non-infringing processes. Simultaneously, India became a centre for generic companies in developed economies to develop, test, manufacture and package generic products for the developed markets. An alternative route was to custom synthesise, develop and produce a molecule on a contract basis for a company to carry out clinical trials. This also involved creating some intellectual property. And most recently, the leading companies have ventured out actively in to new drug discovery. J M Khanna, president of research and development in Ranbaxy, recalls the changes over the years thus, "In the fifties, we were importing everything, in the sixties we started making the dosage form, with the active ingredients coming from outside. In the seventies, we started making our own active ingredients. We excelled in this in the eighties and started exporting the active ingredients, dosage as well as bulk. These exports were initially to the developing countries and thereafter to the developed markets actively in the nineties."

This steady climb up the value chain indicates that the basis of competitiveness, which was initially cost, has changed over the years. The lowest cost rung has already been vacated in favour of China, says R Ananthanarayanan, managing director of Galpharm India, the Indian operation of the British generics firm. He cites the following 2001 costs for paracetamol: US $3.5 per kg, India $2.80–3.10 per kg and China $1.8–2 per kg. According to him, India is still managing to export because of consistency in quality and supply. According to Chaitanya Dutt, director of research and development in Torrent Pharmaceuticals, "We started off with cost as our principal strength but now we are acquiring the expertise to develop unique formulations or value added formulations. As a country we have the strength to produce a good generic and maybe a good formulation which is not necessarily a copy generic."

The journey up the value chain involves various steps and routes. Srinivas Lanka, a director of Aurobindo Pharma, outlines them thus. "The model is by and large similar for all companies, with a difference only in focus. A beginner first looks at being a supplier to top companies for products that are going to go off patent. Second, once you succeed, you try to sell your bulk drug to several companies. Third, you develop a formulation based on the technological support of a company in a regulated market. Fourth, you develop your own formulation. At the next higher level, you try to evolve a non-infringing process, thereby getting an exclusivity and an oligopolistic marketing situation for six months and reaping high margins. At the next level, you become a custom synthesis company. An MNC with a drug model wanting to concentrate on R&D and not the brick and mortar stuff, can determine you have the competence and ask you to manufacture it. Then you synthesise the molecule on a contract, find the best process, do all impurities, develop the characterisations and produce a few kilos for worldwide trials. In this process you develop a sort of intellectual property."

HISTORICAL CATALYSTS

What were the historical catalysts that facilitated this process and what strengths did the sector build on? Interestingly, unlike the element of happenstance that marked the emergence of Indian expertise and competitiveness in software, the progress in pharmaceuticals was almost wholly policy led. First, came the Indian Patents Act of 1970 which recognised process patents and not product patents. This, along with the drug price control order which severely controlled the prices of a range of essential drugs, prompted the then nascent Indian industry to reverse engineer or copy patented products available world wide and also supply them at minimal costs. While the patent regime provided the means to manufacture the drugs in India, the price control regime inculcated in the sector a severe cost control discipline on which its entire survival depended.

Dutt says that the change in the patent law laid open the field of chemistry, giving rise to a lot of innovations and helping companies like Ranbaxy, Dr Reddy's and Cipla acquire an expertise in process chemistry. "The other strength which developed parallelly was in pharmaceutics, converting the chemistry into dosage form. Then in the late eighties came what is called the 'schedule Y', laying down the rules for testing and clearing the introduction of new drugs, imported or domestically produced. This forced the pharmaceutical companies to get their pharmacological or clinical act together so as to conduct proper bio-equivalence and clinical trials. So chemistry strength was followed by pharmaceutical strength which was in turn followed by pharmacological strength."

The next policy change that catalysed the industry was the new economic policies initiated in 1991, one of the first steps under which was a drastic devaluation of the rupee. This made exports profitable and prompted the Indian industry to look outward. But by far the biggest change came over the next few years during which it became clear that India would fall in line with the international patent regime and recognise product patents. The final seal was put with the signing of the TRIPS agreement as part of the Uruguay round in 1994. Well before this, the leading Indian pharmaceutical companies had decided to set their eyes on the highest and most sophisticated level of activity, original drug discovery, which would lead to the acquisition of intellectual property. Thus what started in the early seventies with reverse engineering or copying, culminated in discarding the crutch of other people's knowledge and seeking one's own, made possible by remarkable growth and development in sophistication.

GENERICS

The global competitiveness exists foremost in the generic (off patent) field. "In this, I think we are second to none. I would say the world is looking towards India for more and more generics," says Dutt. Within generics, it is in bulk drugs that India's core competence currently lies. "Bulk production is difficult in highly regulated markets because of environment, safety and technology management reasons," says Lanka. "So the entire bulk drugs industry has to move to countries like ours where technology is available and costs are reasonable. Even God cannot stop the migration of bulk drug manufacturing to countries like India and China," he adds.

Today, around 15–18 generic substitutes are ready when a drug goes off patent in the US. Around 20–25 per cent of these approvals are secured by Indian companies. And in the "vitamins and minerals field, Indian performance is perhaps the best in the world in terms of both quality and cost," says

Ananthnarayana (Charts 5.1 and 5.2). A similar view is held by J De Souza, the Indian general manager of Pliva, the Croatia-based generics company which is the largest player in its field in Europe. India has "world class manufacturing facilities" which have secured regulatory approval from the most advanced countries. These facilities produce "excellent products comparable to the highest international standards," he says.

Echoing the same perceptions, Khanna adds, "reengineering strengths are very good in the pharma industry. The top 10–20 companies have strong chemistry expertise in bulk drugs. They can synthesise any molecule today in a short period. Their chemistry is very cost effective and they know how to scale up. The second strength of the pharma industry is in the conventional forms like tablets, suspensions, liquids, and capsules. These two areas are the backbone of the whole industry. Plus around ten companies have acquired manufacturing facilities which have been approved by the US FDA. The immediate opportunity for the industry is, we have built reengineering and generic capabilities, so let's not limit to only India which is a market of $3 billion (2001). The US market is of $12 billion and the global market is of $40–50 billion. Prices in other countries are higher than in India and by entering their generic markets we can learn to do business there, become familiar with their regulatory requirements."

DR REDDY'S

One of the early successes in bulk drugs was the group of companies that have now all come under the banner of Dr Reddy's Laboratories. It was started in the year 1984 by Anji Reddy, a PhD in chemical engineering who worked with the pilot plant group of Indian Drugs and Pharmaceuticals Ltd, the mother institution for the Indian pharmaceuticals industry. Acknowledging its role, Dr Reddy says, "It is IDPL which gave a thrust to the indigenous efforts in the early seventies." Dr Reddy's and sister company Cheminor Drugs both started off in manufacturing active pharmaceutical ingredients or bulk drugs. Satish Reddy, chief operating officer of Dr Reddy's, recalls that the company started by producing the bulk drug methyldopa, supplying it to the MNC Merck through the Indian company Merind. "Our advantage was strong process development skills which still continues to be the core strength of the company. It is through this that we lower the cost of the drugs."

The folklore in Dr Reddy's is full of stories about the quality of its products. The company sent a sample of its product to Merind and to their surprise, it was purer than their own product. In multinationals, anything deviating from the specs causes concern. They asked if the company could supply something which was closer to their specifications and Anji Reddy's reply was, you are

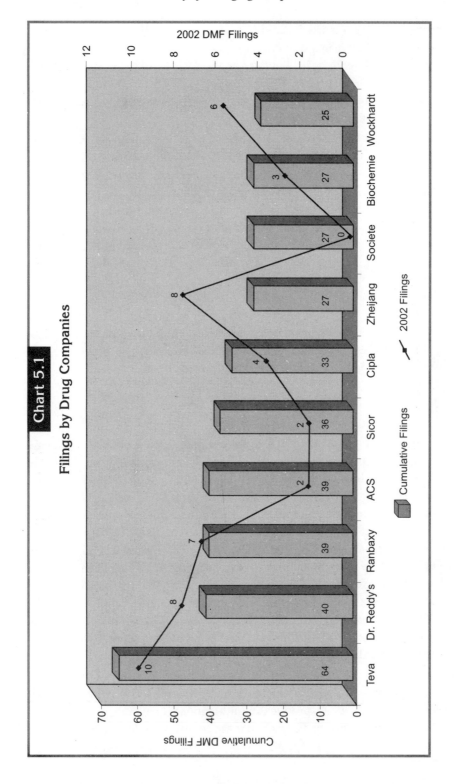

Chart 5.1

Filings by Drug Companies

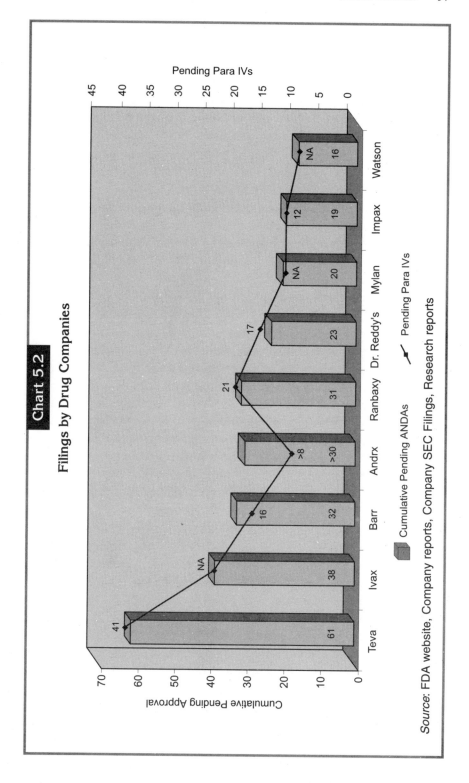

Chart 5.2

Filings by Drug Companies

Source: FDA website, Company reports, Company SEC Filings, Research reports

asking me to add impurities. So the company started off with very high quality standards even while making its products available at a low cost. The next product of the company was ibuprofen. Within two years of existence the company secured US FDA certification of its facilities. This opened up the US market for substantial supplies of the company's products and "other bulk active exporters from Japan and Italy for those products were wiped out of the market and had to down shutters," says Satish Reddy.

One of the major successes of Dr Reddy's was the manufacture of ciprofloxacin, which was in the news in the year 2001 as the cure for anthrax that was in the armory of terrorists attacking the US. When it was imported from Korea, high cost, import duty and formulation margin led to cipro tablets being marketed at Rs 30 per tablet in 1989. Once Dr Reddy's entered the picture and made available the bulk drug to Indian formulators, the price crashed. In the year 2001, during the anthrax scare, it was selling in India at Rs 4 per tablet. Volumes multiplied after prices came down. "Ciprofloxacin was what really made the company," recalls Satish Reddy.

Dr Reddy's entered the formulations business within three years' of inception and although marginal players initially, grew on the strength of being able to bring new products into the market. The story of ciprofloxacin was repeated with norfloxacin, whose price came down from Rs 8 to Rs 3.75 through Dr Reddy's entry. Products were launched in India within a year of their global launch. "Our business model was that we supply a formulation in the Indian market and also provide the bulk drug to all other Indian formulators so that they could also compete in the market at similar prices. This helped us improve our market share rapidly," recalls Reddy. Cheminor over the same period restricted itself to off patent bulk drugs which were exported to developed countries. The business was profitable because Cheminor had dedicated customers among US generics companies.

This state of affairs continued till 1992 when the impact of liberalisation saw the entry of many new players, leading to a squeezing of margins. Smaller, almost single product companies got in, their entry smoothened by the stock market boom of 1993–94. "All that the market needed to be told was that you were a bulk drugs manufacturer from Hyderabad and cash was yours." As this was not a very capital intensive business, almost anybody got in. By the turn of the century many of these ventures were sick. The likes of Dr Reddy's were caught in a dilemma of their own making. They came into their own, because of the laxity in intellectual property protection. But their own margins were under attack because of the absence of protection of *their* intellectual property.

To overcome this, the company decided to reduce its dependence on bulk drugs and get vigorously into formulations. The company, which was number 48 in formulations in 1993–94, decided to build a strong franchise in it. By

1999 it had become number 5 in India in formulations. While using its strength in launching new products quickly, the company began to focus on therapeutic areas. A greater marketing focus led the company to concentrate more on gaps in therapy and build offerings around them. The push to build market share led to the acquisition of brands. This was a period of rapid growth and in 1999 the first acquisition was made, of American Remedies. A new emphasis was also laid on developing non-infringing process routes to add to the company's intellectual property. Then in 2001, all the groups companies were merged with Dr Reddy's and it became the fourth largest pharmaceutical company in the country.

NEW DRUG DISCOVERY

In the early nineties, the major Indian pharma companies, particularly the top two, Ranbaxy and Dr Reddy's, took a major far-sighted decision. Led by Parvinder Singh and Anji Reddy, respectively, they shifted from lobbying to retain India's lax patents regime to arming their companies with a new vision. Ranbaxy adopted a mission statement in 1992 to become an international research based pharmaceutical company and Reddy went round the country saying that it was possible to do original drug discovery work in India. He told the Indian Pharmaceutical Congress in Bangalore in 1993, "The issue before us is not whether to accept the patent regime but a question of when it will be accepted .... The Indian industry ... must make a beginning at new molecular invention. Drug discovery and development in these (developed) countries is estimated to cost between $100–200 million. It is my considered opinion that in the Indian context such an endeavour may be accomplished within a cost of Rs 100 million." This categorical statement, that Indians can do research, and also discover drugs, was met with a lot of scepticism.

Reddy put his money where his mouth was. His was the first company to set up a basic research facility in the private sector. Dr Reddy's Foundation started operations in 1993 as the discovery arm of the company and in 1997 it had its first breakthrough by outlicensing a new molecule to Novo Nordisk in return for upfront and milestone payments. The facilities were set up at a cost of Rs 20 crore and at the turn of the century the annual expenditure was Rs 25 crore. It employed 227 people, of whom 36 were PhDs. Dr Reddy's spends around 6–7 per cent of its revenue on R&D expenditure, in line with other top bracket Indian companies. But this is a far cry from the 15–18 per cent that global pharmaceutical companies from the first world spend. The conceptual breakthrough that Reddy made was to demonstrate that basic drug discovery was possible at far lower budgets in India than the hundreds of millions that drug MNCs traditionally utilise (Chart 5.3).

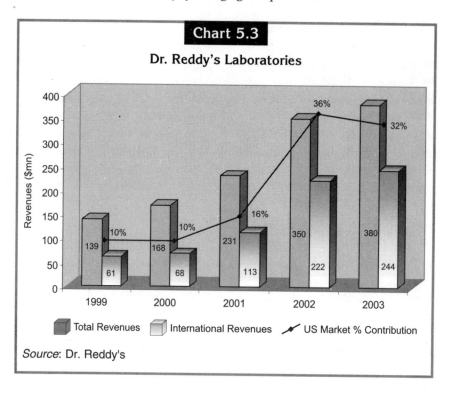

Chart 5.3

Dr. Reddy's Laboratories

Source: Dr. Reddy's

What is his model or the low cost emerging India model? It consists of three elements:

- low cost,
- high productivity and
- selective action.

In research, manpower costs are the most important. Indian competitiveness lies in first having a large pool of trained scientific manpower and second, being able to access it at a fraction of developed economy costs. A PhD degree holder in the US could cost a company $100,000 a year, whereas the same could be accessed in India at a tenth of the sum. As a result of the efforts of Dr Reddy's and Ranbaxy a reverse brain drain of sorts has also started whereby they have been able to relocate in India, key scientific personnel of Indian origin for working with them. Such scientists have been present in the developed economies for decades and constitute an exploitable talent pool.

The second element is productivity. Scientific talent being cheaper, Indian companies are able to get a bigger bang for their buck spent on R&D. Satish Reddy refers to a study in *Script*, a trade publication. It measured the number of patents filed for every $10 million of research spend. For large pharmaceutical companies it is high, i.e., around nine patents; for average companies it is 2.7 patents; and for India it is 21 patents. The third element is selective action. Only one-third of the cost of discovering a new drug, developing it and bringing it to market is accounted for by the basic research part that synthesises a molecule and establishes the proof of concept. It is the clinical trials that come thereafter and the ultimate marketing that accounts the major part of the cost. Significantly, the highest amount of intellectual input and most of the intellectual property creation takes place at the research level itself and this is where Indian companies are the most cost effective.

It is on the basis of this entire argument that Anji Reddy was able to foresee an Indian capability in original drug discovery. In 1997, when Dr Reddy's had limited financial resources, it licenced out its discovery. By 2001, it was going up the value chain. With the proceeds of its American depository receipts, it proposes to undertake the first stage of clinical trials, establishing proof of concept in humans. "Once one of our products reaches the market, post-2004 and we get significant income from discovery, we have intentions of taking a drug all the way through the development stage," says Satish Reddy.

RANBAXY

Ranbaxy Laboratories is another leading Indian company which has actively undertaken new drug discovery and proposes to have this as its future focus. It began its drug discovery work in 1994 and is currently working on a BPH (benign prostrate hypertrophy) product which should be in the market by 2005. But there are several other strands in its effort to acquire intellectual property and convert itself into a research based company. Along with its drug discovery effort, it has also initiated its own clinical research programme. Their experience is that doing it in house is not only cheaper but also quicker. Another IP area, in which it is a leader in India, is devising novel drug delivery systems which also started in 1994. In 1999 it licensed the novel drug delivery system for ciprofloxacin to Bayer. "We have built up this capacity in the last 5–6 years and are bringing one product to the market every year. This is a medium term strategy and we are doing this work exclusively and have got international fame," says Dr Khanna.

But Ranbaxy's major strength, like that of Dr Reddy's, is in generics. It was the first Indian company to enter the US, in the mid-nineties and had in half a decade built up a basket of 40 approved products. But even before that it was able to enter into a supply agreement with Eli Lily in 1992 for its generic cefaclo. This proved to be a great money spinner for it, just the way ciprofloxacin was for Dr Reddy's. Along with novel drug delivery systems,

Ranbaxy has also taken the route of developing non-infringing processes which give it six months' exclusivity on its generic substitute after a patent has expired.

But even more than the generics business, what has marked out Ranbaxy among Indian companies is its conscious and aggressive decision to go international and thereby increasing its global competitiveness. D.S. Brar, managing director of Ranbaxy, says that "at the heart of the (internationalisation process) is brand building." As building individual brands in individual markets is time consuming and expensive, Ranbaxy believes that "building the corporate identity as a brand is the best, most intelligent way to leverage your presence in international markets. We have built this blue R brand. It is our endeavour that this blue R packaging will be in every single drug store in the US. We have centralised R&D, semi-centralised manufacturing and totally decentralised sales, marketing and distribution."

It rationalised its corporate structure in 1994 by creating a holding company for its 25 subsidiaries worldwide. It has paid particular attention to the US market where, it has, by far, the best marketing setup among Indian companies and projects its US sales to overtake Indian sales by 2003 (Chart 5.4).

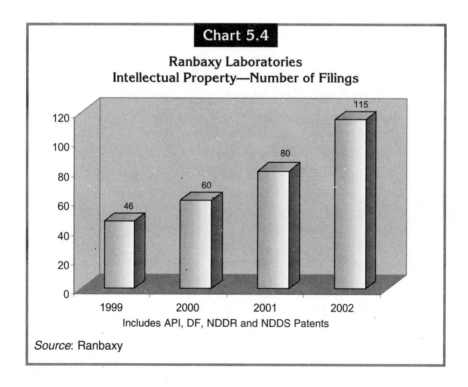

Chart 5.4

**Ranbaxy Laboratories
Intellectual Property—Number of Filings**

Includes API, DF, NDDR and NDDS Patents

Source: Ranbaxy

CROs

From the foregoing, it is clear that the only area in drug development, from bulk drugs to patented products, in which India has not yet achieved global competitiveness, is clinical research (testing drugs on humans). But this is also changing. India is well on its way to emerging as a very attractive place to conduct clinical research and contract research organisations (CROs) which conduct such research for others are sprouting in India. Successful Indian CROs are growing rapidly and with time, hope to go up the value chain.

Most Indian CROs are currently only into bio-equivalence studies (clinically testing a new generic product to see if its attributes matched those of the patented original) but a few have also gone into testing and developing new drugs and others are planning to follow suit. That's where higher value addition lies.

Clinical research began rolling in India when the international contract research organisation, Quintiles, set up shop in 1997. While the bio-equivalence end of the market, which it describes as the low-margin commodity end, has been peopled by Indian CROs, Quintiles has concentrated on research and development of new entities. All its 30-odd clients were initially international ones and the first Indian client was signed up in 2001. Quintiles has been associated with the development work on many high profile global products going on in India, its USP being its own international standards and the fact that it costs a third of global levels to develop a drug in India. By including India in the development of a drug that is to be globally marketed, the whole development process is speeded up. This is because of the size of the patient pool in India and middle class Indians, who make up a fair number by international standards, having acquired the typical disease profile of an advanced society.

Speeding up of research and testing has a huge bottomline implication. The patent clock starts ticking from the day the application is filed, so a year saved on bringing to the market a billion dollar drug means a billion dollars more in sales. Says Farzaan Engineer, managing director of Quintiles Spectral (India), "In this business international quality is the cost of entry. We wouldn't have lasted if we didn't have it. Doing work here is globally competitive, emphatically so. Slowly, the research infrastructure is improving so that pockets of excellence are being created and Indian research is getting globally integrated."

Among the more dynamic Indian CROs is Lambda Therapeutic Research which began in 1999. Nearly 70 per cent of its orders come from overseas and the company is planning to expand from bio-equivalence study to clinical research in which the margins are much higher. Lambda is growing successfully because its quality is acceptable and its costs are 50 per cent of the US benchmark. According to Ashish Dasgupta, one of the two founding directors of Lambda, "Indian CROs can be very competitive but must not be complacent. The global market has a lot of expectations from India."

The views of CROs operating out of India are echoed by their customers, those who outsource research and testing to India. J De Souza of Pliva, an important user of India research, also points to the winning combination of low manpower costs, easy availability of volunteers and large patient pools. Contract research is progressing both in industry and academia. A good part of drug research in India is conducted by the foreign companies themselves, through their Indian subsidiaries. Ivax India Pvt Ltd is part of the American generics Ivax group. The Indian subsidiary supports the parent's product development to bring out generic substitutes for drugs going off patent and also develops complete dossiers which the parent uses to apply for the generic's clearance. Dr Parizad A Elchidana, director of health and product development of the Indian subsidiary, indicates the progress that has been made in India when she says that the next step for them is to have a pilot plant. Once that is set up, the products can be developed in house right till the stage that they can be passed on to the manufacturing licensees.

Some British companies have gone one step further in India. Not only are they developing, testing and manufacturing their products for sale in the UK, even the packaging and printing is being done in India. As one industry expect points out, the entire range of pharma services for generic products, conforming to global cost and quality standards—bulk drugs, product development, manufacturing and now clinical research—is on offer from India. Says Ananthanarayanan of Galpharm India, "the US is about two and a half years behind the UK in outsourcing. As the UK is already here (2001), the next two to three years are likely to be very exciting for Indian companies ready and willing to walk in step with global practices."

CROs in India are engaged not just in clinical research but in the entire range of drug related services from contract research (devising the chemistry), to custom synthesising (making the first few kilos of the drug), to contract manufacturing (producing large quantities of it). There is a global rush to introduce fresh products into the market. This is because a whole host of patented blockbusters are in the process of going off patent. This creates an opportunity for generic players who are rushing in with substitutes. Furthermore, the IP strong companies have a whole lot of new molecules with which they seek to replace their blockbusters of yore. And India is emerging as a key cost effective place where the entire range of drug development can be done by CROs specialising in various parts of the whole process. Says P Hari in *Businessworld*, "One of the best things about chemical services in India is the extraordinary low cost at each step, all the way up to manufacturing." The Indian strength in process chemistry and increasingly drug discovery is enabling these companies to take a molecule from the proof of concept stage to actually synthesising it and then making larger and larger quantities of it needed as the drug progresses through the various stages of clinical trials.

Even a company like Dr Reddy's which is a full range pharmaceutical company is trying to double up as a CRO. In 2001 it started work on custom synthesis, contract research and drug discovery services. It set up a new company, Aurigene, in Bangalore for drug discovery work. Says Satish Reddy, "Custom synthesis gives us a strategic advantage. It builds relationships with innovator companies and makes us the preferred partner for outsourcing." Syngene, part of the Bangalore-based Biocon biotechnology group, was perhaps the first drug research, as opposed to drug development, company to get off the block in India in 1994. The next year Baroda-based Rubamin started a division for drug services division and Kolkata-based Chembiotech began in 2001 with its scope covering the entire range of drug research work.

So, the seed sowed by IDPL in Hyderabad four decades ago has made India an accomplished player in every branch of the pharmaceuticals business, not just in manufacturing but also development and finally research or drug discovery. Because of the high quality and low cost of scientific skills, Indian companies are contracting work in every sphere. What they do not have is size. In contract research and services size is immaterial; in fact innovator companies are typically small, techno-entrepreneur run businesses.

The small size of the larger Indian companies is the result of two reasons. One is the poor growth of business in general in India through the entire period of planning. Two, the government of India has kept Indian drug prices among the lowest in the world for the better part of four decades. This has made Indian drug companies very cost competitive globally. This low cost manufacturing culture plus the low cost supply of scientific skills makes for global competitiveness. Indian software skills are now globally known; the Indian software brand has arrived. The Indian pharma brand is nowhere near as well known globally but is likely to be in a few years.

6

Germinating Competence

India's success in software and pharmaceuticals has kindled expectations that the next frontier of biotechnology will also be conquered. The logic is simple and appealing. Firstly, there is at present, a familiar Indian proficiency in scientific skills; secondly, there are the big strides taken in basic research in biotechnology and thirdly, there is the way in which the discipline has changed in the last few years. The future of biotechnology is being rewritten with the onset of genetic mapping and the primary tool that powers this new era is bioinformatics. Since India has a proven competency in information technology, a competitive edge in biotechnology is within reach via the bioinformatics route.

Unlike software, biotechnology has had direct government support right from day one. The department of biotechnology was set up way back in 1986. Through these years around a score of government funded laboratories, both under the department and the Council of Scientific and Industrial Research, have taken basic research in biotechnology to internationally noticed levels. So while software began only with trained manpower, the biotechnology odyssey has a scientific research base to go with it. All this should make success in biotechnology only a factor of time. But global competitiveness remains a somewhat open ended potential. A long way remains to be covered and not everyone can say with certitude that it will be.

The stakes have been piled up high—both because of the central government investment already sunk in basic research and also because of the most progressive state governments developing a stake in the area. Karnataka, Andhra Pradesh and Maharashtra have announced the setting up of biotechnology parks. Several other states have adopted biotechnology initiatives which will probably culminate in the setting up of parks. Further, the discipline has an enormous developmental role in a poor and predominantly agricultural country like India. Its nutritional health and environmental sustenance are closely linked to achieving a minimum capability in biotechnology. Against this imperative, what analysts are willing to readily grant is that biotechnology has become a buzz, if not a vogue. The ambiguities begin right from the basics—marking out the perimeter of the industry without which there can be no clear picture of its size.

DEFINING BIOTECHNOLOGY

The broad definition of biotechnology includes anything that deals with living things. It covers conventional areas like fermentation, brewing and even bio-fertilisers. By this definition the Indian biotechnology industry has a turnover of $2.5 billion (Rs 12,000 crore; Chart 6.1). On the other hand, the turnover of the new biotechnology sector, that which deals with the manipulation of genes and bioinformatics, accounts for less than $100 million (Rs 500 crore). And what is more, it is not expected to grow at the 50 per cent plus rate of IT enabled services. The Association of Biotechnology Led Enterprises, using a comprehensive definition, estimated that the industry which clocked Rs 2,345 crore turnover in 2002–03 (revised), grew by 39 per cent in 2003–04 to reach Rs 3,265 crore.* But global experts are constantly surprised by the level of energy that the Indian biotechnology industry displays and strongly affirm its initial advantages. India is readily considered an emerging player in the industry along with countries like Korea, China, Australia and Israel.

Dr John Fagan, CEO of Genetic ID, an American company at the forefront of identification of genetically modified objects, describes the whole biotechnology spectrum thus, "At one end it is high tech—dealing with genomics, pharmacological drug discovery, transgenic crop development. At the other end are biopesticides, biofertilisers, composting, enzymes, control agents. In between you have the marker directed breeding. So, biotechnology stretches from high end genomics to agriculture itself. Companies in India are using cell culture to generate elite varieties of crops, virus free propagation materials, biofertilisers and biopesticides. These technologies yield products with a horizon of not 7–12 years but 6–18 months whose market already exists. The gestation period for providing enzymes for food and textiles and brewing is shorter and regulation lower than in pharma. Biotechnology does not need to be flashy or high tech. There are intermediate values of it. There are systems for composting that can convert a wide range of bio-mass into very valuable fertilisers. You can also produce in six months beneficial insects in insectories that attack pests".

---

* *BioSpectrum*

Chart 6.1

Top 20 Biotechnology Companies
2003–04 Biotechnology Sales
(in Rupees crores)

Rank	Company	Sales
1.	Biocon	502
2.	Serum Institute of India	491
3.	Panacea Biotec	149
4.	Nicholas Piramal	130
5.	Novo Nordisk	110
6.	Venkateshwara Hatcheries	88
7.	Wockhardt	84
8.	GlaxoSmithKline	80
9.	Bharat Serum	79.7
10.	Eli Lilly	76.4
11.	Novozymes	65
12.	Quintiles Spectral	62.6
13.	Krebs Biochemicals	56.9
14.	Indian Immunologicals	56.7
15.	Zydus Cadila	55
16.	Mahyco-Monsanto	54
17.	Shantha Biotechnics	40
18.	Syngene International	38.5
19.	Biological E	38.4
20.	Span Diagonostics	35.6

Note: In some cases industry estimates have been taken.

Source: BioSpectrum

There is indeed a new and old part to biotechnology but if you are talking about a frontier science that is exploding with the arrival of genetic mapping and sequencing of the human genome, then it is the new biotechnology that is the main focus. And it is here that the potential is far greater than the successful business models on the ground. Indian capability in bioinformatics, needed to crunch the avalanche of genomic data so as to derive benefits from it, is assumed simply because of the Indian success in software. But one does not automatically flow from the other, says Lakshmi Venkatesan who heads a consultancy that specialises in the biotechnology area. Had it been so the IBMs and Infosys' of the world would have automatically gone into the field is not the staple of conventional software services companies. Also, it is slowly being realised that "bioinformatics cannot exist in a vacuum" or as a stand alone business model. It is difficult for a firm to be just into bioinformatics. Those in the field "have to have backward and forward linkages". The bioinformatics effort, churning and mining the mountains of data that genetic sequencing and mapping have yielded, has to be part of the entire drug discovery and therapeutic research effort. The startups are into it but larger firms will have to commercialise the leads and identifications that bioinformatics firms throw up.

All these facts do not mean that India does not, or will not have the opportunity to become a globally competitive player in biotechnology, only that it is a long haul. And some have already successfully started out on the journey. Says Kiran Mazumdar-Shaw, founder and managing director of Biocon India, the foremost and oldest of Indian biotechnology companies, "Biotechnology has the potential to become a very important business segment for India but right now (2001) it is in its infancy. Its advantage is in scientific resources but things are still in a very nascent stage of development. At the lab level, a lot of research is going on but we have not really focused on commercialisation. That orientation is missing. We have never been known to innovate." The same sentiments are echoed by Khalil Ahmed, director and one of the founders of Shantha Biotechnics. "There is a great amount of scientific skill in India to do the initial part of the research for drug discovery. But nobody is doing that except Shantha and Biocon. Hence a great part of the hype about biotechnology is unjustified."

Global experts feel the same way. Says Prof. Marc von Montague, "A major Indian advantage is very good universities and training. Second is success in information technology. No developing country has such good IT capabilities as India does and if they integrate with what is needed in bioinformatics then they will have a lead immediately. There is indeed a hype about biotechnology. But it is in pointing out how essential biotechnology will be for the future. Either you are in it or you will have to face the consequences of having to buy all the products. If it is the latter, you will not be present in the development, as you have been in information technology. There is as yet no biotechnology industry in India but I am convinced that it will come, just as good evolution is currently taking place in China."

Adds Mazumdar-Shaw, "Biotechnology is a vast and exciting field where India has a potential in each and every area. We need to take advantage of the opportunities in all the three segments—discovery, development and validation. One of the easiest ways of getting into this whole sphere is to become the outsourcing arm of a lot of innovative companies so that in the process you learn to innovate. That itself is a very big need. A lot of people get deterred by the time it takes to get results in biotechnology. So I say, learn while you earn. As in pharma, mimic the discovered molecules and learn how to upgrade and commercialise. We should tie up with American companies for commercialising as we are very good at commercialising others' concepts. If we can do through the biological route what we have done through chemistry knowledge in pharma, that itself will give a lot of experience in manufacturing and discovery proper. India should to able to produce every single generic coming off patent in two to three years. The reengineering skills are very much there. It is a matter of being good in a few molecules and the rest falls into place. What we have done in 15 to 18 years in pharma we should be able to do in five years in biotechnology, starting now (2001)."

Mazumdar-Shaw has put in practice the business model she has just outlined, while combining with it some special strengths. Its main pillars have been generic drug development, R&D and clinical research and of course low cost. Biocon India was set up in 1978 by its eponymous Irish partner and Mazumdar-Shaw. Its first milestone was the development of the Koli fermentation process which was till then, known only within Japan. In the nineties it developed a "revolutionary new fermentation technology" which was christened the 'Plafractor' and won a US product patent in 2000. This gave it the capability to produce speciality enzymes. In 1994, a contract research arm of the company, Syngene, was floated. Thereafter it went into manufacturing high quality pharmaceutical bulk actives through non-infringing processes derived from its own fermentation techniques. In the late nineties the company went into biopharmaceuticals and scored a success with statins, used to fight cholesterol. A subsidiary, Clinigene, has also been floated to conduct patient studies in selected therapeutic areas. In 2004 Biocon became a listed company with a highly successful public issue which greatly raised the profile of the industry (Chart 6.2).

One of the earliest starters on the biotechnology road is Wockhardt, a leading pharmaceutical firm. Says Habib F Khorakiwala, chairman, "We were the first movers in biotech. We have developed our own capability to construct genes and their different expression systems in our recombinant technology." Insulin, Hepatitis B vaccine, Erithropoeitin and Interferon Alpha 2B are products which Wockhardt has introduced. "We have invested in 7–8 biotech products, (the patents for) all of which are expiring around 2005–07. We intend to be there in all those (regulated) markets in addition to India. We are looking at a $15–17 billion market and even in the global context we do not expect much competition, both in the regulated and unregulated markets. This can transform the way you look at our company in five to seven years."

Shantha Biotechnics, a startup which has launched its first recombinant product, a hepatitis B vaccine, has been clearly focused on R&D right from inception. It began in 1993 and commercialised its first product, the vaccine, in 1997. But what it did with the next round of funding, through the private issue of equity, was more unique. It bought a controlling stake in a California company that was totally focused on original drug discovery. It already has a patent on a lung cancer drug and proposes to file three more patents. The raw material for it is a transgenic corn being grown in France. And to finally circumnavigate the globe, it is conducting clinical studies in Japan. Among its more recent developments, is the acquisition of a marine biotech company. It has teamed up with the Indian Institute of Science for basic research for a tuberculosis vaccine and licensed an anti-malarial from a scientist of the same institution.

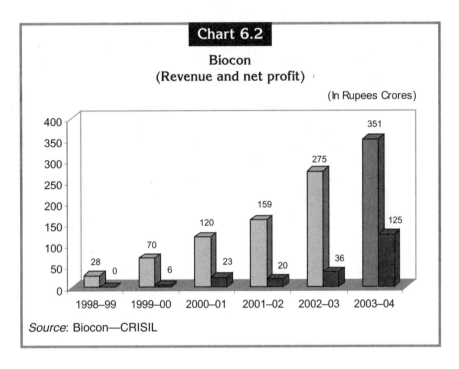

Chart 6.2

Biocon
(Revenue and net profit)

(In Rupees Crores)

Source: Biocon—CRISIL

The Indian industry is using its generics business to fund its basic research and Ahmed foresees that the industry will continue to rely on generics for most of its revenue. Currently, the hepatitis B vaccine in which Shantha Biotechnics leads a clutch of players, is the major revenue earner in recombinant products. But the company's success does not deter Ahmed from having a slightly sceptical view of the industry. Looking at the software success, he observes that, "It really didn't require much investment. But in biotechnology you cannot make a product in six months like pharmaceutical formulations and churn it out at the marketplace. And when it comes to healthcare products, apart from delivering your proof of concept, you need to produce it in a good place and get it through the regulatory system which takes a long time. For biotechnology to prosper, what is really needed is not real estate which the biotechnology parks promise but a different type of mindset among banks and institutions, and venture capitalists."

AGRIBIOTECH DEFICIT

The most important gap in Indian biotechnology is the absence from the market till 2001 of any genetically engineered agricultural biotechnology product, thanks to the intense campaigning by consumer interest and environment protection groups. It took six years for the regulator to clear BT cotton developed by Monsanto and Maharashtra Hybrid Seeds Co. (Mahyco). Both India and China began work on biotechnology in the eighties but the Chinese use of biotechnology products is miles ahead of India's. Says Dr T M Manjunath, director of Monsanto Research Centre, India, "A lot of research is being done in a number of private companies and government labs in agricultural biotechnology. The crop in which advance has been made is BT cotton, proofing it against the bollworm disease. Mahyco took the technology from Monsanto and developed it since 1996. It conducted field trials for five years under the supervision of the department of biotechnology. They generated a lot of data. The Indian regulatory system is very stringent, maybe even more stringent than in the US! In the commercialisation of agricultural biotechnology products, India is at least six years behind. The first biotechnology product was commercialised in the US in 1996. China introduced BT cotton in 1998. As far as R&D activity is concerned, India is at par with most of the developing countries but most of these are confined to the laboratories. We are lagging behind in taking the technology to the farmers."

Who can do this? Says Montague, "There are only limited products for large scale agriculture but more important are all the developments in the universities. The major problem is always to integrate fundamental and applied research. A lot of the applied research cannot be done at the universities and that is why India needs startups. They can try to focus on applications. I am not sure they will make products which will reach the markets. Industry has to do it. Startups have to work for seed companies or industries that will develop in the coming years. So it is a learning process." Then he adds pointedly, "You have to be present there otherwise you will never be there. I would agree that there is a lack of industry focus in Indian post graduate programmes in biotechnology as opposed to information technology. There also you have the good teaching plus the companies that can select the best. There is not yet a biotechnology industry in India. It has to come. First comes good teaching and research at universities. Then startups take knowledge from universities upto a point and pass it onto larger companies for exploitation. Otherwise a lot of knowledge stays at universities and is not applied."

Avesthagen is the sort of startups that Montague talks about. Set up by Dr Villoo Morawala Patell, a doctorate from the University of Louis Pasteur, Strasbourg and a member of the New York Academy of Sciences, it is a fully integrated biotechnology and bioinformatics company dedicated to creating its own intellectual property and is in the business of contract research. Tata Industries has taken a stake in the company and venture capital funding has also come from ICICI Ventures. It has already filed several patent applications and plans to license or sell its intellectual property and also get into strategic alliances. Among its current list of alliance partners is Wipro, Icrisat, AstraZeneca and Genetic ID. A key focus for it is to develop processes for discovery made possible by the genetic revolution and the resultant release of sequential information.

Avesthagen is working on rice varieties like Basmati, trying to identify genes that give them special characteristics which are important for breeding new varieties. It is also setting up contacts with IT companies to work out programmes that bioinformatics needs. Adds Montague, "The whole world needs this and when you do this you bank on IT in which you are strong. If biotechnology companies can convince IT companies that they need a programme for analysing DNA then the IT companies can commercialise such programmes and sell them globally. I am convinced that Avesthagen, which is setting up a basis for dialogue with IT companies will bring in contributions. In bioinformatics you can generate revenues quickly but for that you have to interest the IT companies to outsource such development. They are not yet convinced, just as the general public is not yet convinced, that biotechnology is important for this century. Some people will believe in it only if the business is there and there are others who have the vision that it will be there. If there is a hype about biotechnology, then it lies in pointing out how essential it is for the future."

We have dwelt at length on Avesthagen because its role is illustrative. Dr Srinivas Seshadri, a former chief technology officer at Lucent Technologies, and four Indian Institute of Science professors, have founded Strand Genomics which has the slogan 'Algorithms for life'. Another startup is Metahelix Life Science which has been founded by, among others, some scientists who were with Monsanto. Its main focus is gene discovery for agronomic and nutritional enhancement of commerical and food crops. Algorithm design and software development for various applications in bioinformatics is another business area for it. Both Strand Genomics and Metahelix will do contract research to initially keep the pot boiling, as both will be straddled with negative cash flows for several years.

Where exactly is Indian biotechnology and which is justified, the hype or the scepticism? As it hangs in limbo between the two, the change that Avesthagen is undergoing providers a pointer. Says its CEO Villoo Patell, "Our vision of discovery and product development needs huge sums of money which are not available in this country. Initially we established enough IP positions so that tomorrow, when our products come out, we will have enough freedom to operate. The discovery work has evolved into a convergence of food and pharma type products. Our products can be put into genes, the genes can be expressed into food and eaten as food as well as pharma products. We are saying, to eat right is to live right. We have both—seed for food and food for medicine."

Avesthagen has built a solid discovery base and credibility but it has not made any significant revenues. So the agenda now is to focus on services through the 'research process outsourcing' model (it has copyrighted the phrase) and raise revenues. "We are absolutely focusing on raising revenues significantly and closing the deals in the pipeline which we have at the moment." It is now seeking to become the research process outsourcing partners of companies and has entered into strategic alliances with Genetic ID and Wipro. In the latter case, it is addressing knowledge management systems. Its aim is to integrate into companies right from discovery to clinical trials and basically write packages for them.

INADEQUATE FUNDING

Funding in biotechnology is inadequate because of two reasons—lack of vision among venture capital entities and the inability of Indian biotechnology to show sufficient results. "Whatever you are creating has to be packaged to the world. There is a funding dimension which is missing here. The credibility to package and sell to the world is also missing. Unless we get these things in place foreign investments, big money is not going to enter into biotech," explains Patell. But while these hurdles remain, the Indian biotechnology sector has made considerable progress. Patell maintains that, "The picture is very bright and we have all the ingredients to make a big success. In the last three years India has gained ground as a biotech force. We have created awareness that some real companies are out there and a real biotech initiative exists in the country."

She also places the pace of progress made so far in the context of US and Eurpoean firms taking 18 to 24 years to break even. "From 18 years earlier, today it takes seven to eight years for a company to succeed. We are unprepared in this country to take the risk and are trying to dull the face of biotech by saying it hasn't shown any promise. It is a long-term venture, a very risky venture. You have to back up the biotech companies. We are missing the point that we can very quickly herald the leadership. It is ten times cheaper here to undertake biotechnology work. We have the people, we retrain them, we have natural resources. There is infrastructure but the connectivity between them is missing. In the west, biotech companies have succeeded because they have been paid an upfront fee to be partners with larger companies line Monsanto. The big companies in the US and Europe are becoming sales people, just marketing. The link [in India] between biotech and big pharma, biotech and big IT companies is missing."

What is the recipe for quicker progress? According to Patell, the biggest need of the hour for Indian biotech is funding and access to international markets. For that India has to streamline its policies and patent structures. To reach international markets you have to establish credible partnerships. Strong laws need to be in place to govern these partnerships. Indian legal and patent systems have to be very tight and make Indian companies credible marketing partners with companies out there. She feels, "there is a big misalignment here. How do you strengthen the systems within the country that can make you credible in the public eye? Patents are still an issue. People are really afraid that when projects arrive and are sent for clearance up there, they are stolen. All this is perception. This may not be true any more. But we have to take enough missions, do enough lobbying to convey the new message." Thus, for the Indian biotechnology industry to make a mark globally, both the government and the industry have a major selling job to do.

Khorakiwala adds his own words of caution. "The chemistry of conventional pharmaceutical manufacturing was at no time as complex as biotechnology is. There were enough technical people, chemistry PhDs, moving around even then. Entry barriers (cost of plant and regulatory requirements) were low. This is not the case in biotech. Even in India, environmental requirements are very rigid. Cost of entry is very high and skills are very limited. It is going to be a tough proposition and not too many understand the technology. Besides, today the patent regime is different, the window to commercialise will shortly not be there."

He does not wish to rationalise the hype or buzz about biotchnology. He bluntly asserts, "We have to be worried about the hype over biotchnology. It happened with dotcom companies worldwide. Biotech will remain a powerful force in the pharma industry and will play an increasingly important role. In the last two years 40 per cent of applications received by the US FDA for new drugs were for biotech products. The very fact that the human genome is being decoded, 30,000 proteins have been identified and monoclonal antibodies have emerged as a new treatment point to biotech. There are diseases where biotech alone can provide a solution. Obviously, some companies will come in but you can't get carried away." Thus the potential, the skills, fledgling companies and serious minded generics players are all there in Indian biotechnology. These are all ingredients of success. But some more potions are needed to make the alchemy work. Only then will the promise of India becoming a global player in biotechnology, just as it has become one in pharmaceuticals, be delivered.

7

The Cooperative Exception

A key element in the Indian dairy sector (milk and milk products), the Anand type cooperatives, makes it one of the most globally competitive. Over 50 years ago, a group of farmers in the villages around the Gujarat town of Anand set out to get a better price for their milk. They came together to form a successful cooperative, the Kaira District Cooperative Milk Producers' Union—better known as Amul—and eventually grew into the Gujarat Cooperative Milk Marketing Federation. The Amul enterprise shot into national fame and became a symbol of success, both in grassroots development as well as a commercial enterprise. This made the then Prime Minister, Lal Bahadur Shastri, seek out the architect of the success, Verghese Kurien, in 1965 to set up and head the National Dairy Development Board with the mandate to replicate the Anand model in the rest of the country. This was achieved through the three stages of Operation Flood.

Today, India is the world's largest milk producer and the Amul brand has branched out from milk, milk powder and ghee into ice cream and cheese. In ice cream, it posed a formidable challenge to Kwality, the ice cream brand of Hindustan Lever, forcing it to change its marketing strategy. It has launched its own brand of pizza, as a vehicle for its cheese, which aspires to challenge the supremacy of global brands in India. In some other milk products like condensed milk it is taking on Nestle. There is an overriding irony in all this. Something designed basically as a marketing project, has created a cooperative alternative to the private ownership model of dairying.

MILK OUT OF LEFTOVERS

With hindsight, rise of the Anand type cooperative seems all so rational. But when the battles were fought one by one over the years the outcome of many a struggle was far from certain. How did Indian milk emerge as one of the cheapest in the world? Kurien explains it all with a simplicity of logic, born out of decades spent in the company of farmers. India has the world's second largest human population and the largest cattle population, both almost equally impoverished. So, it was necessary right from the beginning that man and beast were not in competition. If they were, then man would win and that would be the end of dairying. For dairying to win, you had to feed the cattle what man could not consume, like straw, rice and wheat bran, rice polish and oil cake. Hence the first unique feature of the Indian dairy revolution, which also gives it such a low cost structure, is that it is built on the foundation of feeding the leftovers to the animals.

Verghese draws a comparison with the typical New Zealand farmer and his dairying. He has 120 to 150 cows, which are left to graze in the outdoors in fenced out paddocks because the weather is mild, and allowed to feed on abundant grass. This has all the protein and so there is no need to feed the animals concentrates. All that the farmer has to do is ensure that his dog collects the animals and brings them to the shed for milking by milking machines. "This type of dairying is very cheap but even the New Zealand farmer cannot compete with us because our milk is a byproduct. We do not even cost the labour of the farmer's wife, who looks after the cattle and milks them, as we do not know her opportunity cost. That is why our milk is the cheapest in the world."

MEANS TO AN END

The second distinguishing feature of the Anand model is that producing and selling milk is really a secondary concern, a means to an end. The first concern is creating incomes and jobs for India's rural poor. Dairying caught on because it provided an excellent subsidiary occupation, probably the most important, for India's rural women. India's milk production has quadrupled in the last 20 years, even though the farmer is paid only his out of pocket expenses and a little more. This is because the meagre amount he is paid is sufficient incentive for him to produce more. The typical member of a milk cooperative has 3.5 acres and 1.5 cattle. His income from the latter equals his income from the former if you do not take into account his wife's labour and the straw the cattle is fed on. The only thing he has to buy from the cooperative system is cattle feed concentrate. The rest is imputed cost.

"India's milk production is now 86 million tonnes, compared to 20 million tonnes in 1976 when Operation Flood started. To achieve this, we spent Rs 100 crore per year for 20 years, that is Rs 2,000 crore. From this I get Rs 66,000 crore (the value of the additional milk produced as a result of Operation Flood). There is no project in the whole world where the input is so low and the output is so high. This was the finding of the evaluation team of the World Bank. Today there are 175 Anands (Anand type farmers' milk cooperatives). We are a global dairy power and we are growing at 4.5 per cent per annum in milk production. Our philosophy is the best product at the lowest price. Now nothing will stop us," declares Verghese triumphantly (Chart 7.1).

PROVIDENCE

Even nature seems to have helped in achieving this. Milk becomes spoilt (goes bad) if it is not chilled within four hours. The village women milk the cows and bring the milk to the collection centre within half an hour while the froth is still there. Chilling plants are now being set up in the villages, but in the past the Anand movement got a divine grace, so to speak, of 20 minutes, allowing a little more time for transportation of the milk from the collection centre to the dairy without chilling. It has been found that the keeping quality of Indian cow's milk is a little more than that of milk from cows elsewhere in the world. The keeping quality of buffalo's milk is even more. The bacterial count of milk goes up exponentially with time after it leaves the udder, eventually causing it to be spoilt if not chilled in time. But the bacterial count goes down in the first 20 minutes because of what is called the bactercydal quality of milk. It is here that milk from Indian breeds scores and manages to remain unspoilt longer. The major logistical challenge before the Anand experiment was to collect the milk and first transport it to the dairy (in the absence of sufficient numbers of chilling plants) and the longer keeping quality helped in making do with a cheaper collection system necessitated by meagre budgets.

OWNERSHIP

Important as these were, the Indian cooperative dairy movement was most crucially helped by both a sense of ownership on the part of its participants and professional management. Verghese personified both the relationship and the management model. In his own words, "There was Tribhuvandas Patel (an enlightened leader among farmers who made Verghese stay on in Anand), a leader of great integrity and wisdom. There is a lot of wisdom among our farmers. What I have is knowledge acquired by going to college. The creation of Amul was really because the two got together—Tribhuvandas' wisdom and my knowledge. And my knowledge was made subordinate to his wisdom and the leadership of farmers. The challenge was to get professional managers who would subordinate their knowledge and recognise that there was wisdom in India. The challenge was in deploying that knowledge in such a manner as not to lose the farmers' initiative, sense of ownership and pride in the institution

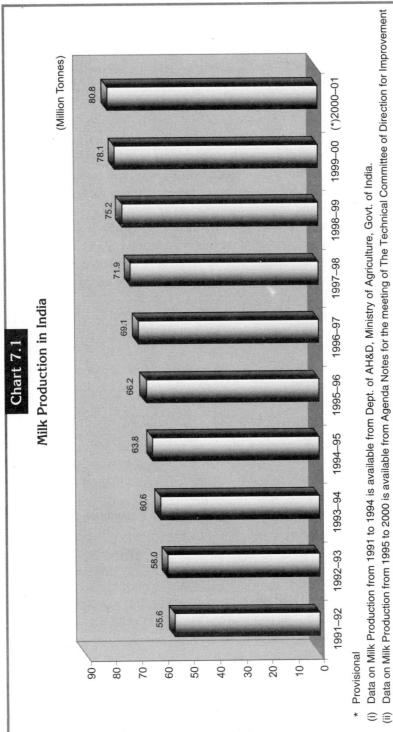

Chart 7.1

Milk Production in India

(Million Tonnes)

* Provisional

(i) Data on Milk Production from 1991 to 1994 is available from Dept. of AH&D, Ministry of Agriculture, Govt. of India.

(ii) Data on Milk Production from 1995 to 2000 is available from Agenda Notes for the meeting of The Technical Committee of Direction for Improvement of AH&D Statistics dated 19–20th February, 2002 at New Delhi.

Source: NDDB

(the cooperative). Shastriji asked, What's the secret. I said the secret is very simple. The dairy is owned by the farmers and they in their wisdom have appointed me as their manager. If I can't satisfy my board I will lose my job. It is a combination of the farmer, his wisdom, and my knowledge. He said, if that be so then it is replicable. All other conditions (breed of cattle, fodder, tradition of animal husbandry) exist everywhere in the country. All we have to find is managers and get them employed by farmers' cooperatives."

Shastri created the National Dairy Development Board and made Verghese its first chairman to replicate the Anand experiment all over the country. To deliver, Verghese needed and obtained major policy concessions. Milk is a highly perishable commodity that has to be marketed within a few hours of production. Quick and smooth procurement is essential but the additional challenge is to procure from a large number of farmers who mostly have 0.5– 1.5 litres to sell at a time. The cooperative structure is tailor made for the smooth running of an operation in which such large numbers of small players are involved. But for the cooperative model to succeed in a situation in which the price to the consumer cannot be raised unduly, the farmer has to gain the maximum share of the consumers' expenditure. For that he has to gain command over the procurement, processing and marketing of the milk. Finally, costs can go out of kilter if the cooperative has to bid for the milk along with private dairies. Verghese explained all these reasons to the policymakers who created the necessary policy regime for Operation Flood to succeed.

COOPERATIVE MONOPOLY

The germ of the cooperative movement was sowed in Kaira district when farmers rebelled and went on strike because they were being shortchanged by the private company Polson, which had monopoly procurement rights in the area. Now, cooperatives were given a procurement monopoly through the Milk and Milk Products Order of the government which allowed a milk cooperative exclusive procurement rights in a particular area, without any competition from the organised private sector. This monopoly procurement by farmers' milk cooperatives was dedicated to paying a good price to the farmer. In fact, once NDDB was born, dairying became virtually reserved for the cooperative sector. Existing players like Nestle and Glaxo, which were mainly in the north, were allowed to expand their capacities at a restricted rate. So, a good part of the north and the entire south of the country was left to the cooperative sector.

Starting NDDB with a government fiat was one thing. Getting funds for it was another. Kurien was a zealous guardian of the cooperatives' distance from the regular government machinery and suspicious of direct government funding. Recalls Amrita Patel, the current chairman of NDDB, "When we came, there was this one successful cooperative but in every state there were government dairy schemes which lost money. When states were asked to contribute from their dairy funds for an Anand type cooperative, no money was forthcoming. That's when we negotiated with the World Food Programme for butter oil and milk powder to be reconstituted into milk. It was the first example in the world of food aid being used for development. Having negotiated that and brought it in as a gift, the government took an important policy decision. The structure made responsible for promoting dairying and leading us to self-sufficiency was also made responsible for the imports."

IMPORT CONTROL

Adds Patel, "The next decision was, irrespective of the price at which we imported (import prices were much lower than those prevailing in India because of producer country subsidies), the product made from imports would not be sold at prices lower than those prevailing in India. These two decisions ensured that at least for the first two phases of Operation Flood we did not allow imports to come in indiscriminately." The country had just come out of the experience of accepting grain aid from the US under the PL 480 scheme. There was keen awareness that cheap imports which killed local initiative and created permanent dependence on imports would not be allowed in the dairy sector.

In NDDB, Shastri had set up a government body to rescue dairying from the government by taking advantage of market forces and channelling them in the chosen direction. This was the first example in the country where increase in the production of an agricultural commodity was led not by scientists and technologists, but by the market. As the market grew there was the incentive to produce more. Recalls Patel, "The experience of Anand was not just farmers coming together in a cooperative, but the recognition that unless you have the market of Bombay, Anand will not grow. There was a limit to local consumption. In the first phase of Operation Flood we selected the four best markets—Bombay, Delhi, Calcutta, Madras—and developed cooperatives in the hinterland of these markets. The only way to succeed in a difficult project is to first take up what is likely to succeed. It is important right from the start to demonstrate success. In the second phase of Operation Flood, we took over markets with a population of one lakh and above, and the milkshed area around them."

COST COMPETITIVENESS

We have recorded the reasons why Indian dairying is globally cost competitive. Deepak Tikku, managing director of NDDB, gives the numbers to establish it. 85 per cent of global milk output is accounted for by the US, EU, Australia and New Zealand. Production is highly subsidised in the US and EU, but not in Australia and New Zealand. US and EU costs work out to 26 cents per litre. Australia and New Zealand costs work out to 16–17 cents per litre, and Indian cost 18 cents per litre. How is India able to compete with low cattle productivity and zero high value input by farmers in terms of enriched cattle feed? 75 per cent of the cost of milk production is feed, 5 per cent is labour. As explained earlier, the Indian farmers' feed cost is negligible, compared to the international competition, and his cost of labour, provided by his wife, is almost none at all. The Indian farmer's land holdings have mostly remained static, 1–3 acres, his herd size 1–3. This enables him to meet most of his fodder needs from his straw and some other waste products like rice bran and oil cake. Thus, he is able to survive but is beaten by a whisker by the Australian and New Zealand farmer whose herd size is 500 and who is able to keep feed costs minimal by allowing the cattle to graze in the open.

WHAT NDDB DID

We have listed the reasons and statistics of success in Indian dairying. But how exactly did NDDB go about achieving it? Once an area was selected, NDDB assessed the market to determine its dairying capacity and built a dairy. It then put in place an organisational structure, helped recruit people to man it and initiated training. Where there was an input gap, it devised a long term solution. It set up Asia's largest animal vaccination plant and brought down the prices of vaccines. It organised the manufacture of dairy machinery by setting up the Indian Dairy Machinery Manufacturing Co to first bring down equipment prices and then create the infrastructure to indigenously manufacture dairy machinery. And to meet the shortage of managers it set up the Institute of Rural Management at Anand.

The engineering and veterinary solutions in particular, devised by NDDB, give an idea of the scale of what it attempted. A particular challenge was the logistical one created by there being milk surplus and milk deficit areas in the vast country. To overcome this, a milk grid was needed to cover the entire country. This was done during the second stage of Operation Flood. The key hardware used for this was insulated milk tankers for both rail and road transportation of milk, designed by NDDB. It also standardised equipment specifications and provided detailed designs for small scale industries which made it possible for 95 per cent of dairy equipment to be manufactured in the country. And one of its unique innovations has been the bulk milk vending machines, now ubiquitous in metro centres, which have eliminated packaging costs.

As Operation Flood succeeded, NDDB realised that for milk production to keep increasing, the quality of Indian cattle had to be improved. The buffalo and indigenous good milch breeds had to be upgraded and nondescript cows had to be cross-bred with exotic semen to increase their milk production. Hence NDDB stepped up research in animal husbandry. Today, artificial insemination and quantitative genetic techniques, embryo transfer and embryo micro-manipulation techniques, biotechnology and genetics engineering make up the initiative in animal breeding.

Finally, NDDB has initiated a process whereby all the cooperatives come together to promote the mnemonic so that it is seen to be a symbol of quality and quality products coming from cooperatives. Every cooperative milk pack is uniform, the shop design is the same irrespective of which part of the country you are in. So, as far as the Indian consumer is concerned, he sees it and knows it is a cooperative product. The latest effort is directed to convert Amul into a powerful brand so as to combat the private sector challenge.

CLOUDY FUTURE

Given all the achievements listed above that have given Indian dairying such a low cost structure, there should be a good export market but, as is well known, the global market for dairy products is highly distorted. Not only are there high import tariffs, 60-200 per cent, guarding the US and EU markets, their surpluses are exported with high subsidies, thus keeping international prices low. The advent of WTO-mandated reduction in support and trade barriers should have created markets for Indian dairy products but a new barrier has emerged through phytosanitary standards. The new line is that not only is the quality of the final product important, so also is the way it is produced, from the farm right up to the consumer. For example, it is being mandated that only products from entirely machine handled milk will be allowed in. WTO allows states to have their own phytosanitary standards. If there is a dispute, WTO will benchmark to international standards. These have been the Codex standards evolved by WHO and FAO. Explains Tikku, "From being designed for consumer protection, these standards have now become counters in trade disputes. The US and the EU are laying very high standards for water and residues like lead, arsenic and antibiotics. The Indian position is that these are indeed important but they should be measured in the final product. But that is not acceptable."

MILK IS STILL KING

With export prospects thus being not at all bright, the focus of the Indian dairy industry has shifted inwards. It is concentrating on how to face import competition in the domestic market and keep improving health standards in dairying in a practical and common sense way. "Our simple schedule is clean udders, hands, water and stainless steel containers, quick journey to the collection centre and to the chilling plant in four hours. The farmer is even being paid a small premium so that he does not sell to the *gowala* but to the cooperative while maintaining these standards." As for import competition, the issue is import duty on the two main components of milk, fat and milk powder. On fat the import duty is 15 per cent (2002) and on powder it is 15 per cent for the first 10,000 tonnes of imports and 60 per cent thereafter. But despite these low import duties, imports have been minimal. "I don't think they (the rest of the world) are competitive," declares Patel definitively.

But within India, a new battle is also emerging. The MMPO, which helped the cooperative sector to grow and prosper has now been withdrawn, partly because the cooperative sector is perceived to have come of age and partly because continuing with monopoly procurement rights for a particular sector is today anachronistic and non-WTO compatible. Hence, a battle is looming ahead for the cooperative sector with organised private dairying and the *gowala* over the purchase of fresh milk. The battle is only marginally at the product level—over ice cream and cheese in which there is greater value addition and private competition can be expected to be keen. Fascinatingly, everyone is focused on the one object, that is, purchasing cheap raw milk. The cost of raw milk is so important even for a value added product, that the whole economics of dairying and milk products hinges on it.

If the cooperatives are to grow they need to hold onto the liquid milk market. That is the market which provides working capital to the farmer. So their milk should ideally be sold as liquid milk, so as to turn around the capital quickly. It is the leftovers, whatever cannot be sold, which are converted into products. They take a backseat as it is milk that matters. Patel says, "We must make sure that the maximum sale is of liquid milk. Ninety per cent of our cooperatives' turnover of Rs 7,000–8,000 crore is liquid milk. All MNCs are now going into liquid milk. So far they were only into products. But now they see money in liquid milk."

THE DOMESTIC CHALLENGE

Thus, the key issue is expanding the supply of liquid milk. "The challenge," as Patel sees it, "is not to be competitive in exports (market distortions rule it out) but to be competitive to expand our market which has limited purchasing power. Those (consumers) who are buying milk today are not going to be buying much more. For those who cannot afford it, we have to bring prices down. Only if we do this will we ensure that imports don't come in. The real challenge is how to bring prices down, how to reduce costs at the village level, in transportation. Every paisa now counts. Some say we are not competitive because our herd size is too small. We should copy the model abroad. But I don't think it is going to work. The farmer who has two, three or five animals can feed them on byproducts and keep costs down. That is our unique competitiveness."

We have explained the following—how the Indian dairy sector is globally competitive but market distortions have prevented it from exporting, and how it is having to fight for its domestic space in a new era when its monopoly rights have been taken away. But one more explanation is necessary—how the cooperative sector is today fighting back by posing a competitive challenge to the private sector. How is Amul combating Kwality, the ice cream brand of Hindustan Lever, when the latter has the most high powered management and marketing backing? The answer to this question becomes even more complex when we note that the farmer gets a far higher share of what the consumer pays from the cooperative (80 per cent) than is the case with the private sector (47 per cent). That this income generation lies at the root of the phenomenal increase in the milk supply in the economy has been already established earlier. But how is the cooperative sector able to market this milk as cheaply as it does despite paying such a high share of the earnings to buy raw milk?

LOW MARKUP

One major difference in the cost structure between the two sectors is the brand royalty and technical knowhow that the multinational parents take out of their milk business in India. "This amounts to around 5 per cent of their costs," estimates B M Vyas, managing director of the Gujarat Cooperative Milk Marketing Federation, which owns the Amul brand. Markup also depends on the length of the supply chain, the number of middlemen. In the cooperative structure, it is the primary cooperative which sells the milk to the district cooperative which produces the value added products. The brand building, marketing and distribution are done by the state cooperative federation. These operate at a minimum surplus, which ultimately goes back to the primary member, the farmer, in the form of dividend. The farmer who gets a good price for his milk is not complaining about the low dividend. Much of the technology has been developed by NDDB and passed on to the cooperatives at a minimal cost. This is over and above the initial investment in infrastructure also made by NDDB.

If raising the supply of raw milk while keeping a watch on prices—keeping it low even while not allowing it to go down in real terms—was a great achievement, another was logistics and marketing. Today, milk produced by 11 million farmers is collected from 100,000 villages and in good part marketed within three hours. But, a lot of it also travels across the country. NDDB designed special railway milk tankers and entire milk trains first made trips from Anand to Mumbai and thereafter, to Delhi. Flagging off these milk trains became national events. Then a more sophisticated challenge came up after the consumer revolution occurred in the country from the late eighties. The major task became one of building the Amul brand. This has also been done very successfully. Amul has had some memorable advertising campaigns to its credit which have won prizes and is today one of the foremost brands in the Indian market.

Such has been the success of Amul in a value added area like ice cream, that Hindustan Lever has been forced to change its strategy. Once Amul's challenge became serious and the ice cream business of Hindustan Lever made minimal on no money at all, the company made a drastic change. It stopped trying to market everywhere in the country and concentrated on the metros for its ice cream. This has made the business turn around. Amul products today are successful above all because they are perceived to be able to provide enormous value for money. They are unbeatable in price but also score very well in quality and are riding on the back of a packaging and marketing effort which is the envy of many private sector companies.

SECURING COOPERATIVE DAIRYING

We now address the last issue. Cooperative dairying in India has fought and won handsomely but is its position sustainable? The answer to this is not at all clear. The greatest threat to the future of cooperative dairying is its success. It grew and prospered because Kurien and the system he built up, managed to largely keep government interference out of the cooperatives, allowing them to run professionally and making the professionals answerable to the farmers. The various state governments' animal husbandry departments were already there with their own setups, when Operation Flood was initiated. But these did not deliver because they were not oriented to serve the farmer as the Anand type of cooperatives were. At the village level, any person who owns an animal has the right to become a member. Over 90 per cent of village cooperative societies work well and make a profit. At that level, government interference has not crept in to the extent of destroying the structure. The problem comes in at the district level. People get elected as office bearers of cooperatives, taste the power that flows out of a successful grassroots commercial orgnisation, and then aspire to become MLAs. That is where politics comes in. And the law of the land allows these politicians and bureaucrats to give a role to themselves as soon as there is a chink in the farmers' defence against outside interference created by those from within with political ambitions.

Realising the danger to the cooperative movement, at a time when internal and external opening up will require it to be run with the highest level of professionalism, NDDB and the leaders of the Anand type cooperatives have devised a two pronged strategy to keep politicians and bureaucrats out of cooperatives. The simpler one is to encourage women to join cooperatives in larger numbers. Says Patel, "We are anxious that over the next ten years women membership will rise from 20 to 50 per cent. Women at the village level care about their family first and then the world beyond. If we can prepare her to come into governance—she is very good at looking after her animal—if we can take her where she can understand simple accounts, test the milk and manage that little milk collection center, then we can at least ensure integrity at that level."

But that is not enough. The cooperative leaders intensively lobbied politicians and went up to the prime minister for legislation under the Companies Act for the introduction of a new category of companies, producer cooperatives where the shareholders are the producers. The amendment was eventually passed by Parliament. All the principles of cooperation remain, but under the discipline of the Companies Act and taking it into the central government's domain, so that state level politics is kept out. The status of these producer companies is that of a private limited company.

So far, the privately owned firm has proved to be the most durable form of business organisation in the recorded history of commerce. There have been rare and transient examples of cooperatives running as successful businesses. The Anand type cooperatives fall into the latter category, with their future wide open. If this structure does not reform and survive, it is unclear if dairying in India will continue to be as low cost as it has been in the past.

8

Tata Steel:
Least Cost Challenger

We begin our study of Indian companies in the old economy which are globally competitive, by taking a look at Tata Iron and Steel Company. Steel is a traditional industry, and also one of the most durable. But, despite there being a long term demand for steel—not the least in developing countries which are yet to build all the roads, houses and bridges they need—it was one of the brick and mortar industries which totally fell out of investor favour during the boom in technology shares in the late nineties. McKinsey, the consultancy, advised the Tata group that Tata Steel should diversify into telecommunications which promised higher returns and hence was more likely to retain investor interest.

The investment scenario has undergone a sea change since the technology bubble burst at the turn of the century. But this decline in technology stocks did not automatically revive investor interest in steel. It came much later in 2003 with recovery in steel prices. A key reason for this is global over capacity in steel which led to an OECD initiative in 2001 to rein in further addition to steel capacity and shutting down non-competitive steel mills all over the world. State support to steel mills in trouble has virtually ended but still the global market for steel remains far from free. The United States, the largest and most accessible steel market in the world, first imposed and then confirmed, in 2001, 33 per cent anti-dumping duties on hot rolled coils, the benchmark steel item manufactured by Tata Steel and other Indian producers. The Indian market itself remained one of the most protected in the world with a 30.8 per cent import duty till end 2003.

Thus it is difficult to establish the international competitiveness of an Indian steel company by looking at either its export performance or presence in the home market. While it could, Tata Steel achieved a realisation of $245 per tonne on its export sales in 2001 but domestic sales were far more remunerative at $310 per tonne. There was thus very little incentive for a company like Tata Steel to become internationally competitive and every incentive to lobby for the retention of high tariff protection at home. It is therefore remarkable that it should have followed a strategy through the nineties that first made it a global least cost producer of hot metal or iron and eventually steel in the new millennium.

Tata Steel's claim to be a globally competitive steel maker rests on the following factors. First, it remained one of the few highly profitable steel makers of any size in a situation in which most steel makers lost money. In financial year 2000–01, Tata Steel turned in its most profitable year in its history, clocking a net profit of Rs 500 crore. The protected Indian market did not provide the sole explanation as most other Indian steel companies lost large amounts of money in the same year. While new companies with high operational efficiencies lost on account of high energy and capital costs, a public sector giant like the Steel Authority of India, of earlier vintage, lost on account of high manning levels and incomplete and costly modernisation.

WORLD CLASS

World Steel Dynamics, the New Jersey, US based consultancy, in its June 2001 report on Indian steel makers, described Tata Steel "as a true world class steel maker". It attributed this to several factors. A key factor was low input costs. It has its own iron ore and coal mines and needs to import only a third of its coking coal requirements. From this partially stems its low fuel costs. But Tata Steel has taken considerable technological initiatives to realise the low cost opportunities that its raw materials endowment has provided. To this has been added low manpower costs, which at $2.70 per hour in 2001 was one of the lowest in the world. To build on this it has added (cold rolling) and plans to add (long products) new facilities which will result in higher value addition and respond to emerging market needs. All this has been made possible by a stable management being in place and a good human relations environment.

Tata Steel scores the highest in World Steel Dynamics's comprehensive ranking of 12 world class steel makers which includes Nippon Steel of Japan and Posco of South Korea. WSD does the ratings with two disclaimers— many of the individual ratings are subjective and some of the factors could have a higher weightage than others. Tata Steel scores the highest (ten on ten) in ownership of low cost iron ore and coking coal and favourable location for procuring raw materials. In operating costs, it scores nine on ten, beaten by CSN and Severstal. In skilled and productive workforce, Nippon Steel, Posco and Severstal score the highest whereas, Tata Steel scores seven. In price paid for electricity, it is at about the same level as the leaders. On ongoing cost cutting measures, all the companies score eight, with only Unisor scoring nine. This would imply that the world leaders are all equally eager and adept in cutting costs. Also, they all boast of the same high quality of management. In balance sheet and cost of debt and equity, with scores at seven and eight, Tata Steel is behind the best. It is not among the best in high quality and niche products and scores the most poorly when it comes to its own downstream and steel using businesses.

During the planning era, when Indian industry operated under strict licensing conditions and the steel industry was additionally under price and distribution controls, Tata Steel was a market leader and a blue chip. Its main grouse then was, it was not free to invest and grow. The first break came with the preliminary stirrings of liberalisation when Mrs Indira Gandhi returned to power in 1980. Since then the company has gone through successive 'modernisation' programmes, the fourth and last of which was completed in 2001. Important as these changes were, they were quite basic, like switching to continuous casting (thus skipping the ingot making stage and saving on materials and energy) and switching from the open hearth process of steel making to the basic oxygen furnace route. But this was adopting technology that had globally arrived even in the seventies.

DECONTROL

The big change came in 1991 when India's economic liberalisation agenda was rolled out in earnest and pricing and distribution controls on steel were removed in early 1992. Dr J J Irani, managing director of Tata Steel until 2001 and credited with leading the transformation of the company, recalls that the outsized workforce of the company was brought home to it by prospective investors when the company went on its first global road show after decontrol to raise capital. A workforce of 78,000 was a drag even after taking into account the fact that it ran its own mines and town administration at its works in Jamshedpur. It thereafter embarked on a systematic and carefully structured plan to cut its workforce which by the financial year 2002–03 had come down to 43,200 (Chart 8.1). As simultaneously the company had increased its output, in about a decade its productivity, tonnage per worker, went up three fold (Chart 8.2).

Pinpointing the key focus that transformed the company through the nineties, Irani says, "In this day and age we have actually been able to reduce our operational cost of steel making by a few percentage points every year. And I think that is the basis on which our profitability has improved over the last two or three years". The global slowdown in 2001 worsened the impact of

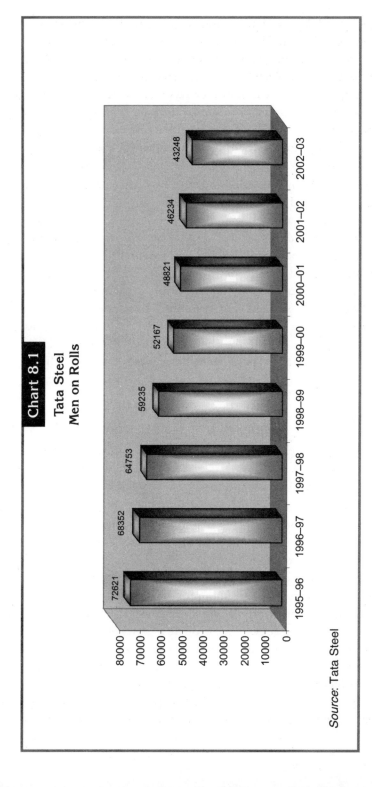

Chart 8.1

Tata Steel
Men on Rolls

Source: Tata Steel

the excess capacity and depressed prices, thus affecting profits in the financial year 2002. But, he feels that, "The realisation from the improvements that started coming in the mid-nineties are continuing," enabling the company to easily weather the downturn which further heightened the distress in the global steel industry. Emphasising the continuity, he says that, "In the beginning we cashed off the low hanging fruits, so to speak, but even coming back to the same department after say a cycle of two years we can see further ways of reducing costs." This is through efficiencies like improving yields, fuel rates, material consumption rates, and reducing the supply chain, deliveries.

Describing the difference in mindset before and after decontrol, Irani recalls how "earlier material was cheap, labour was cheap and we were living in a cost plus situation. That was obviously not conducive to improvements in efficiencies. Then came decontrol and we were on our own. I always told our people, look we can no longer control prices. But profit is the difference between price and cost and we *can* control our costs. We have to bring our costs down to improve our margins." The control mechanism bred other aberrations. The government's joint plant committee fixed prices for primary material but not defectives. These, being outside of the controlled JPC price and in conditions of scarcity, would fetch a higher price than the prime material! So Tata Steel was not very active in reducing defectives and seconds. Today, with a surplus in the market, a severe control is maintained on any defectives.

BENCHMARKS

The tonnage of material used to make one tonne of steel, has been cut down by 25 per cent over the latter half of the nineties (Chart 8.4). A major gain has come from the way coal is charged into coke ovens. Earlier the ovens were top charged, which needed higher quality coal. Now stamp charging is done, which allows the use of medium quality coking coal to produce high strength coke. This has lowered the coke rate for the blast furnaces. This not only has an impact on material costs and energy costs but transportation costs also, which are a key factor in the total cost of steel in India. Costs have also been cut by making the plants totally free from the import of liquid fuel. Jamshedpur now is a totally fuel balanced plant. The gases coming out of the steel melting shops and blast furnaces are reused. Some of these gases are being used to generate power also. Thus, energy costs have been significantly lowered (Chart 8.3). Refractory consumption has been cut down to a third of what it was earlier through better practices. For example, regular small improvements are made through critical examination of the heat profile of a vessel through thermo-vision camera, thereby strengthening the portion more prone to

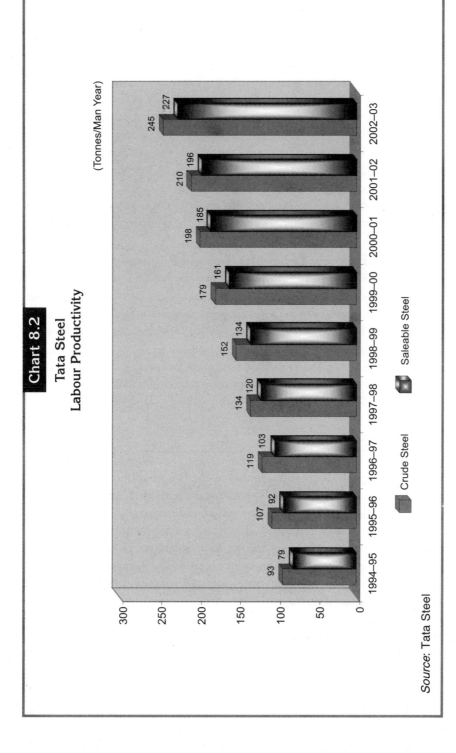

Chart 8.2

Tata Steel
Labour Productivity

(Tonnes/Man Year)

Crude Steel   Saleable Steel

Source: Tata Steel

erosion. The tar that used to be sold earlier, is now being injected into the blast furnaces.

When Tata steel first looked at its costs it realised that it did not have a proper measure of them. So around 1990, it engaged Arthur D Little, the cosultancy, to help design a proper management information system and thus came about the company's 'executive information system'. Different cost centres were identified and the responsibility of operating people in controlling costs was clearly outlined. A new department called 'operational cost and research' was started around 1991–92 and paved the way for benchmarking Tata Steel's costs with those of the cost leaders in the world. The benchmarking showed many weaknesses and gaps. This started the process of determining the enablers that had helped the global leaders improve their costs and further deciding which would work for Tata Steel and which would not. The major gain from this whole exercise was finding out what were the company's main sources of cost competitiveness and how to leverage them.

The next input came from McKinsey which, around the mid-nineties imparted to the company the methodology for looking at and improving efficiences in various ways. This gave an idea as to how each item of operation had to be looked at and how costs could be chipped away on a continuous basis. Having its own iron ore and coal which yielded hot metal were the strong points with which the company started off. So the production of blast furnaces was raised and as a result, the company became a net seller instead of a net buyer of scrap. Hence, the proportion of use of hot metal to scrap has gone up from 70–30 to the present 95–5.

TECHNOLOGY

Describing the way Tata Steel went about the task of bettering itself and the spirit that evolved, Dr T Mukherjee, deputy managing director, says, "In innovation you have to seize the unknown, challenges that you feel are not impossible, no matter how great. When you see a benchmark and find the Japanese have done this, you feel we have to do it. Then we are under psychological pressure to find a way of doing it. We have broken down our major targets to smaller and smaller targets and assigned them to individuals (from the managing director, to the executive directors there are probably 500 individual targets). When the consultants said you have to reduce your compressible costs by 40 per cent, find ways of doing this, from officer to worker all came forward with suggestions. So, innovation has been more or less forced on people. Our 2.5 million cinter plant is now producing 4 million tonnes. We have not followed someone else in this, the productivity of our cinter plant No. 2 is the highest in the world."

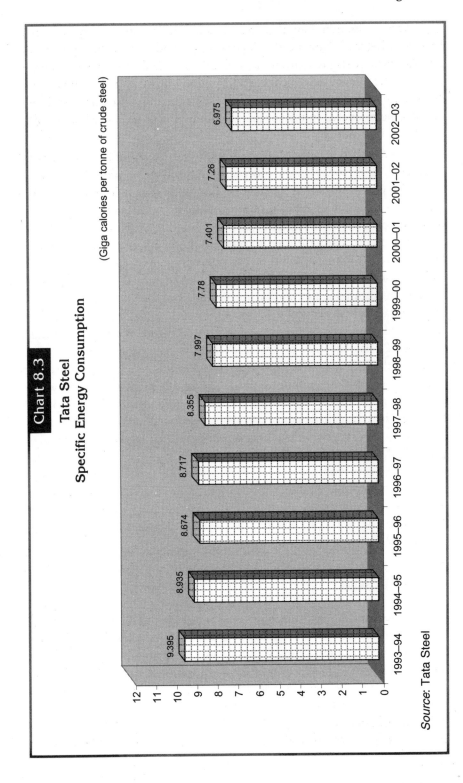

Chart 8.3

Tata Steel
Specific Energy Consumption

(Giga calories per tonne of crude steel)

Year	Value
1993–94	9.395
1994–95	8.935
1995–96	8.674
1996–97	8.717
1997–98	8.355
1998–99	7.997
1999–00	7.78
2000–01	7.401
2001–02	7.26
2002–03	6.975

Source: Tata Steel

"Waste utilisation is another area. As waste utilisation has gone up, costs have been reduced. Now nearly 70 per cent of solid waste is being used. All our blast furnace slag is used, all our mill scale is used, all our coke oven sludge is used." The mines used to generate a lot of iron ore fines which could neither be used nor sold. Now the fines are used in cinter plant production. So mining has become balanced. Instead of fines being surplus, there is sized ore surplus which can be exported.

Then Mukherjee narrates a remarkable story. "Reuse of LD slag has also saved us a lot of money. In the process we are making low phosphorous steel from high phosphorous hot metal." For Tata Steel, along with the advantage that comes with having its own iron ore, has come the disadvantage of that iron ore being high on phosphorous. This has to be removed during steel making at a cost. Earlier it used its own limestone for cinter making and in blast furnaces. For some reason there was a disruption in the supply of limestone and everyone was asked to find a solution. "Ashok Kumar—he is at present head of our technology group for iron making but then was quite junior—said LD slag had 50 per cent calcium oxide which comes from limestone. It has high silicon, phosphorus, but it can be used. So, by 8 o'clock we started moving LD slag in place of limestone for the cinter plant. But that left unattended the problem of removing phosphorous. All LG slag uses flux dolomite to supply magnesium oxide to the slag. Then, I proposed that we do not use magnesium oxide but dunite as that will help remove phosphorous. It took over three years to convince everybody. No one in the world had done it. Even doing a trial run was a big thing as it involved making 100,000 tonnes of cinter. Today we are the only steel company in the world who do not use magnesium ore in the blast furnace. This helps in the removal of phosphorous and reduces our cost. We had to struggle with the idea because we have our own dolomite mines, whose output we are now supplying to Steel Authority. This use of dunite alone has resulted in 7–8 per cent improvement in productivity."

MARKETING

The change from controls to open market conditions and free imports under steadily reducing duties has produced a sea change in the marketing operations of the company. Earlier, selling was more akin to distribution and there was no attempt to develop a relationship with customers except for a few large and special ones. The change in marketing, says Irani, has been greater than in operations as it started from a very low base. Earlier, a customer in a place like Bangalore would place an order which would go to the head office in Kolkata and then to the works in Jamshedpur. And only after Jamshedpur accepted the order would the buyer get to know the date and price at which the order would be supplied. This process would normally take three weeks. Now the whole company is wired up, order generation and fulfilment have been brought under SAP and a customer's order is confirmed in minutes, in 90 per cent of the cases.

Earlier, the window for executing an order was around four months. Sometimes, in the control days it could be infinity. You paid and got your material later. It improved from the earlier nineties and today there is a very narrow window for delivery, maybe even less than a week. Earlier, there used to be stockyards all over the country for stocking saleable materials and traders who would intermediate between producer and buyer. Today, stockyards and traders are gone. The material is held at the customer's end by a consignment agent so that the saleable inventory is on the books of the company. The customer will draw according to his need, once a day or maybe even twice a day. Tata Steel has now introduced customer accounts managers at the customer's premises and they are the ones who place the orders with the works on their assessment of the customer's likely needs. They have to ensure that the customer never runs out of material. So, if there is a high inventory on Tata Steel's books then it is the fault of the customer accounts manager.

The company has also initiated a customer satisfaction index, which is compiled twice a year by a market research agency. It has in a way helped to measure the dynamics of change and cultural transformation. Recalls Irani, "We were always a few percentage points higher than the best of the rest. Then when we introduced SAP, the wiring up, for one half year our customer satisfaction index went plunging. There were hiccups, people thought this would not last and went on with their old ways. But we made it clear that it would not go away. I got an urgent message once that certain materials for Telco next door were held up as the computer would not issue an invoice. Without the invoice, the material couldn't be loaded. So could we short circuit the system, which only I could authorise. But Telco was informed that they had exceeded the limit and so, they had to pay up. Whatever had to be done to satisfy the computer programme was done. So after the hiccups were sorted out and the customer realised it was for his own good, the satisfaction index has shot up again".

The change in approach and emphasis is best highlighted by the fact that even as the company is drastically reducing its staffing levels, its sales and marketing force has gone up in strength. The company's goal is to build relationships, through relationship marketing. This has paid the company dividends by way of a premium over what the competition realises even in a depressed market. To Irani, the Tata name is a pick-me-up, the first step to getting into a saddle. Then once you are in the saddle you have to provide the service. The marketing effort and ability to earn a premium is closely linked to the changing product mix of the company. The product of its new cold rolling mill, which will meet the requirements of such high value and high profile items as cars and consumer durables, has taken the company one step higher in the value chain.

GLOBAL STRATEGY

A lot of what Tata Steel has done, downsizing its workforce, e-enabling itself and adopting modern marketing techniques is not unusual and is staple for any company that seeks to remain in business in today's competitive global markets. What is more unique, is the way in which a traditional successful company, just the sort which finds it difficult and has little urge to change, changed and reinvented itself with a vengeance. One explanation may lie in the change of management in the early nineties with Irani, becoming the managing director. A metallurgist by training, who had earlier run the operations in Jamshedpur, he was well placed to appreciate the need for the company to technologically upgrade itself and was best able to make the right technological choices. The changes in the marketing setup of the company were fairly obvious and resulted from the compulsions emanating from the new emerging marketplace created by decontrol. The decade also saw several new players enter the steel making scene in India and there was a severe competition between the old and new players. The willingness to change may also have been triggered by the compulsion to prove itself.

Tata Steel, with a capacity of 4 million tonnes, is a small to medium player by international standards. It has to grow and establish a presence on the global scene. The fact that it is hardly known globally, gives it a lower score on 'high quality and niche products' in the WSD study. It has the correct cost composition to enter the arena of global competition, but it has to build on that to eventually earn a premium. "To earn a global premium we have to be a niche player. Our volumes dictate that", admits Irani.

Explaining the company's strategy, he says, "We get a better price in India than our competitors for most materials. We don't have an export grade, only one grade for domestic and export customers alike. We would make the maximum profit if we were to sell all our products in India. But to protect ourselves from currency fluctuations and meet the need for imports we have targeted 15 per cent exports by volume. Our costs are coming down, prices of imported materials are coming down and Indian import duties will also come down. From 25 per cent they will go down to 15 per cent which is the WTO norm under our conditions. If tomorrow the government issues a diktat and says it will be 15 per cent I won't lose much sleep over it." This is the self-confidence created by achieving global competitiveness.

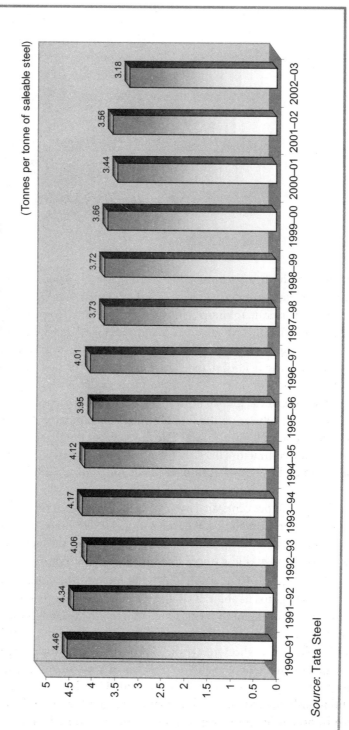

Chart 8.4

Tata Steel
Specific Raw Material Consumption (Net & Dry)

(Tonnes per tonne of saleable steel)

Source: Tata Steel

9

Larsen & Toubro:
Engineers Indian

Larsen & Toubro is a unique Indian company. Its name sounds foreign. Its eponymous founders were, in fact, Dutchmen, but it comes as close as a private company can, to enjoying the status of a national company by partnering the government in strategic areas like defence and aerospace. In its chosen field, it is technologically the only one of its kind between Italy and Japan. Its fabrication yards at Hazira and Powai are among the best half a dozen such facilities in the world. Yet, its bottomline is under pressure. There has been little addition to the global stock of manufacturing capacity since the Asian crisis of 1997, subjecting the manufacturers and erectors of industrial plants like L&T to a prolonged slump. Life for Indian capital goods manufacturers and turnkey contractors like L&T has been even worse, with the slowdown compounded by a growing international competition on home turf because of the gradual opening up of the Indian economy. Many of its plants are working at a 40 per cent capacity (2002). This has taken its toll and L&T has had to divest its cement division, the national leader in size and technology in that industry, as it was unable to carry the division through the prolonged slack in demand and low prices that hit the cement industry.

This widespread slowdown which has revealed the vulnerability of L&T has also highlighted its ability to fight back. The company presents a fascinating picture of a set of engineers trying to reorient themselves into business managers first. But, more than that the fightback has underlined the perspicacity of its CEO, A M Naik, who foresaw the slowdown and set the company off on a strategy of going global as the only means of survival and the only route to prosperity. The story of L&T is twofold. One is, how it has sought to continuously upgrade the technology of the goods and services that it sells. Two is, how it has also used technology to modernise its own running and thus turn itself into a globally competitive business.

This is how Naik says it in his own words, "I had foreseen seven to eight years ago that we would have a hard time growing in India. Once India becomes a part of the global economy, there is no way we will be able to earn the margins we did earlier. So, in the first week I took over (as CEO) I said, forget dependence on India. I started pushing for competitiveness, global benchmarking. I said, transform the whole company to look outward. It takes time. It will take L&T five years to transform itself. By the year 2006, we want our global turnover to be 20 per cent of total turnover. The internal target is 20–25 per cent from zero. And this does not include software. In 1999–00 it was one per cent." But there is an ironic twist to this rapid progress in the ratio. "For the last three years (1998–2001) before we could transform the company, suddenly there is a huge slowdown." So the slowdown in the denominator has been matched by the slowdown in the numerator, thus keeping the percentage intact. But within this and despite the slowdown, much progress has been made. "In fact, the pendulum has swung the other way. We are slightly more competitive abroad than in India." (Chart 9.1)

The mindset in the company is changing nevertheless. An important message has gone out in the organisation: We are not interested in growth for the sake of growth; we want qualitative, profitable growth. At a job site today, more often than not the supervisor will talk of ROC rather than technical issues. Value systems in the company have changed to give more importance to terms like free cash flow, bottomline, as opposed to topline, and of course ROC. The recent emphasis has been on how to create business managers from engineers. K Venkataramanan, president operations who heads the turnkey business, recalls his own career to underline the transformation. He was in R&D from 1970 and moved out in 1980 to set up the famed Hazira facilities. And then he has spearheaded the concept of business managers. Venkataramanan recalls, "A lot of business managers emerged from hardcore engineers. More recently we have been wanting to get more IIM people, more of a blend of the managerial and engineering types." Reflecting the same transformation that is taking place in the leading software companies in the country which have been set up by engineers, he adds, "As we go forward the business orientation is going to take over much more, using your foundational engineering, but with a lot more of business orientation."

BEGINNINGS

L&T made its initial money at the end of the second world war by reconditioning and reselling construction equipment. Its traditional advantage lay in its skilled work force which could be trained very fast in any new technology which the company decided to introduce. It had a unique practice of a four-year training for a workman and never took in anybody except through this route. Says Venkataramanan "We had young, committed, skilled manpower who could quickly grasp the changes in technology." It realised very early that if you want to be good in fabrication you have to be good in welding, fixturing, tooling and with time, operation of CNC machines. First you must have the hardcore skills and practices that enhance productivity at the shop floor. Then comes planning, systems and progress monitoring.

"As a company we went in early into production engineering." The production manager was not just a slave driver but had to think of better ways of doing things. In the early days (1969–70) project work meant putting together small systems. Then came the integration of these small systems into the bigger task of managing the setting up of an entire project. The journey up the value chain can also be captured in the transition from making non-pressure vessels to eventually making ultra high pressure vessels. "We began with residual engineering, then developed capability for detailed engineering. Now we have set up a group for front-end process and design engineering. In the process we are trying to cover the entire gamut of the value chain."

The importance of R&D was realised very early. Along with it, went the need for modern tool rooms and testing labs. L&T's electrical testing laboratory was the first to be set up in the country, before even the government's Central Power Research Institute. As engineering and technology are the key differentiators in L&T's chosen area of business, it has heavily invested in R&D. There are centres in Mumbai and Baroda for this. It also formed two joint ventures, L&T Chiyoda and L&T Sargent and Lundy which helped it upgrade its skills and provided a source of low cost engineering to the collaborators.

L&T had technology, understood it and kept continuously upgrading itself technologically. This eventually led to an extensive use of IT in the running of the company. The domain knowledge of the various businesses L&T is in, combined with extensive use of IT created great strengths in e-engineering. Out of this has grown the decision to make e-engineering a separate profit centre and eventually a separate business, maybe a subsidiary. L&T was one of the first in the country to leverage IT internally. It introduced ERP nine years ago. It uses e-commerce to improve productivity by finding new procurement sources. It has undertaken an extensive knowledge management exercise internally with initiatives like the use of Lotus Notes, document management and a strong networking. It raises general staff IT literacy through two training colleges in Mumbai and Baroda. A key milestone was crossed when it decided in 1988–89 to do away with drafting boards and entirely adopted 3D engineering software and workstations, the first Indian company to do so. Then in the mid-nineties, it travelled much higher into ERP. "IT development in the last decade has been a big differentiator for us. From 1991 onwards we first moved to engineering oriented IT, then to communications oriented IT, then total resource planning for all our transactions and now to the finer side of knowledge management and sharing like e-commerce and customer relationship management."

L&T ultimately seeks to build an India brand in engineering. Naik is acutely conscious of the fact that you don't need to sell the India brand in software. But that is not the case with Indian engineering yet. Says Venkataramanan, "We began with residual engineering and came to the core. The absolute brain is process design. We can build a process design because we are very competitive individually in each of these elements—engineering, fabrication, construction." Which is the space India is seeking to get into? "The trend is we can beat the Koreans in India and not run away like the Japanese and Europeans. People have stopped doing hard work of this type in America—making a pressure vessel, slogging it out welding it. Today America is largely becoming an aerospace, IT and bio-industry country. The skills first moved to Japan, then successively to Korea, Spain and Italy. If tomorrow I am recognised in the Far East as I am in India, I can be very effective. Today we have to break the barriers of being Indian."

L&T's strategy is to defend its core business, then build its international business which it is currently doing and in future have operations like L&T Middle East, L&T Far East. Those will become growth centres as Hindustan Lever is for Unilever in India. That will be the path for the next ten years. "There is some advantage in the India brand which is conceived as a low cost one, with a lot of skilled manpower. We believe we have the ability to offer products and services matching global standards." L&T is transiting from building things to more and more creating the value that is there in designing things.

THE STATUS OF VARIOUS BUSINESSES

We have seen how L&T has set its sights on going global and is using technology and IT to achieve that end. But the company is extensively diversified and these various businesses are running at different paces. To see where it is going and the chances of its overall progress, it is necessary to look at the businesses one by one. Like most diversified firms which are eager to go forward, it is shedding peripheral businesses and focusing on what it considers its core businesses. And to that it has added a smaller list of thrust areas. First, let us look at the cement business which until the year 2003 was the most autonomous and had the least symbiotic link with the rest of the business. It could well have been a different company and it is the low return on capital employed in cement that eventually compelled the company to hive it off.

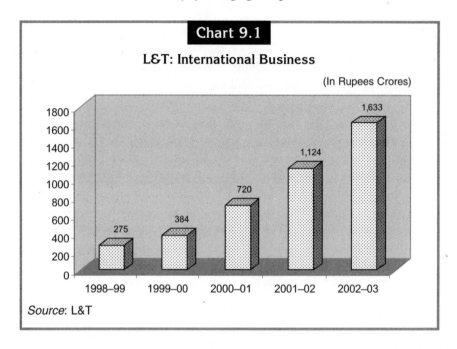

Chart 9.1

L&T: International Business

(In Rupees Crores)

Source: L&T

One reason why it was difficult for L&T to give up its cement business and why it is useful to study it even though it is not a part of L&T any more is because its strengths in cement flowed from L&T's typical strengths. "We are the number one in terms of volume and quality, our plant and equipment are among the most modern in the world and of global economic size," said J P Nayak, president operations and head of the cement division, in early 2002. The quality flowed from its technology in which its leadership was unsurprising as it was the major producer of cement manufacturing plants in the country. Nearly all of the country's cement plants have switched over to the modern dry process and in this energy intensive operation most of Indian manufacturing is fairly energy efficient. Fascinatingly, L&T first went into producing cement manufacturing machinery and then into cement itself. This is the reverse of what most competitive companies do. They go into manufacturing the machines that produce something only after they excel in manufacturing the item in the first place.

L&T's cement manufacturing capacity was globally cost competitive, technologically modern and environmentally up to the mark. The quality of its product was also very satisfactory, enabling it to command a premium on the basis of its brand in this commodity business. "We can justifiably claim that this industry is edging towards world class standards in operations," says Nayak. But L&T's besetting weakness was the poor location of its capacity. Cement is bulky; carrying it across distances is prohibitively costly. So, a company with a large capacity has to have it distributed all over the country. Otherwise it cannot deliver the cement to consumers at competitive costs.

Ironically, some of the cement division's troubles stemmed from its attempt to be ambitious and forward looking. It set up a massive four million tonne capacity on the west coast industrial centre of Hazira, complete with a modern jetty, to send the cement straight from the plant into the hold of ships at the right temperature for export. But unfortunately, from the 1997 Asian crisis, the bottom fell out of the global cement market. From a pre-1997 price of $42 per tonne, prices still hovered at $22 per tonne till 2001. At this price, it was not profitable to export. L&T's misfortune was compounded by the slump in the domestic market also. Investment in new plants is now sharply down and infrastructure projects like ports are not taking off in sufficient numbers. The only bright spot is the government's ambitious road building programme (Chart 9.2).

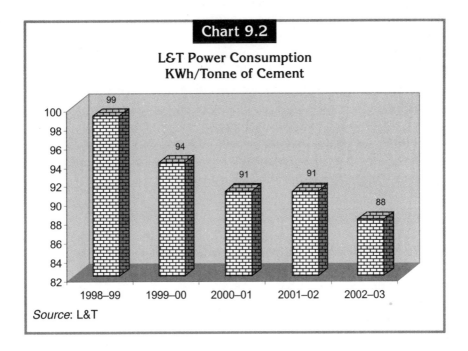

Chart 9.2

L&T Power Consumption KWh/Tonne of Cement

Source: L&T

SWITCHGEAR

The other business in which future global prospects are unexciting is one of L&T's most traditional businesses, low tension switchgear, with which it is often identified by the average non-technical Indian. Domestically, the company is doing fine, with a 40 per cent share of the market. International players like GE, Siemens and Schnider have an Indian market share of between 10 and 20 per cent. Despite earnest efforts through the nineties, the international players have not been able to take away L&T's market share. It scores because of the strength of its distribution and customer services network. In terms of basic technological competency, it is not behind its competitors and claims to have an edge because of the robustness of its design which takes into account the dust and heat of the Indian environment. But internationally, it is non-existent. This is mainly because of its size. The global players are between 25 and 40 times its size and their manufacturing facilities are totally automated.

Within India, the global players have acknowledged L&T's strengths—largely in distribution and a little bit in technology also—by offering to join it in collaboration, even as a minority partner. As for L&T, it is scouting for global partnerships that involve shared branding and product development. Possibilities for this are opening up because the international players now take L&T's ability to develop technology seriously. Operationally, L&T's switchgear is equal to its competitors', though until recently, it suffered from being too bulky. With a third range of products now in the market, this shortcoming has also been overcome. But, still L&T is mostly able to catch up with cutting edge global technology rather than create it in the first place. Considering all this, the share of the electricals division's output—it mainly produces switchgear but also some medical electronic equipment—in the company's total output is not expected to go up from the present 10 per cent by the year 2006 and exports are likely to be 10 per cent of this. But within the country the switchgear business fetches high margins of 17–18 per cent.

CONSTRUCTION

L&T's construction business, popularly known as ECC, is in some ways a simple multiple of its switchgear business. If some know L&T through its switchgear, then many more know it from the many prestigious construction projects that bear its name and whose solidity and durability does much to underpin the image of the company. It contributes a significant part of the company's topline, like E&C (turnkey projects). But the margins in the business are not the greatest. Internationally, L&T is competitive in construction in selected geographical areas where it can manage the risks which are high in such projects. In these areas, the company has an advantage if it can take the labour from India. But so can other such contractors. The same holds for management and supervision where imports from India help but others can do the same. There is some real saving in the cost of the top project management, if sourced from India, but here also CEO Naik says the higher cost of hiring a non-Indian manager more than pays for itself if he has experience in working in that environment and can therefore effect significant savings. But where there is an unqualified competitive edge is in the supply of materials, particularly prefabricated steel items from the Hazira yard. All this, according to Naik, translates into a 2–5 per cent cost advantage.

But even this has to be qualified. There is not much of an advantage or competitiveness in civil construction works which are low skilled. The edge is in mechanical and electrical works, setting up large plants like nuclear power plants, refineries and petrochemical complexes. The company has identified a few thrust areas in this like water projects (pipelines and treatment plants), ports, airports, power transmission lines and buildings and factories. But despite the large presence of the company in many new road projects, there is not much of a competitive edge in it. L&T can get priced out in a business in which there is no pre-qualification and the contract goes to the lowest bidder. But it is different when there is some value added in a project. It can be a road that has to be completed with speed and according to exacting standards. In buildings, L&T has established its forte in putting up intelligent buildings with most of the software technology parks being made by it like the Tidel Park in Chennai, the International Tech Park near Bangalore and the Hightech City in Andhra Pradesh. Overall, L&T considers itself to be only moderately profitable in this field.

TURNKEY PROJECTS

L&T's operations get more distinctive and competitive when it comes to turnkey projects. The margins in this area are higher than in construction but the key issue is risk, which is the highest. There is little advantage in overseas projects from what is sourced from outside India. Correspondingly, the advantage rests in what can be sourced from India. This is where heavy engineering comes in. Increasingly, customers in developed countries prefer as much as possible of the fabrication work to be done off site because of material risk and people risk. L&T's great plus points are its two facilities at Powai and Hazira which are in many ways state of the art. Heavy engineering equipment that is constructed in these places in modular form has high margins. The only downside of this is the freight element, which, when it comes to metal fabrications that mostly make up plant and machinery, can account for as much as 25 per cent of cost. The way the company gets around it is to send the material in shiploads, made up of both critical and non critical equipment, thus bringing down the freight to 10–12 per cent of total cost.

After all the gains and losses are worked out—the latter being material procured from outside India—the overall advantage that L&T would have vis-à-vis a multinational would be around 3–5 per cent. "It is a very very small band of competitiveness," says Naik. But India scores when, say, L&T and Bharat Heavy Electricals (BHEL) get together. There is a sizeable saving in sourcing the turbine generating sets from BHEL, rather than GE. This is what has happened in the case of the power plant that L&T is executing in Sri Lanka, but that has not happened in the case of the power plant that is being set up in Oman. "You have to be super smart at every stage of the work, from conceptualisation to engineering to procurement to construction to commissioning. We have just started in this area."

"In turnkey or EPC (engineering, procurement and construction) projects, L&T's profitability compares very well with that of its global competitors," says Y M Deosthalee, chief financial officer. In this business, many global companies have lost their shirt, millions of dollars. But its problem is the overall cost of capital, which is higher for an Indian company. Hence L&T is trying to reduce its gearing from the present 1:1 to 1:0.7. It has also in the last five years gone up the value chain. He places the company's current capabilities in this field at five on a global scale of one to ten. The jobs the company has been able to do at home, while competing with international bidders, have been both an invaluable learning process and also helped establish its credentials in the respective fields globally. Foremost is the massive desulphurisation project undertaken by the Indian petroleum refineries. L&T, the only Indian bidder, won 40 per cent of the project though it had to spend months making presentations that it could qualify to bid even though it did not have any experience in handling similar work. "We did a fantastic job. All except one project was completed on time and all to the customer's satisfaction. As a result, we have now been qualified to bid for the Oman refinery." Similarly, the company has gained a lot in recent years through its handling of a host of other power projects and offshore projects for ONGC.

HEAVY ENGINEERING EQUIPMENT

The other area where L&T excells is in manufacturing heavy engineering equipment. In some of these like equipment for nuclear power, aerospace and defence where there are no exports, it is difficult to judge the level of competitiveness, though with the opening up of defence to private participation some scope may also emerge for exports. But, by using the technological excellence it has achieved in these areas, it has been manufacturing very high technology equipment like reactors and high pressure exchanges. For this, after five years' effort, it has secured all the qualifications. It is now one of the five to seven companies in the world which manufacture these equipment for a variety of industries and from the beginning it has scored well on quality. "Last year we installed three polypropylene reactors in the US, using a

Union Carbide process, one of the four companies in the world qualified to do so," says CEO Naik.

The entry barriers the company has been able to overcome are best captured by the number of qualifications it has to secure in this field before entering it. In the heavy industry field you need four qualifications even before you manufacture a single equipment. The owner of the process technology, say Union Carbide, has to certify to the customer, say Exxon, that L&T is allowed to build the equipment to manufacture polypropylene. Then come the contractors who take on projects on a turnkey basis, to whom the likes of L&T will have to supply the equipment. These 35–40 global turnkey contractors have to qualify L&T as a supplier of equipment. The third qualification has to come from the quality surveillance agencies like Lloyds for L&T's manufacturing facilities. This qualification has to be renewed every three years. Lastly, qualification has to come from the ultimate owner of the plant being set up like Exxon. All this has to be done before a reactor worth $2 million is supplied.

Says Naik, "Over 30 contractors, over 60 major clients, over seven inspection agencies and over 30 process consultants yield over 400 qualifications. We have more than 2,000 building procedures qualified under one roof, the highest anywhere in the world. It is really a very tedious task, but because it is so we have a chance to be competitive. The Koreans, for example, are not in the space for very high tech reactors because they find the headache too much in relation to returns. In the last six months we have sold reactors and similar equipment worth Rs 180 crore to Norway, Australia, Brazil, US, Canada and Qatar. Fortunately for us, our on-time completion, which is the most critical aspect, has gone to 97 per cent." In this area L&T is highly competitive because it is able to engineer and deliver on time and with quality and the margins are also high.

L&T is also competitive in the field of manufacturing plastic machinery and rubber machinery. The latter—hydraulic and mechanical presses—is going to grow as it is very strong in it with its designs and products. Engineering, machining and fabrication costs are competitive. By the year 2006, 60 per cent of the turnover in this line is expected to come from exports. Another highly successful manufacturing area is industrial valves in which exports have gone up from Rs 27 crore in 1996–97 to Rs 100 crore in 2001–02. These products are exported all over the world and a warehouse has been set up in Houston, US. Exports are targeted to account for 40 per cent of turnover in the year 2006. By then, the entire heavy engineering division—it also includes nuclear, aerospace and defence where exports are negligible—is targeted to have a turnover of Rs 1,800 crore with exports accounting for 35 per cent (Chart 9.3).

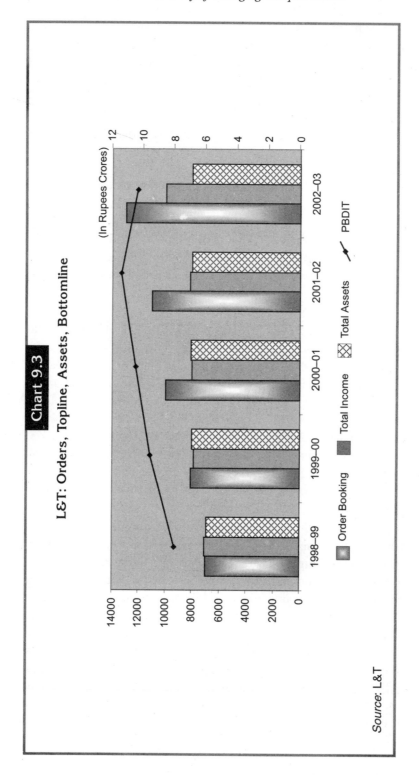

Chart 9.3

L&T: Orders, Topline, Assets, Bottomline

Source: L&T

Perhaps the most promising area is IT services and e-engineering for overseas customers. L&T's capabilities in this are rated as topmost in the country. In this area it has gone into product design and system design where it wants to become partners in interactive and collaborative R&D. It is focusing on select 40 to 50 companies and creating 40 to 50 dedicated centres in four verticals—industrial products (like switchgear), heavy machineries (like tractors, hydraulic excavators), aerospace engineering and automobile engineering. Another initiative taken by the company, is in embedded software because its switchgear, medical electronics, remote energy metering and petrol pumps, all need it. End to end solutions are offered. Software is developed, tested, validated, matched with the product and operated. It is also trying to get into IT in manufacturing which is really its forte. The entire software operations, which currently account for Rs 300 crore are slated to go upto Rs 1,000 crore, with exports accounting for 90 per cent of its turnover.

The engineers who run L&T have sought to put business first but they remain engineers first. Their plans to get the company out of the slump are driven by technology. As the Indian economy picked up in late-2003, prospects of manufacturing capacity expansion—orders for new plants which L&T makes—brightened. The company, minus the drag of its cement division, saw light at the end of the tunnel. With a revived home market, it would be able to better leverage its competitiveness to gain international business.

10

BHEL: Half a Global Player

Bharat Heavy Electricals Ltd, better known through its acronym BHEL, is that great oddity. It is a child of the planning era when the nation staked its developmental future on building heavy machines. That era is gone but BHEL continues as a profitable, publicly listed company which is able to stand up to global competition. Its bottomline is not exceptionally attractive and its price-earning multiple suffers from the common public sector discount but its competitors treat it with the utmost respect. Despite being hamstrung by its public sector status from being able to offer the most attractive compensation packages, in a 2002 Hewitt study* it made it to the list of the ten most attractive Indian companies to work for. In fact, the issue that we will address towards the end of the chapter is not whether it measures up to international benchmarks, which it does, but why it is not beating them and becoming a true global leader.

BHEL is a highly diversified electrical engineering company with power equipment like turbines, generators and boilers accounting for 60 per cent of its business. There has been an enormous global consolidation in this sector and the total number of original equipment manufacturers has shrunk from 10–12 to five, BHEL being one of them. The others are General Electric, Siemens, ABB and Alstom. 80 per cent of BHEL's business is won by competing in global tenders. Since 1978, it has won over 86 per cent of the multilaterally funded orders for power equipment mandatorily placed through public tendering in India. It has supplied 76 per cent of the power equipment installed in India since it came into being. It is difficult for a foreign power equipment supplier to competitively sell in India after the 15 per cent import duty that the World Bank allows. Hence BHEL does not have any problem in licensing

---

* 2nd BT–Hewitt Best Employers in India Survey, *Business Today*, March 3, 2002.

the latest global technology. It is their owners' way of securing a part of the Indian market. The downside of this is that it cannot compete with technology licensed from GE in the United States or from Siemens in Germany. But where it can—for example in the Asean, Middle East and Mediterranean regions—it has on occasions beaten another bidder with the same technology.

What will happen when duty levels are reduced as they will be under WTO disciplines? K G Ramachandran, chairman and managing director of BHEL, has two answers to this: one is that effective protection levels tell a different story from nominal duties. There was an inverted duty structure in the pre-liberalisation days. This still continues. Pre-liberalisation BHEL paid 88 per cent on what it brought in. Today, it pays duty on raw materials in the 5–35 per cent range and the finished goods competing with BHEL's products attract duty in the 0–22 per cent range. If nominal duty rates are lowered while anomalies are removed, then BHEL has confidence in the future as far as the domestic market is concerned.

PLANNING TO GO GLOBAL

But it also has a clear strategy to slowly become a global player by enlarging its global business. The strategy has two parts. One is to raise exports from India. These went up from 2.5 per cent of turnover in 1997–98 to 8.5 per cent in 2002–03, against the 10 per cent target that had been set. Two is to locate manufacturing facilities abroad. There are three ways of raising exports—through projects, products and services. Project exports fetch the maximum value and have so far contributed the bulk of export earnings. But they involve setting up local establishments—having to handle local staff, becoming conversant with local labour laws and learning how to deal with the local authorities. Markets which can be conveniently entered, given the technology licensing restrictions the company works under, have been identified. These are the Middle East, sub-Saharan Africa and East and Southeast Asia (Malaysia).

Product exports involve no such complexities and are short term operations. Hence a plan has been chalked out to promote product exports, by adding a new product and a new destination every year. For this, a market-product matrix has been developed. Products in which BHEL perceives to be within 90–95 per cent of its competitors in terms of cost, quality and delivery have been identified. These products have been modernised and their manufacturing process cleaned up, so that they become 100 per cent globally benchmarked. Product exports, which are currently (2001–02) earning Rs 170–180 crore annually, have been targeted to go upto Rs 250 crore in two to three years (Chart 10.1).

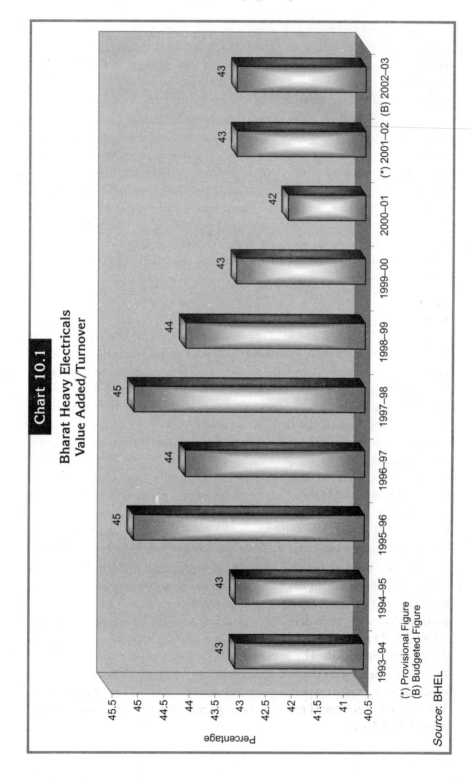

Chart 10.1

**Bharat Heavy Electricals
Value Added/Turnover**

(*) Provisional Figure
(B) Budgeted Figure

Source: BHEL

Another way to go global, is to become sub-suppliers to global majors. BHEL's global competitors do not manufacture all the elements of a power plant. GE makes only turbines, not boilers or transformers. It is the same with Siemens. The exception is Alstom which, like BHEL, is into all aspects of power plant equipment. Hence in the Asian region BHEL can become sub-suppliers to them. It is trying to form vendor relationships so that they can source from it what they do not manufacture themselves, particularly for East Asia. For example, Foster Wheeler makes boilers but while tendering for a particular order, it sought to source the boiler from BHEL instead of shipping it all the way from the US. Foster Wheeler eventually did not win the order, but BHEL had given it a competitive quote for the boiler. Conceptually, the country's cost competitiveness in the heavy metals based sector can be leveraged into a regional advantage because of the importance of transportation costs in the heavy machines business.

BHEL is also laying particular stress on service export by leveraging two advantages—its stock of good service manpower and India's IT skills. It plans to go into IT enabled and service solutions for the power sector and remote maintenance of power systems. It sees a market for this in the Middle East, where it has already executed several high profile power projects successfully since 1978. The area in fact has a larger promise for BHEL. It, along with the Asean, are the two regions where the company is contemplating setting up manufacturing facilities. It did not think along these lines till now, as a global oversupply of power plant equipment persisted through the better part of the last decade. The world entered the nineties with the developed countries feeling they had not just adequate capacity but in fact, an excess of it to take care of even preventive maintenance shutdowns. Then came deregulation and globalisation which ended the protected markets for national companies and forced an extensive consolidation on the industry (Chart 10.2).

GLOBAL SUPPLY DEMAND BALANCE CHANGES

In the last two to three years the supply demand balance has changed, mainly because of new concerns in America, particularly on its west coast, after the famous Californian brown outs. Today, Americans feel that what they thought of as surplus capacity may not be there at all. Hence, there has been a tremendous surge in capacity addition in the US, putting an end to earlier notions of over capacity. The US, which was earlier adding 1 per cent capacity per year, in the year 2001 raised it by over four per cent. Global manufacturing capacity is placed at 139,000 mw. Pre-1999, demand was running at 85,000–100,000 mw. But in the year 2001 capacity addition went up to 177,000 mw, thus taking demand ahead of supply. The present demand and supply balance

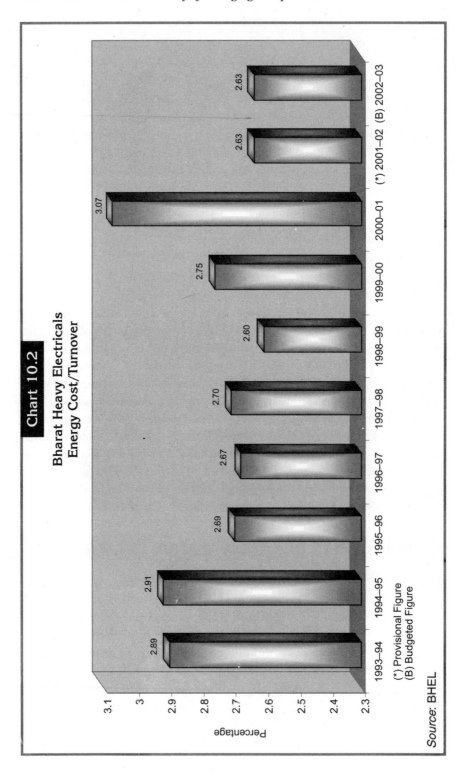

Chart 10.2

Bharat Heavy Electricals
Energy Cost/Turnover

(*) Provisional Figure
(B) Budgeted Figure

Source: BHEL

should continue till 2003, says Ramachandran. Deregulation is continuing, with Europe jumping onto the bandwagon. This may add to a demand for fresh capacity. The US had earlier decided to 'rusticate' nuclear and coal based power plants but the Bush administration has a different attitude, particularly towards nuclear power.

This new demand and supply balance is prompting BHEL to look at setting up capacity abroad. The situation in one of the areas identified for this, the Middle East, may also be changing. So far, the focus area was the Gulf Cooperation Council countries which, with a combined population of 25 million, was not so attractive. But now there is talk of a pan-Islamic group of 170 million people, taking within it Iran, Iraq, Egypt and Yemen which could make a viable market. UAE could be the manufacturing location to supply this market and Malaysia, where BHEL has successfully executed projects, could be the location for supplying the Asean region. "We will certainly have these overseas facilities in the next two to three years," says Ramachandran.

COMPETITIVE ADVANTAGES

What are BHEL's own perceived competitive advantages which make it draw up plans to go global? Ramachandran outlines them thus: it has integrated manufacturing facilities and capabilities developed over the years to provide almost all the main plant and equipment required by a power station. This integrated manufacturing gives the customer a cost effective solution. Second, it is technologically absolutely uptodate in its field. Third, its fixed costs tend to be low. Its factories, set up in the seventies or earlier, have been renovated, upgraded and modernised continuously. Thus it has modern facilities which are nevertheless heavily depreciated. "We have historically valued, fully depreciated assets which continue to be useful."

Fourth, prudent financial management has kept working capital requirements low (these have been under some pressure lately). Still, interest costs currently account for no more than two per cent of total costs. The result is that "fixed costs, interest and depreciation do not figure in the costing of the company," making it globally very cost competitive. Fifth is low manpower costs. Throughout the nineties, the company has not been adding to non-executive manpower and replacing executive manpower judiciously with highly qualified engineering skills. As it is a 40-year old company, with a large recruitment in the sixties and seventies, separation through superannuation is reducing numbers speedily. These, plus a voluntary retirement scheme in the last three years, has enabled it to bring down its total manpower strength by 22–23 per cent, from 62,000 to 48,000 (February 2002) (Charts 10.3 and 10.4).

How has BHEL come to acquire these competitive advantages? A look at how the company started and grew is useful as it is quite unique and has in many ways been a pioneer, able to shake off some of the routine maladies afflicting the Indian public sector. V Krishnamurthy, who headed BHEL through the seventies and is acknowledged as the key architect who gave the company its present shape, recalls that it was started at about the same time as Heavy Engineering Corporation, Ranchi. While the latter has virtually met its end the former is still alive and also very much in the reckoning. "Not a single person who worked in HEC rose to a leadership position over the years. On the other hand, 25 BHEL managers of the seventies became chief executives of other public and private enterprises. A case study at Harvard of these two organisations brings out clearly the fact that the reengineering of BHEL in the seventies made all the difference. That too when reengineering as a concept was hardly popularised by US management gurus".

It is not as if BHEL was successful right from day one. Between 1970 and 1971 were dark days for both BHEL and Heavy Electricals Pvt Ltd, which had till then, not been merged with BHEL. They were considered "white elephants" because of the losses they were suffering and this had eroded confidence in the public sector's ability to run such large operations. In the year 1972, Krishnamurthy was made the CEO of both HEIL and BHEL and in the year 1973, the two entities were merged under the identity of BHEL. By 1977, BHEL was considered the largest and best managed public sector enterprise, among the top half dozen designers and manufacturers of engineering equipment in the world. Structurally and in terms of its business profile, it is today largely where Krishnamurthy had left it and ready for another close look at the fundamentals.

The Trichy unit of BHEL manufacturing boilers always faced domestic competition from AVB. But to face competition on turbo-generators, the company had to look overseas. It scored its first notable success in the mid-seventies by executing its projects in countries like Libya, Saudi Arabia and Malaysia. In fact, the first turnkey job the company undertook was outside the country, in Libya. It looked outward at a time when it did not have to, in the belief that you must test your competitive abilities away from home turf. This commercial policy was matched by suitable personnel policy that sought to limit recruitment only to qualified people and prevented a clerical setup and culture from developing. A sign as to how seriously exports were taken was by placing export operations under the director finance so that quick decisions were available. And to achieve competitiveness, the company has had a productivity drive in place right from the early eighties. Every unit has to identify productivity improvement projects every year. These projects are funded by the company's budget, thus ensuring their monitoring.

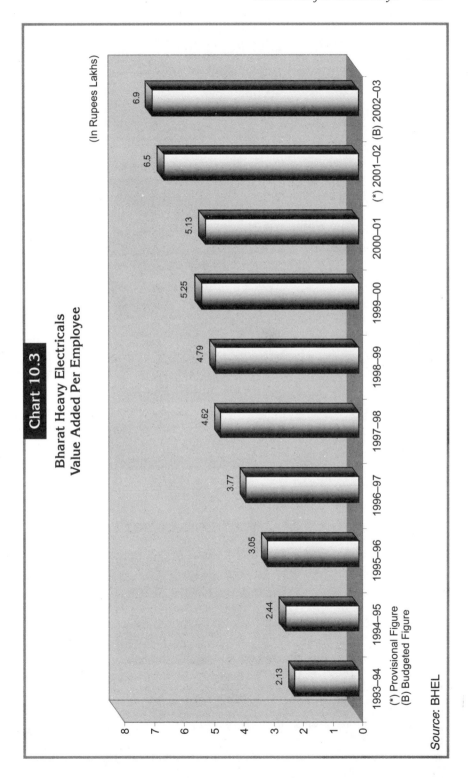

Chart 10.3

Bharat Heavy Electricals
Value Added Per Employee

(In Rupees Lakhs)

1993–94: 2.13
1994–95: 2.44
1995–96: 3.05
1996–97: 3.77
1997–98: 4.62
1998–99: 4.79
1999–00: 5.25
2000–01: 5.13
(*) 2001–02: 6.5
(B) 2002–03: 6.9

(*) Provisional Figure
(B) Budgeted Figure

Source: BHEL

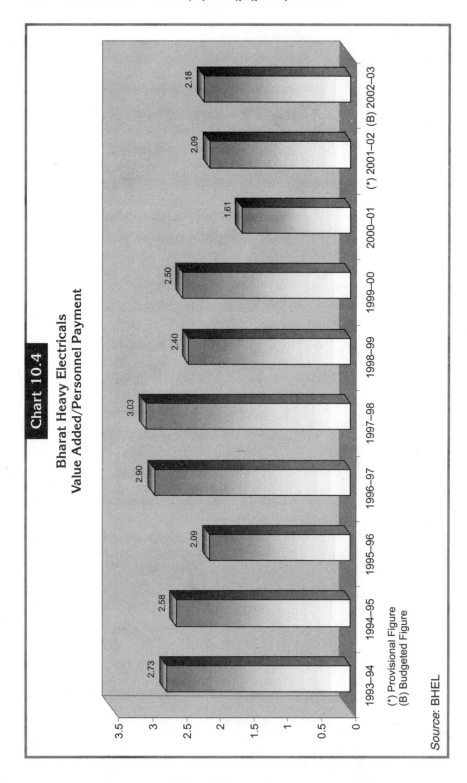

Chart 10.4

Bharat Heavy Electricals
Value Added/Personnel Payment

1993–94: 2.73
1994–95: 2.58
1995–96: 2.09
1996–97: 2.90
1997–98: 3.03
1998–99: 2.40
1999–00: 2.50
2000–01: 1.61
(*) 2001–02: 2.09
(B) 2002–03: 2.18

(*) Provisional Figure
(B) Budgeted Figure

Source: BHEL

Domestic competition came first in the early eighties when the newly set up National Thermal Power Corporation (NTPC), which obtained World Bank funding, had to go in for international tendering to place its orders. BHEL failed to win the first NTPC order, for the Ramagundam project, losing to Ansaldo. It was a shock which made it review and tighten up its tendering and pricing policies and quote successfully. Today domestically, BHEL's bids have become benchmarks which international competitors seek to match. Then when NTPC went in for 500 mw units, the government let BHEL supply the first five with loans from KFW and technology from Siemens. Other than this, BHEL has had to compete for all multilaterally aided projects. The World Bank has allowed it a 15 per cent rate of protection from import competition but, with one exception, BHEL has never had to use this price preference to win contracts.

GOING BEYOND COST

Like all firms and industries that begin by first having a cost advantage, BHEL is seeking to transit into a more durable basis for its competitiveness, based on quality, timeliness, after market service and providing comprehensive solutions. First is quality. The track record of BHEL power plants, particularly those run by the NTPC, has been well established through the very high plant load factor achieved consistently over the years. Second is timeliness of delivery. On this also BHEL considers its record satisfactory. What is more, it has managed to considerably reduce the delivery time cycle so as not to miss a delivery deadline even when some time has been lost through disruptions. The time taken for commissioning a 210 mw thermal power unit has been reduced from 42 months to 28 months and that for 500 mw thermal power units from 51 months to 44 months. This reduction in time cycle has enabled it to reap an additional cost advantage; taking less time to do the same job invariably means doing it at lesser cost.

Third, it is seeking to differentiate itself on the basis of its ability to provide field services. The quality of its service manpower and their knowledge base are the primary capabilities to achieve this. Fourth, more recently it is seeking to provide solutions to customers' diverse energy needs. For example, a customer may want the option to use, in addition to coal and fuel oil, some other fuel. Hence BHEL has been developing boilers which can use corex gas, a byproduct of the steel making process. Then boilers using bagass, the waste residue after sugar has been extracted from crushed sugarcane, have already become very popular with sugar mills. This not only reduces their energy bill but at times, enables them to become net energy suppliers to their adjoining power grid. Also, BHEL's hydro power generators have achieved world-wide acceptance.

As a result of these strategies, BHEL has begun to command a premium in some product areas like boilers. But Ramachandran says that its attempts to reap a pricing advantage based on these features and not costs have been stymied by the global oversupply in power equipment manufacturing capacity existing till the last three years, as has been detailed earlier.

Now that there is a more favourable demand and supply balance, BHEL is seeking to relook at some of the basics. Its first mandate was to make India self-sufficient in power plant equipment supply. "It has achieved this and as a result become a virtual supermarket in power plant equipment," says Ramachandran. But today, global deregulation has reduced the premium on self-sufficiency and upped that on profitability, which cannot come without competitiveness. Hence it has adopted a policy of rationalising its product lines. This involves giving up low tech products and those where other more competent solutions, available externally, can be outsourced. The company offers a menu of 176 products which come under 30 product groups. Hence, it is trying to identify 'star products' in which it will have a market for 8–10 years, has the necessary technology, manufacturing competence and competitiveness in the marketplace. All its investments, process improvements and modernisation effort have been undertaken keeping these star products in mind.

It conducts annual product profitability studies to identify where it is becoming marginal. Once this list is prepared, it is relooked from the strategic angle. If outsourcing a key product from a competitor can affect the profitability of the final product, then its production is not given up on strategic grounds. The areas where BHEL wishes to remain and which constitute its star products are steam turbine and generating set, gas turbine, hydro turbine and generator set, transformer, large electric machine, pump, control equipment, switchgear and control gear, valve, compressor and traction machine. And some of the products that it has given up are trainer aircraft, meters, small telephone exchanges, foundry products (metal parts) and electrolytic capacitors.

BHEL has the Indian market under its belt. It is targeting the Middle East, Mediterranean, Asean and sub-Saharan markets. The US and most of the European markets are beyond its reach because of technology licensing restrictions. That leaves out perhaps the biggest power equipment market of the future, China. But the Chinese market presents certain formidable entry barriers as China does not import what it produces. For example, it has a venture with GE and Westinghouse for gas turbines, but they go only upto frame six, i.e. 39 mw capacity. So for gas turbines of a higher capacity for which BHEL has the capability, there should be a market in China. The other option, under existing arrangements, is to enter into a joint venture with Chinese power equipment companies. But that is not feasible as BHEL does not have the kind of technology to offer that a GE does. Further, China has its own BHELs which produce equipment of sufficient quality. Things may change of course with China joining the WTO and coming under its multilateral trading rules, but that is an era that is just beginning. A third option is for BHEL and Chinese companies to join hands and access third country markets. Even within these constraints, BHEL has made a fortuitous breakthrough in China. It secured a merchant order for three gas turbines for a power plant promoted by AES Transpower, the largest utility in the world, in Western Australia. But this project ran into some environmental difficulties and AES is relocating the project in China. Consequently, BHEL's first power plant will be exported to China.

KEEPING TECHNOLOGY UP TO DATE

Other than cost, quality and timeliness, what has enabled BHEL to remain in business is its ability to keep equipping itself with current technology as it has emerged globally. The BHEL success story is a good example of how to remain technologically competitive without being a frontranking innovator. In this it has been partly like the Japanese who also have not been the primary innovators, but have managed to keep apace with incremental improvements. Since the eighties the Japanese have of course gone much further and this is what BHEL has to aspire to be in the future. But let us first see how the company has fared so far.

Conceptually, BHEL's technology strategy stands on four legs. First, where the technology already available is considered adequate. This applies to transformers and hydro power. Barring a couple of other areas, the technology for what it produces is mature, not changing very rapidly. Coal based power plants, for example, have been around for a hundred years. On the other hand, the earliest gas turbines are around 20 years old. In gas turbines, GE has moved very quickly and occupied a globally commanding position. It owns considerable intellectual property in this area and has captured 45 per cent of the global market and 77 per cent of the US market. The growth in the gas turbine market is confined more to the US and thus GE is open to licensing its technology to prominent players in non-US markets. Consequently, BHEL has employed its second strategy, a technology tie-up with GE in gas turbine technology till 2006. In 2001, BHEL signed two agreements for outright purchase. Such technology, once purchased, is carefully absorbed and put to extensive use. According to one estimate, India's gas resources will last another decade and so BHEL feels that for the market where it matters, it is technologically well covered. By then alternative sources of energy will have become more viable (however, recent gas finds in India and its offshore areas may create a technology gap). Another area where technology has been purchased is supercritical technology which improves boiler efficiency and reduces pollution.

The other area where technology is developing fast and needs to be accessed is control and instrumentation of power plants. Technology in this field was acquired from ABB in the year 1986 but the agreement expired in 1994. BHEL improved the software part of C&I operations on its own and it served the company's needs till 2000. But there was a limit to such improvement and ABB was unwilling to supply developments it was making as a market for the technology was opening up globally. So BHEL has now adopted a two-part strategy. One, it is developing its own technology so as to have its own technology platform for C&I in power plants. But parallelly it has also tied up with Metso Automation MAX Controls of the US for the most advanced platform. This ten-year-long technology tie-up has just begun. Says Ramachandran, "As we are armed with all the technology updates that MAX will give us for nearly a decade more and as our own platform will be ready by 2003, we have started discussions with customers to try out our platform as a backup. Once this product is standardised, we will be technologically self-sufficient in this key area. Here the country's store of software skills has been a tremendous advantage."

Third, where outright purchase is not possible, the route taken is joint working so as to give the technology supplier a share of the business and absorb the technology through the process of working together. Fourth, where none of the foregoing options is available, BHEL develops its own technology in toto. A case in point is gas insulated switchgear which has technological advantages in comparison to vacuum switchgear in terms of compactness, user friendliness, maintenance and environmental acceptability. As the two or three global players in this area will not sell such technology to BHEL, it has developed it on its own. It has already supplied switchgear of 36 kv using the gas insulated technology. Switchgear of 145 kv is being developed and the next step will be to work on 245 kv capacity.

As opposed to gas, India's coal reserves will last two more centuries. Power equipment using such coal faces two challenges—high ash content and environment cleanliness. The technical challenge of using such coal has already been overcome internally, as the technology obtained from Combustion Engineering would not have served the purpose. What remains to be tackled is the disposal of the ash and the environmental angle. The lion's share of the 107,000 mw of new capacity envisaged by the power ministry by the year 2012 will be coal based. By that time, BHEL foresees that its ability to handle coal from the environmental angle will have also improved. In two other areas also BHEL has tied up the sources of the latest technology. One is supercritical reactors, of 660 mw, for which an agreement has been entered into with

Babcock. Technology for 1000 mw plants is academic because the first hurdle that India has to overcome to make use of such large generating capacity is grid and transmission capacity. The technological angle in two other areas have also been taken care of. For steam turbines a ten-year extension, from 2001, of the agreement with Siemens, has been concluded. In blade design, an incremental improvement is taking place.

BHEL has also been active in another technological frontier—non-conventional energy sources. It has been carrying out continuous development in solar photo voltaic cells. Systems have been developed not only for homes, hospitals and hotels but also for stand alone, grid independent power solutions. A 700 kw solar photo voltaic power system has been put in operation in Lakshadweep. A similar 100 kw system has been set up in Mausami island in Sundarbans, West Bengal. More importantly, work is going on in amorphous silicon which is also a source of non-conventional energy technology. From a 'single junction' stage the technology has progressed to the 'triple junction' stage. A pilot plant for it, set up for the government, is being transferred to the company for continued research in the area. Wind turbines for wind energy have also been developed with the help of technology from the Danish company Nordex. The non-conventional energy business already accounts for 3–5 per cent of the company's revenue (2002–03). Costs are going down but non-conventional energy is still not commercially viable without government subsidy. BHEL's aim is to keep a foothold on this technology frontier so that when such technology becomes commercially viable, it will have the wherewithal to be a player in it.

THE FINAL GOAL

With all this development, has BHEL done all that it could and ought to have on the technology front to maintain a role as a competitive player? Krishnamurthy thinks not. It could have done much better. With the headstart it had and the amounts sunk in R&D expenditure and facilities, it should be standing alongside a GE or a Siemens as a global technology provider. For example, it was a pioneer in the use of information technology but never exploited it as a business area. To better global benchmarks and become a leader, BHEL, Krishnamurthy says, must focus itself better. In products it should concentrate on hydro turbines and generators, transformers and traction equipment in which it can become a global leader. Second, it should lay greater emphasis on services. Third, it should use the WTO regime to reenter global markets that have been barred from it. To be able to do this, it will have to reduce production costs and also improve on providing composite services. That is the real challenge. Otherwise, BHEL will remain half a global player (Chart 10.5).

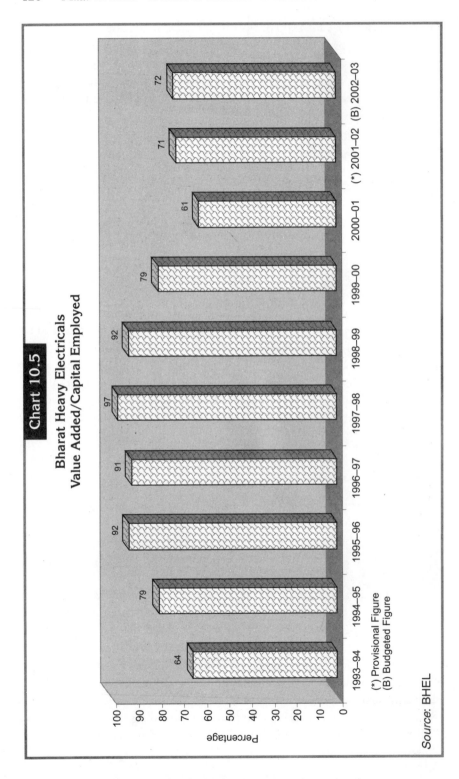

Chart 10.5

Bharat Heavy Electricals
Value Added/Capital Employed

Source: BHEL

11

Reliance: Startup to Global Big League

Reliance Industries, India's largest private sector company, lays claim to being one of its most competitive. It exports close to a fifth of its turnover. It is also one of the youngest large companies in the country, being beaten in this regard only by the software companies. Till its founder, Dhirubhai Ambani, who began earning a living as a petrol pump attendant in Aden, died in 2002, it was a first generation company, with all the energy and aggression that mark a startup.

The company began in the early sixties as a merchant trader with emphasis on exports, then went into manufacturing textiles, grew phenomenally through the seventies and eighties to become a petrochemicals company, first producing polyester and then a whole range of petrochemicals. In the late nineties it added a massive refining capacity, and subsequently entered oil exploration, thus making the story of Reliance into one of remarkable backward integration. Thereafter, in the new century, the Reliance group traversed the old-new divide and entered the fields of life sciences and telecommunications. It first became a mobile service provider in a small way and started to lay a braoadband network across the country. Then in early 2003, it introduced limited mobility phone services in a big way in the entire country. At the same time it also became a player in the power sector by gaining control of a leading Indian utility Bombay Suburban Electric Supply.

Reliance's exponential growth, which was wholly unparallelled in Indian corporate history, was initially attributed in part to its founder's ability to manage the political environment during India's era of planning and strict government control of industrial investment. Dhirubhai Ambani himself never sought to downplay the role of the government in Indian business or the need to influence it. According to him, convincing the government meant adopting a flexible approach. "The most important external environment is the government of India. You have to sell your ideas to the government. Selling the idea is the most important thing, and for that I will meet anybody in the government. I am willing to *salaam* anyone. One thing you won't find in me and that is an ego." The absence of an ego extended to taking pride in his very humble beginnings. He would often ask journalists to write about his rags to riches story. He told one journalist, "Please mention this in your magazine because I am proud of it and people should get inspiration from this." Or to another, "I am only a matriculate and I would like you to particularly mention this fact. People will have hope that they too can become successful." He would often joke that he belonged to the 'Zero club' because he started with nothing.

But fascinatingly, the pre-1991 growth, attributed to managing the political environment, pales into insignificance when compared to the growth registered during the nineties, the decade that began with an end to licensing of industrial capacity. Between 1991 and 2002, Reliance's turnover grew from Rs 2,100 crore to Rs 57,000 crore, 28 times or by a compound annual growth rate of 40 per cent. The biggest jump came with the amalgamation of Reliance Petroleum, which was the vehicle for the new world class refinery, with Reliance Industries in 2001. Anil Ambani, vice chairman and younger son of the founder, recalls pointedly, "In 1991, when India's economic reforms really began, the verdict out there even before you gave time to anybody was, Reliance will collapse, Reliance will become history. Reliance is a creation of the licence permit raj. I said in 1991–92 that half the industry groups that are there right now will not exist in 2001. Look at 2002. It is pretty much a reality."

ACCOLADES AND ATTRIBUTES

Over the last couple of years, Reliance has won plaudits from a wide range of industry organisations, analysts and business publications, and personal recognition for its leaders.* In a survey conducted by the American Chemical Society, Reliance Industries (prior to its merger with group company Reliance Petroleum) ranked 31st among global chemicals companies in terms of year 2000 sales. A survey conducted by European Chemical News in 2001 adjudged Reliance Industries as the tenth most profitable chemicals company in the world. In 2001, Reliance Industries became the first Indian private sector company to enter the Forbes list of the top international (non-US) companies. And the group's petroleum refinery at Jamnagar, when it came on stream with a capacity of 540,000 barrels per day, became the fifth largest refinery in the world in a 2001 listing of the Oil and Gas Journal.

---

* It features in the Forbes Global list of the world's 400 best big companies.

The foregoing recognitions give a measure of the company's size and profitability. What of its competitiveness? The company cites an Arthur D Little study of 4,000 Asian companies, based on the Michael Porter model, to claim that Reliance is among the top ten competitive companies in Asia across all sectors, alongside Sony, Honda, Toyota and Acer, and also the most competitive chemicals company.

What made Reliance competitive? Says Anil Ambani, "Achieving competitiveness in what you do is clearly a state of mind. Even prior to economic reforms, it was my father's vision to be globally competitive. So, whenever he spoke about building a plant, he spoke about economies of scale. In the sixties when we started with four knitting machines, we were exporting 100 per cent of our production. Vimal as a brand got known first in the international market and then in the Indian market. The Indian customer got to know of it from the domestic sale of 'export surplus'. What was this paranoia, this great love for exports? It was only a dimension to saying, if I can be a quality producer, if I can understand fashions, trends, designs, colours which are acceptable internationally, I know I have set a benchmark. As you trace back the history of Reliance, it all started somehow with the bug in my father's mind for quality. The other thing that drove him to create large capacities was the belief or gut feeling that if our per capita consumption in India is so low, then it has only one way to go, which is up. So, long before people spoke about competitiveness, it was a *mantra* in Reliance."

Mukesh Ambani, now chairman of Reliance, traces the growth of the company to the 'irrepressible' desire of its founder that India should be second to none in the world. This had created a passion for world class businesses and facilities and a global outlook. Dhirubhai Ambani measured performance by two simple tests: are we able to earn more from one rupee of investment than others and can we execute a business plan in lesser time than anywhere else in the world? "This has created a commitment to achieving the highest level of capital and operating productivity."

ASIAN LEADER

By the late nineties, as the global surveys cited earlier have shown, Reliance had become an acknowledged Asian player in the chemicals business, largely through its petrochemicals operations. These received a massive investment boost since the mid-nineties which took the output from 1 million tonnes to 10 million tonnes in 2000. The new facilities in Hazira and Jamnagar, both in Gujarat, made it the world's second largest producer of polyester filament yarn and polyester staple fibre, the third largest in parazylene, the fourth largest in PTA and the sixth largest in polypropelene. Handling such a large expansion and investment would have been daunting for any company. But during this period it simultaneously undertook another massive investment. It floated a separate company, Reliance Petroleum, and set up a grassroots world class petroleum refinery at Jamnagar in Gujarat that doubled the group's turnover. The company now has under its belt the largest greenfield refinery business in the world. The history of how it was done explains the basis of the global competitiveness of the company better than anything else.

For a petrochemicals company that was so wedded to backward integration, a refinery was the next logical step. The strategic fit was perfect, recalled Mukesh Ambani, but expert opinion was not so encouraging. International management consultants indicated that the refining business had matured and would generate no more than 6–8 per cent returns in dollar terms. Even under India's then prevailing administered prices regime, a refinery would earn no more than a marginal rate of 10–12 per cent. This did not make it economically viable. "In this context we took the first daring plunge. We decided to build a new business at the intersection of petroleum refining, petrochemicals and power generation. The integration of these businesses would generate value that no single business can generate alone." As integration with petrochemicals and power generation could help build a refinery that fetches superior rates of return, Reliance decided to build one "in defiance of conventional wisdom and against expert advice."

Earlier, refineries were designed to process a limited range of crude oil. The first innovation that Reliance introduced was to design for the processing of virtually every type of crude oil in the world. This raised capital costs but would allow the company to capitalise on price differentials in crude oils and earn higher returns. The second innovation was to so configure the product mix as to have a higher proportion of lighter fractions that are of a greater value (among a refinery's products, furnace oil or naphtha are some of the heaviest products which fetch the least value, whereas kerosene and aviation fuel are the lightest that fetch the highest value). The heavier products would get converted to lighter products which would add more value. While older refineries produce two per cent of high value liquified petroleum gas, Jamnagar would produce 12 per cent, and while the former produce 15 per cent of fuel oil products, the latter would produce none of that at all.

SETTING GLOBAL BENCHMARKS

The third innovation, and perhaps the most important, was to set a new benchmark for the capital cost of a refinery. This was crucial for the viability of the project as refineries are capital intensive. Reliance first completed the project at a 30–50 per cent lower cost than similar refineries around the world and then went on to commission the project in 60–90 days as against the normal 6–18 months. "Thus Reliance redefined programme management, project execution and start up," claims Mukesh Ambani. The dramatic reduction in commissioning time was achieved through actions on a range of areas like engineering, procurement, construction, fast track project management and financial engineering. Reliance acted as its own managing contractor with responsibilities for supplies, resources and infrastructure. In sum, it took a lion's share of responsibilities on its own shoulders which reduced costs but at the same time heightened risk.

The 30 per cent plus capital cost advantage, complexity of the project, low crude delivery cost and good product fit have combined to enable the Jamnagar project to achieve one of the lowest per tonne conversion costs in the world. According to data made available by the company, the Indian Oil refinery at Panipat, commissioned in 1999, has achieved a $8.2 per barrel per day processing cost, Star Petro of Malaysia commissioned in 1996, $12.1 and Jamnagar $5.9 (Chart 11.1). The capital cost is matched by a globally low selling cost and rock bottom costs for a highly skilled workforce, the latter derived from the country's competitive skills base. The average age of Reliance employees is 37, 44 per cent of the professional workforce is below 35, 83 per cent of them are engineers, eight per cent are MBAs and two per cent are PhDs. A study of Jamnagar, made in the year 1999 by Solomon Associates, compared the refinery with its Indian peers, Asian peers, European pacesetters and US pacesetters and placed it "among the top ten per cent of companies in the world in terms of capital and operational efficiencies and generating superior returns for its investors," says Mukesh Ambani.

The emphasis on competitiveness is there in the statement of Dhirubhai Ambani at the last annual general meeting of Reliance Petroleum (it has not till then been merged with Reliance Industries) which he addressed in 2001. "RPL's objective is to become amongst the lowest cost producers of petroleum products globally. RPL benchmarks itself against its global peer group on all operational parameters. RPL intends to continuously enhance its global competitiveness by: optimising crude oil procurement and the product mix; improving refinery production yields; enhancing product quality; reducing operational costs; improving operational productivity and efficiencies; focusing on energy conservation; and strengthening logistics management further."

RELIANCE BRAND

With the exception of the Vimal range of fabrics which accounts for only a minuscule part of the company's turnover, Reliance has been mostly into producing commodities like synthetic fibres, petrochemicals and refinery

Chart 11.1

Lowest Capital Cost Refinery in Asia

Company	Commissioning Year	Capacity (Mbpsd)	Capital Cost ($ million)	Cost per Unit Capacity ($ per bpd)	Nelson Index
MRPL, India	1996	60	760	11.2	6.5
Shell, Malaysia	1996	125	1,978	15.8	4.14
Star Petro, Malaysia	1996	150	1,820	12.1	–
IOC, Panipat, India	1998	120	986	8.2	6.31
RIL—only Refinery	1999	540	3,209	5.9	9.93
—with petrochemicals	1999				13.77

Source: Reliance

products (Chart 11.2). Its margins have come from cutting costs and raising operating efficiencies, rather than reaping brand premiums. But Reliance and brand equity go together, argues Anil Ambani. "Reliance is a strong brand by itself. It attracts capital, attention, goodwill, it has its own aura at the marketplace from an employee, lender and investor perspective." The Reliance brand was both promoted and used through the late seventies and eighties when Reliance raised, by Indian standards, unprecedented sums from the capital market which provided a cornerstone for its growth. In the process was born the equity cult in India and also the Reliance brand among the investors. "If we as Reliance did not have access to the capital of our 6 million investors who built Reliance, we wouldn't be here. They have put in equity capital, which is venture capital as far as we are concerned, and they have made their returns." In the process the Reliance brand has been fortified.

Chart 11.2	
Reliance: Global Ranking in Major Businesses	
	Global Rank
Polyester (fiber and yarn)	2
Paraxylene	3
PTA	5
PP	7
Refining	4th largest at a single location
Source: Reliance	

Reliance's financial innovativeness has further extended to the global capital market with the opening up of the Indian economy and the opportunity for Indian firms to raise funds outside the country. "In 1993–94 we became the first company to issue GDRs and opened up that market which has now raised billions of dollars for the government of India and the private sector. Opening up the debt market, issuing 10–20–30–50–100 year paper, getting Moody's and S&P rating, those were all very cutting edge decisions" which helped introduce the India and Reliance brands globally. The long term debt created an yield curve for Indian paper in global markets where none had existed earlier (Chart 11.3).

Chart 11.3

Reliance: Refining Margins

(US$/bbl)	Last 3 years' average
Reliance	5.2
Singapore	2.4
Delta	2.8
Rotterdam	1.1
Delta	4.1
NY Harbor	1.8
Delta	3.4

Source: Reliance

Moving forward to the new century, Reliance is banking on the strength of its brand, created by 30 years of growth and the millions of investors, to change from being only a manufacturing company into one that is also into information, communication and value added services. "I think we have a pretty good feel and understanding of the Reliance brand equity in going forward. Where are the telecom revenues coming from? Who are they? They are the same whom we sell something or the other to. We already have an interaction with them and they are the guys who are going to bring in the telecom bucks. So it is only a question of extending that brand equity, leveraging that to capture a larger part of the revenue of the future," adds Anil Ambani.

ENTERING THE NEW ECONOMY

Reliance's venture out of manufacturing into the new economy ICT space is in three areas—laying a broadband network in the entire country, offering a GSM mobile phone service in several states and most ambitiously covering the entire country with a CDMA mobile service. The GSM service is being offered through Reliance Telecom and the CDMA service and the broadband network is being offered through Reliance Infocomm. The rollout for the GSM mobile services got extensively underway from the year 2001 and by 2002–03 it covered 15 states and accounted for over 400,000 subscribers. Through Reliance Infocomm, Reliance has connected 115 cities through 60,000 km of a broadband network. It also holds licences for national and international long distance services.

At the year ending 2002, Reliance Infocomm revealed its hand by announcing CDMA mobile services in 673 cities at virtually half the rates offered by GSM service providers. It also threw in free incoming calls and low STD rates. At the time of writing, the CDMA service has got off the ground at a very fast pace but is still plagued by regulatory uncertainties (its right to offer 'roaming' has been referred to the Supreme Court). Earlier its marketing model suffered a setback as Reliance Infocomm decided to dispense with the services of most of its newly appointed selling agents who had failed to bring in the requisite customers and rely instead on its own distribution network. But few doubted that eventually the service would settle down and usher in a new cost paradigm in Indian mobile telephony.

The features of the CDMA mobile telephony, which were evolved under the guidance of Dhirubhai Ambani, bear the hallmark of Reliance's business model that Indians have become familiar with. It principally rests on economies of scale, made possible by mass coverage, and ensures low cost. Dhirubhai's understanding was that a long distance phone call would not be attractive to the common man who would bring in the volume unless it costs about the same as a *paan*. It then fell upon the project team to bring down capital costs suitably to make such pricing possible. They sought to achieve this in two ways—develop a part of the enterprise software in house and beat down the international vendors reeling under the slump in demand brought about by bursting of the technology bubble. And as if inevitably, Reliance Infocomm's decision to offer roaming facilities to its subscribers under licences allowing for only limited mobility was seen by its GSM competitors as its long term ability to shape policy to suit its business ends.

If Reliance is able to successfully stabilise its ICT business, it will have traversed the old-new economy divide. This will reaffirm its competitiveness which rests on its ability to achieve international quality benchmarks and beat international price benchmarks by going in for economies of scale and innovatively cutting down on project costs.

12

A Deming Family in India

Countries have usually developed global competitiveness in individual industries (nobody is good in everything) which have grown up in identifiable geographical clusters. An Indian competitiveness seems to be emerging in auto components and two wheelers in the state of Tamil Nadu. But what is unusual is that there is an additional synergy among some of these globally competitive auto companies in the south Indian states—they are all run by members of one family and belong to the eponymous TVS group. There is no group oversight of companies but those who independently run them are the first to acknowledge that they belong to a common tradition and share certain values which have gone a long way in making these companies what they are today. In this chapter we will take a look at Sundram Fasteners which is run by chairman and managing director, Suresh Krishna, Sundaram Brake Linings which is run by chairman and managing director, K Mahesh and TVS Motor Company which is run by its managing director, Venu Srinivasan.

The most defining common attribute of the TVS family is that firms run by its members have monopolised all the three Deming awards that have come to Indian companies. Sundaram Clayton won the highly prestigious Japanese quality award in the year 1998, Sundaram Brake Lining in 2001 and TVS Motor in 2002. Sundram Fasteners has not won a Deming award as yet, but belongs firmly within the Japanese quality tradition. The Deming award was instituted by the Union of Japanese Scientists and Engineers in 1950 and its recipients have come to represent the highest standards of quality in manufacturing—a field in which Japanese companies have come to be acknowledged as world leaders. A company that wins the Deming award is automatically acknowledged as a global leader in terms of quality and that is the firm foundation on which global competitiveness is built. Three out of these four companies are medium-sized and the fourth, TVS Motor, is small as auto assemblers go. We will examine how these companies, which were so firmly placed in the backwaters of global manufacturing, came to acquire global class.

SUNDRAM FASTENERS

Let us first take a look at Sundram Fasteners which has been in the Indian corporate limelight the longest by virtue of having become a star OEM supplier to General Motor. The story of Sundram Fasteners' association with GM goes back to the year 1988, when it landed a sizeable order from Opel, the European brand of GM. A couple of years later, GM came to Sundram Fasteners and asked if it was interested in buying a radiator cap plant in England, which GM was closing down, and supply the entire output to it. Sundram Fasteners successfully bid for the plant, set it up in Chennai and has for the last eight years been supplying its output to GM. It has been awarded five times now for being the best supplier of radiator caps to GM. GM has around 30,000 suppliers and around 150 of them are so honoured every year for being the best suppliers. Being a persistent winner "has given us tremendous confidence as not only are we the best in terms of quality but also cost competitiveness," says Suresh Krishna.

Sundram Fasetners' journey down the road of excellence in quality began in the mid-nineties when it took the help of the Japan Institute of Plant Maintenance to introduce the total productive maintenance (TPM) process. The company opted for this as TPM, which addressed manufacturing, would most suit the company's needs. TPM put a lot of emphasis on zero or hundred—zero breakdown, zero consumer complaints, zero accidents and hundred per cent consumer satisfaction. In just four years, the company won the institute's award for TPM excellence. It now exports a little over 20 per cent of its output and, Krishna says, "our goal is 50 per cent of our revenue should come from non-rupee areas. We have become convinced over the last ten years that we are extremely competitive globally in terms of price, knowhow and sustaining customer satisfaction." So, the company has now started looking for acquisitions or even setting up greenfield ventures overseas in order to become truly global. A key consideration driving this is the local content requirement rules that exist in China and the Asean region.

It was only in the early seventies that Sundram Fasteners started looking globally. "We felt we needed to measure our quality against the world's best," and the company landed an order from Mercedes-Benz in Germany. "We got reasonably good orders for one and a half years from Mercedes-Benz in Manheim for critical items like connecting rod bolts. Then we had a problem as the German suppliers thought we could be a threat and told the company that you either buy everything from Sundram Fasteners or cut them out. What was important was not the value of what we supplied but the fact that our quality had been accepted." (Chart 12.1)

That was the end of a chapter but not the end of the company looking globally. In fact, it was goaded on to do so by the sluggishness in the Indian automobile market. As soon as it started seriously looking outward, treating exports not as an additionality but as a regular business, it realised that it had to change its entire organisational structure which was till then geared only to the domestic market. It got into initiatives like 'war on waste' and 'policy deployment' with the help of Lucas Engineering Services, UK. It was at this juncture, between 1988 and 1999, that the company won the order to supply Opel and started its journey outward in right earnest (Charts 12.2 and 12.3).

SUNDARAM BRAKE LININGS

Sundaram Brake Linings, the second TVS company that we are examining, was also outward looking from a very early stage. It started exporting in 1978 to meet an export obligation given to the government. After 25 years it is now exporting 54 per cent of its turnover to 56 countries. "We got hooked onto exports because it gave us an exposure to what was happening in the rest of the world," says K Mahesh, chairman and managing director, adding with amusement how difficult it was to pinpoint on the map, for the benefit of the workers, Croatia which had just been added to the list of export destinations. When the journey down the road to global competitiveness began in earnest in 1987, it was a "typical, traditional, floundering Indian company." Today it is confident of meeting the challenge of global competition. "By 2005, we should be ready for a zero import duty regime. That's what we are working for," asserts Mahesh.

The transformation of Sundaram Brake Linings can be broken up into two phases—from 1987 to 1996 and from 1997 to 2001, when the company won the Deming prize, the only brake lining company in the world to do so. The initial phase began with the adoption of statistical quality control tools and continued in an exploratory fashion by picking up ideas here and there, often from books, and trying to implement them in a do it yourself fashion. A key landmark happened in the year 1989 when the company took the help of Lucas Engineering Services of the UK and set itself certain goals to improving its manufacturing practices. These goals were all over fulfilled and a point to point comparison, between 1989–90 and 1996–97, captures some of the change. Sales per employee rose from Rs 3.4 lakhs to Rs 8 lakhs, the stock turn ratio rose from 10 to 30, the order book fell from one month to three

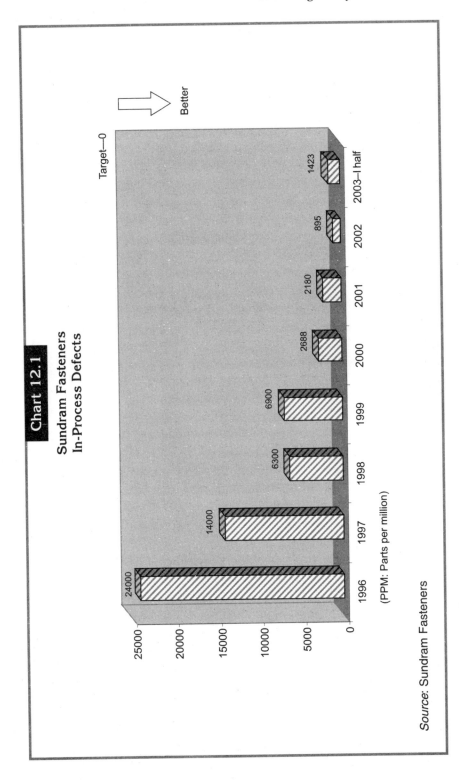

Chart 12.1

Sundram Fasteners
In-Process Defects

(PPM: Parts per million)

Source: Sundram Fasteners

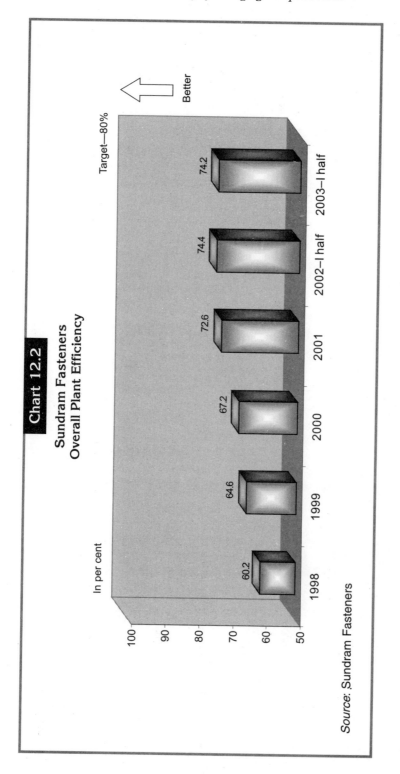

Chart 12.2

Sundram Fasteners
Overall Plant Efficiency

Source: Sundram Fasteners

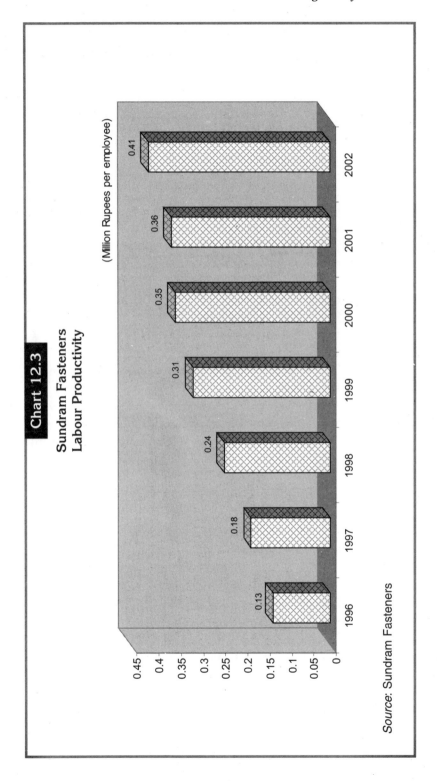

Chart 12.3

Sundram Fasteners
Labour Productivity

(Million Rupees per employee)

Year	Value
1996	0.13
1997	0.18
1998	0.24
1999	0.31
2000	0.35
2001	0.36
2002	0.41

Source: Sundram Fasteners

days (why sit on orders) and the internal defect rate, which measures quality, fell from 6.2 per cent to less than three per cent. A British consultant benchmarked the company in 1996 and ranked it "pretty close to the British auto components industry" and indicated that "in five to six years we should be world class." (Chart 12.4)

1997, the beginning of the second phase of change in Sundaram Brake Lining, is a key year. That year it began the process of adopting "lean manufacturing", one of the names by which the Toyota Production System is known. Prof. Daniel T Jones, head of the Lean Manufacturing Centre in the UK, " visited our factory in 1997 and lit a bomb, saying your material flow is not smooth. That hurt our pride, as we had worked for ten years and the man walks in and says too much *mooda* (waste). I asked him to rank our company compared to Toyota. He said you will be three out of ten. Toyota would be nine. It will take us three to five years to become world class and maybe we will reach 70 per cent of Toyota." Then, in quick succession the company adopted TQM (total quality management) in 1998 and TPM (total productive maintenance) in 1999. So, the company simultaneously had three sensei (a teacher whose learning curve you borrow)—for TPM, TQM and lean! "We were one of the few companies which were doing TPM on one side and TQM on the other side. Then we realised this is what Toyota had done 38 years ago. After it got the Deming award, it borrowed TPM from Denso which was part of Toyota. So they merged the two to form the base for the Toyota Production System. In my opinion TQM is the right hand and TPM is left hand which together protect the company and make it stable and responsive to the customer." (Charts 12.5 and 12.6)

PLAN, DO, CHECK AND ACT

Recalls Mahesh, "In 1997 Prof. Y Tsuda was our sensai for TQM. He put TQM in a completely different perspective. We were doing elements of TQM, fundamentals, but he made us start thinking differently, the TQM method of thinking. We used to look at production and sales at the end of the month and look at the gap. But, by that time it was history anyway. So he introduced daily work management—everyday, what is it you planned, what is it you did, what is the gap and why did the gap arise, and do a PDCA quality cycle—plan, do, check, and act. So we started doing it every day, now we do it every hour. From a month to a day to a shift to an hour is the change in thinking which has happened. This change took place through 1997 to 2001. But it required 10 to 12 years' preparation before that."

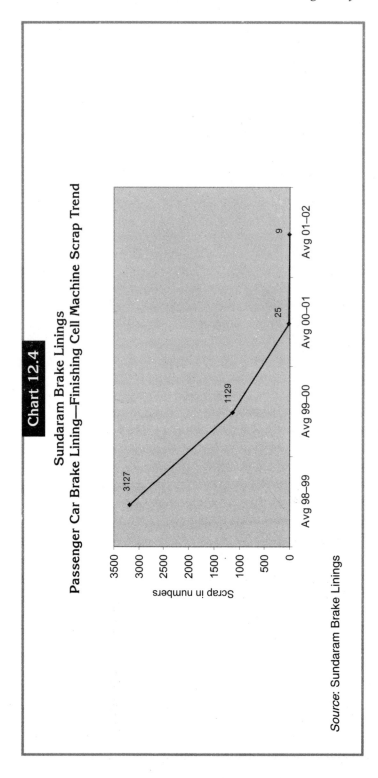

Chart 12.4

Sundaram Brake Linings
Passenger Car Brake Lining—Finishing Cell Machine Scrap Trend

Source: Sundaram Brake Linings

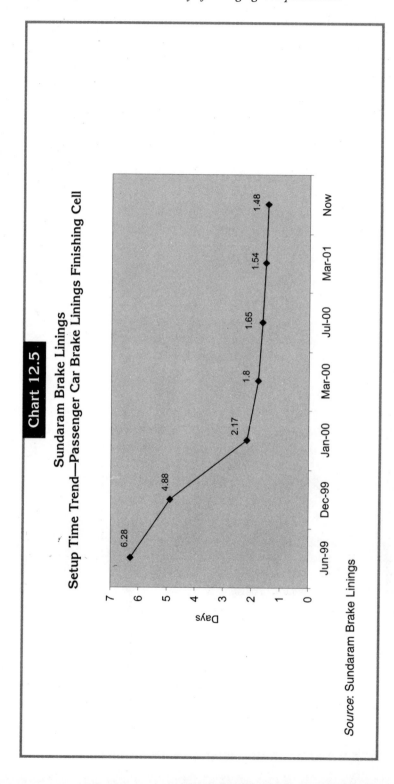

Chart 12.5

Sundaram Brake Linings
Setup Time Trend—Passenger Car Brake Linings Finishing Cell

Source: Sundaram Brake Linings

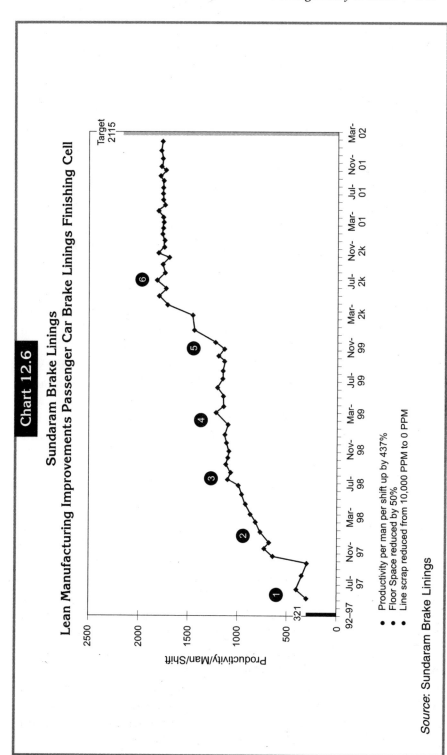

Chart 12.6

Sundaram Brake Linings

Lean Manufacturing Improvements Passenger Car Brake Linings Finishing Cell

- Productivity per man per shift up by 437%
- Floor Space reduced by 50%
- Line scrap reduced from 10,000 PPM to 0 PPM

Source: Sundaram Brake Linings

From its daily work management, the company went in for a deep analysis which involved designing of experiments to optimise the process and reduce the cycle time. This also led to a reduction of scrap. Thereafter, Prof. Tsuda introduced managing points and checking points so that each manager had a set of checking points which are the subordinate managing points. This created a tiered system of controls of what the person is supposed to check and what he is supposed to do. Finally, he "introduced us to what is called policy deployment where you align the company's policy and all departments down the line get aligned. You normally take three objectives for the year and you align every department for the year. So the whole company and all divisions are aligned to one goal of achieving those three targets."

At the end of the second phase, where does Sundaram Brake Linings stand? Between 1997 and 2002, in the passenger car brake lining finishing cell, productivity per man per shift has gone up by 437 per cent, floor space use is down by 50 per cent and line scrap has gone from 10,000 ppm to zero. A longer time perspective makes the change process clearer. For the same cell, a key ratio, value added time to production lead time, rose from 2.9 per cent before 1990 to 8.3 per cent in June 1999 to 22.2 per cent in March 2002. The benefits of the processes adopted can also be gauged from the changes that took place in the passenger car finishing U line—scrap was down by 93 per cent, downtime reduced by 85 per cent, changeover time took four minutes, labour productivity was up by 424 per cent, and customer service level was up 798 per cent. Where was the human element in this? The number of workers in the line was reduced from seven to two and supervision was no longer needed!

Mahesh sums it all up thus: "Our labour productivity is four times. The throughput time has come down from six days to 1.5 days. The velocity of movement through the plant is so high now that no ERP can catch it, and by the time you capture and display it, it is out of date anyway. We have started working with our suppliers and we are now collecting 60 per cent of our material every day. We are also starting to work with our distributors who used to have six to eight weeks' stock. We are trying to first get that down to 10 days, then six days. They believe it won't work. We say, we'll prove it to you that it works. The whole question of *mooda* or waste of inventory starts from the supplier to the end customer. You keep on reducing *mooda*, eliminate waste and reduce your costs. This is the whole principle of Toyota."

What Mahesh is particularly proud of, is the way in which his company has started building machines. "One of the things Toyota practised was, never go and buy a machine because they never build it for you. We were able to make our machines 50 per cent cheaper because we knew exactly what we wanted. So we saved a tremendous amount on investment. In India, the cost of capital being high, this is one of our greatest achievements."

TVS MOTOR

The emergence of the third company in our study, TVS Motor, on the national horizon is the most dramatic. Till well into 2000, it was one of the lesser players in the Indian two-wheeler market whose main claim to fame was its decision to end its collaboration with the global two wheeler leader Suzuki and change its name from TVS Suzuki to TVS Motor Co. The main concern among the company's investors then was how it would be able to source technology, now that the collaboration with Suzuki was no longer there. Then, in late 2001, TVS Motor grabbed everyone's attention by launching Victor, the 110 cc four stroke motorbike that it designed entirely on its own. Victor had an exceptional preview in the technical press and became an instant success from almost the day it was launched. Overnight, TVS Motor became that rarity among Indian players on the automobile scene, one with product development capabilities that would not only allow it to stand on its own feet but possibly help it to chart an international script. Its managing director, Venu Srinivasan, has set a clear goal ahead of the company, "We want to be among the top five two wheeler companies in the world in the next five years."

Looking back, he recalls how in the sixties and seventies, people went to sleep in India when all the doors were closed to competition and the business scenario was marked by MRTP, licensing and severe import restrictions. "Like all companies many of us also went a little soft. So when the eighties came and the markets started opening up, I think this yearning for the past glory broke through and different TVS companies started activities to build back their world class capability. The way we did it was largely through Japanese methodologies of TQM, lean manufacturing. In the auto components business lean manufacturing was the absolute key, and in the larger businesses like automobiles, TQM was more important, not just lean manufacturing. By whatever methodology, TVS companies have striven over the last ten years to get back the original excellence that TVS stood for."

THE JOURNEY

Early attempts made at establishing TQM started with Sundram Clayton in 1987. The pace of learning and implementation was significantly accelerated from 1994 and the company won the Deming prize in 1998. TVS Motor Co also followed a similar schedule and path. The first and foremost task it set before itself was to get the organisation and people's attitudes right. In the interregnum of the sixties and seventies, people's attitudes had flagged. The kind of highly committed individuals that had formed the core of TVS companies many years ago was now somewhat dispersed. "We had to do two things—one, have a certain amount of patience for some people to retire and two, request with incentives the really intelligent naysayers to leave." With a core team back in place, the second step was to take up some simple, not too difficult tasks which were obvious to the eye for improvements to be made in manufacturing, design and sales. "We did the dealer development programme in 1993 and some amount of supplier training from 1996. The focused HR development process was started in 1998, lean manufacturing and TQM in 2000. The new product development process, which was started in 1993 was greatly improved and culminated with the launch of the Victor in 2001. So various things came together to make it possible for TVS Motor to get the Deming prize in 2002."

Conceptually, the whole process can also be broken up into three phases—awareness, promotion and implementation. First came the awareness and consensus building phase which lasted for about two to three years, from 1993 to 1996. Then, came the phase of initial implementation which was really a promotional phase when you started training everybody, started small projects and secured company wide implementation. This phase happened between 1996 and 1998. Then came the real implementation phase which was between 1999 and 2001. "This took eight years but I don't believe the market and economy will allow future companies to take eight years. You won't be there in eight years. So I think the awareness phase needs to be much tougher. We waited to build a consensus slowly but today you need to compress that to a year. It's the same with the promotion phase which needs to be compressed to two years and the implementation has to happen within five years. People say the market will not give you even five years but I don't believe it can be done in lesser time. In any Six Sigma programme you will get significant improvement in three years, but for the programme to be holistically implemented it will take at least five years. I believe the same is true for a complete company-wide TQM."

Having conceptualised and categorised, Srinivasan admits that these journeys were not always as coherent as made out in ex post facto rationalistion. Also, human beings act by intuition and not just by logic, so you make some right and wrong moves and as you go along, the picture starts emerging and then everything comes together. "This, in my opinion is the truth of most organisational growth. But later on history records it in a more logical and rational fashion."

THE ROAD AHEAD

What lies ahead of TVS Motor? "I would believe our productivity needs to be about 30 per cent better than what it is today. To be really at the cutting edge, we have to be 50 per cent better than what we are today. We'll get there. On the productivity front we have completed a significant amount of work on reengineering the manufacturing process. In manufacturing we are today able to get 20 per cent plus improvement in productivity year after year. But on the white collar front—marketing, engineering, accounting and other administrative areas—I don't believe we have done the same amount of reengineering. Even in manufacturing, we have some way to go. That would be the key reason why I say 30 to 50 per cent. Third, we have invested a large amount in engineering and marketing which will not increase as our sales increase substantially over the next three years. This is the input needed for developing our own capability without any partner. There is a greater amount of managerial investment in a company that is building for itself than a company which is a licensee. So this productivity will be made up with time."

In terms of more specific milestones, on the quality status, the company hopes to achieve an internal rejection rate of less than 100 ppm on engines by April 2003 and the goal of good global standards of less than 50 ppm by another six months. Five years back it was five per cent which is 50,000 ppm!

TECHNOLOGY VISION

The vision of the future and the performance of the past are closely related to technology. Profits peaked between 1993 and 1996 when the company used up all its capacity. They fell between 1996 and 2000 because basically it didn't have a four stroke motorcycle. It could have licensed the technology for a 100 cc motorbike from its technology partner, Suzuki, but "we were very clear in our minds that four stroke motorcycles should be designed and made by us. So we only licensed a higher cc bike. We made our own four stroke scooter and then all that we learned from making it was converted into a completely new motorcycle which has succeeded very well." Technology is important not just from the point of view of saleable products but also costs. 67 per cent of the company's selling price is material cost. So, value engineering, design for cost and supplier improvement are the three areas which create the right cost improvement.

But, in the age of converging technology in automobiles when most world class products in the same category have similar technical profiles, R&D has to deliver products that sell. It also determines whether the product is sold at a premium or at a discount. Product design and packaging can deliver the difference between premium and discount. "So it is really new product design that is the key winning competence in the automotive business. You can see it in cars, you can see it in two wheelers," says Srinivasan.

In R&D, particularly the sort that delivers successful models in automobiles, nothing can be delivered overnight. The company already had a moped business before it tied up with Suzuki. It had made its own moped to suit its own design. While in collaboration with Suzuki, it designed its own scooter called Scooty. Srinivasan picks out a critical differentiator when he explains that "because we had a history of our own design, we had the freedom to do our own R&D. Most joint ventures are usually not permitted to do this. As we already had a business, products, we constantly strengthened them, knowing full well that ultimately a joint venture, even if it lasts as a joint venture, must have its own capability. Otherwise the other partner won't respect it and will one day put pressure on you by denying products, saying if you want this product then you better sign on the dotted line, either on costs—they will skim away the profits—or on control. We knew there was an inevitability in a joint venture. So we had always from the beginning invested in an R&D capability. We had engineers sent to the best universities in the world for training, got the best consultants working with us."

Even being able to design appealing products with world class specifications and engineering is not enough in the automobile business. There has to be a sufficient flow of new products. "We have gone from making one product at a time to three products at a time. From doing one or two variants a year, we can now do five or six variants in a year. Our lead time for a product has come down from 30 months to 22 or 23 months and we will bring it down to 18 months by application of simultaneous engineering and design of experiments. The entire planning exercise is made to bring products to market in time. One product or swallow does not make a summer. So next year we plan to launch three or four new products. It is the success of that which will finally put the seal of approval or confidence, saying that this company has come of age and does have the capabilities to become a global company."

With all these products in the pipeline, what are the company's international plans? "These are at this stage only a gleam in our eye. Exports are going to be very difficult. They can be undertaken to the US, Europe and parts of Africa, all of which represent less than 20 per cent of the less than 150 cc market. We believe we have to go to Asean. China, India and the Asean are going to account for 80 per cent of the global two-wheeler market. So in the next ten years we have to be in all these markets. There you will have to manufacture, because they also have a condition in the Asian Free Trade Area that you will have to have 40 per cent local content. Our business will grow by investing in those markets and growing our volumes. We will certainly go to Asean in the first stage. We will go to AFTA which includes Indonesia, Malaysia, Vietnam, Philippines, Thailand, Cambodia and Laos. We will have to set up one or more assembly/manufacturing plants, depending on logic, logistics and costs," outlines Srinivasan.

THE TVS WORM

These are the stories of three TVS companies that have now become world class. A common thread that runs through them—their use of Japanese quality processes to achieve global quality standards and through that route achieve global competitiveness. But why did these companies take this particular route and most of the rest of corporate India, the more well trodden path? All the three companies say that they are where they are because of their shared TVS ethos. TVS dates back to 1912 and through the thirties and forties came to stand for things like productivity and quality. In the forties, it ran a bus service in Madurai which became synonymous with punctuality. Suresh Krishna recalls that when Sundram Fasteners was born in 1966, it was small in size but rich in an inherited tradition. A method of doing things, system of running a company, upkeep of assets—these have all been a part of TVS values since the group's inception.

Says K Mahesh, of Sundaram Brake Linings, "TQM has become a way of life. But funnily enough these practices were a part of the TVS way back in the forties when my father and grandfather were alive. Most of the machines we bought were world war surplus. They were all rebuilt and worked till about 1992–93. There was regular retraining of mechanics, we had a training school. So a lot of elements of TQM were in TVS, which we didn't know. At that time Japan was nowhere in the picture and the word TQM was not even there. But unfortunately, TVS lost that culture when we went into joint ventures with the British and the Americans. They had a very different approach to quality— as long as you could sell it, you got away with it. I went to the UK in 1967 to get trained. I am an IIT graduate. When I realised that all that I had learnt was wrong in terms of methodology, I had to unlearn everything."

Venu Srinivasan talks about the same thing thus, "The milestones go back to 1920 when TVS started the dealership with GM. We ran dealerships which were to world standards in those days in terms of customer service, integrity and sales effort. TVS has a history, a common ethos, key values, that are driving companies, be they Sundram Fasteners, Sundaram Brake Linings, Sundaram Clayton or TVS Motor. The first key value concerns employees who have always been empowered and treated as a part of the family. It is us (employer and employees) versus the market—a single group of people who are committed to the larger cause of the company and its missions. Second, customer satisfaction was the foremost goal of the company, to the exclusion of almost everything else. If the employees are not totally committed to the mission, you cannot really service the customer and he cannot come first. We always maintain trust, with our customers, society and shareholders. So it was always the concept of a larger stakeholding community with which one needs to maintain trust. We always call ourselves, Trust Value Service for TVS."

All have dwelt on the key role that treatment of employees play in the TVS ethos but Mahesh says it most forthrightly, "When we started the change, I told the workers in an open meeting in 1987, management screwed the whole thing up, I apologise. But let us not look back. I assure you any improvement you make, no confirmed employee will lose his job. I have maintained my word and they have never reminded me that it is the management which first screwed it up. Most of the problems in industry, particularly in India, are created by the top management because of lack of knowledge, implementation and a fire in the belly to become world class."

The shared values are passed on long before formal apprenticeship begins. Says Krishna, "Being a business family, I have been subjected to a lot of interactions with my father, uncles, from my school and college days. Many of the value systems of running a company have been handed over more by osmosis than formal apprenticeship." Adds Mahesh, "We talk business all the time. At a TVS marriage, within five minutes after the initial pleasantries, we are back to, how is Telco doing, how are your exports doing. Everything sort of gets shared. Unfortunately, there is nothing called family life, they (work and family) are completely entwined. We get exposed from a very young age, and more so through shop talk. Maybe we are a very unique, or maybe a typical brahminic family."

Such a distinctive ethos must have a name and Mahesh has chosen to give it one: "Fundamentally, Toyota calls it the Toyota worm, the Toyota way of thinking. We would like to think there is a TVS way of doing things which we have rediscovered after a lapse of 20 or 22 years. The TVS culture in some of us who have been exposed to the elder generation is so strong that it is like a TVS worm."

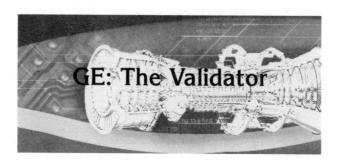

13

GE: The Validator

We have so far examined the various sectors and firms in the Indian economy which have achieved a degree of global competitiveness. We have traced this to advantages which are both national and also rooted in the historical development of individual firms. All these micro studies taken together will enable us to develop a profile of Indian competitiveness—in what way and in which spheres Indian business and the environment for it are competitive. We now submit our evolving profile of Indian competitiveness to a simple test, a proof of concept. If certain competitive advantages are found to reside in India, then in this age of globalisation some global firms should be coming forward to set up bits of their business in India to take advantage of those competitive elements. In this chapter, we take a look at the extensive operations of General Electric in India to answer the question just posed, in the affirmative. Yes, it is indeed correct to say that in India, there is a globally competitive supply of certain skills and India provides a competitive environment to run certain businesses because GE has extensive business operations in those areas in India.

How did it all begin? Here is a bit of anecdotal history as remembered by Tarun Das, director general of the Confederation of Indian Industry. "The GE story is very interesting. In the eighties, Ratan Tata, Jamshyd Godrej, Rahul Bajaj and myself used to go every year to the US as a CII mission. We said we will meet CEOs and talk to them about India. India was closed then. It took us a year to get a meeting with Jack Welch. I remember we left our hotel at 6 am to have a breakfast meeting with Welch at 7.30 am. He said I am not interested in India. India is corrupt, India is closed. We don't want to do business in India. We talked to him for an hour and a half, CEOs speaking for the country without any authority. Eventually, he came here. Every time he came he addressed the CII."

R A Mashelkar, director general of the Council of Scientific and Industrial Research, remembers an equally fascinating story. Since the early nineties, when CSIR started to develop an international clientele, GE was one of the first targets. "In 1992 I had been to their Schenectady, New York R&D centre, to give a seminar. But I had put in a ten minute commercial on National Chemical Laboratory. I was supposed to just lunch with the scientists but by lunch time, the table grew bigger with other people coming in. By afternoon we were discussing what we could do together. In the evening, the senior vice president came in and they made me postpone my visit so that I could talk to him. Within 2–3 months they sent four people just to see whether what I was saying we could offer was true. They were very impressed by what they saw and then we started talking in terms of contract research as a partnership. And when I quoted a price, they said for this we can buy a Russian lab. They had come via Russia, USSR was crumbling at that time. I said you go and buy it but you won't get what I am going to give you. And they came back and our partnership started growing."

That was the time when the benefit of patenting became very clear to both sides. "We had developed a superior process in polycarbonate in which GE have a 40 per cent global market share. When we first filed a patent on it, it was almost like putting a flag on their territory. It was that and a portfolio of two or three other patents which we finally licensed to them. That is how the partnership began. And then their confidence grew and at one stage they asked, do you have the capacity, and I said we can double it year after year for the next five years. So when a presentation was made to Jack Welch he said if NCL is so good then why are we not there. That is how the idea of the Jack Welch Centre in Bangalore was born."

Scott Bayman, head of GE's operations in India, sums up its raison d'etre in the country in these words, "We found that the quality of work done here was as good, if not better, than in the US, as measured by Six Sigma. So, in essence, India offered a good combination of capacity, intellect and quality. And of course at a much lower cost." This has a clear topline implication. "By the middle of this decade exports from India could touch $3–4 billion from a little over $1 billion in the last couple of years," Bayman said in the year 2001 (Chart 13.1).

GE's discovery of India took place in two parts. It first started looking at India seriously in the late eighties as a market for its products. Bayman says, "We saw in India a highly educated workforce and people that were likely to continue to value education. We also saw an inherent entrepreneurial capability in the country. The other plus in India was the wide use of English as the language of business. There was also a familiarity with and similarity to accounting practices prevailing in Europe and the US where we did business. In addition, there was a body of law that gave some sanctity to contracts. Then when liberalisation came we got even more excited and proceeded to establish joint ventures with some of India's leading businesses." But around 1996–97 the realisation dawned that the markets in India were not going to grow as expected earlier. Also, around this time GE needed to expand backroom capacities to support growth, having made some acquisitions in the US. It was boom time in the US economy and the employment market there was very tight.

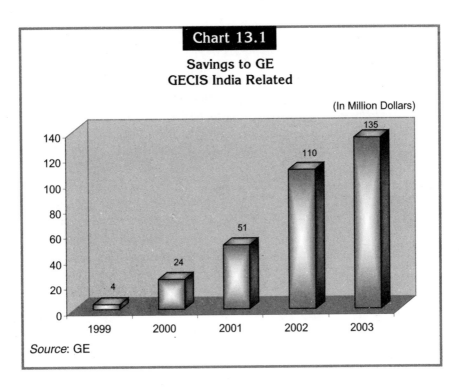

Chart 13.1

**Savings to GE
GECIS India Related**

(In Million Dollars)

Source: GE

At this juncture, when the Indian market was not growing according to expectations and US demand was sprinting ahead, "India presented us with a very attractive alternative," recalls Bayman. The outsourcing opportunity from India was perceived and seized. "It is often assumed that this meant call centres, but the outsourcing also included work like processing insurance and mortgage applications and claims. We found we were able to attract educated people here who sought to build careers instead of looking for something more temporary. All this influenced our decision on what made sense to do here. As we looked into the future we realised that the human and intellectual capital won't go away. Compensation packages may go up but other costs of doing business likely will go down with further liberalisation, privatisation and more competition .... So the overall relative competitive cost position of India may not change that much." Bayman predicts that "India will remain far more important as a sourcing centre and for software and engineering than a market for our products. We love the costs but are also getting the quality and the capacity. We wouldn't be here in this scale just for the costs, that is an added benefit."

MEDICAL SYSTEMS

One of the main areas in which GE has successfully outsourced from India for its global business is medical systems. By 2002–03 GE Medical Systems, South Asia was a $300 million business comprising several arms—Wipro GE Medical Systems, GE Medical Systems X-Ray (South Asia), GE BEL, Global Technology Operations and GEMS Information Technology—and slated to earn nearly $250 million in exports. The medical systems story began in 1990, when Wipro GE Medical Systems was formed with the initial task of launching CT and ultrasound scanners in India. These were launched in 1992 with the help of GE Yokogawa Medical Systems of Tokyo. Recalls Shanker Annaswamy, CEO of GE Medical Systems, South Asia, "We kept introducing new models by bringing the best technology to the local market through local production. We did so well in ultrasound that the Japanese asked us to meet a small need in Korea. The product was so well liked that people said, why don't you design and develop ultrasound scanners for the world market from India? So we worked with GE Yokogawa and designed a product called Logic 100. That, with some variations, sells till today and is very popular in many countries, including Germany."

The next big change came when in the mid-nineties, GE decided to move its manufacturing facilities to low cost countries with the requisite technology skills and the company picked India as a source for key components in medical electronics and detection. So a joint venture was set up with Bharat Electronics to manufacture high tech X-ray tubes, high voltage tanks and later critical devices like detectors for CT scanning machines. These have very high technology content and handling them requires engineering and design knowledge. Over a span of five years, GE BEL has grown into an organisation employing 300 people and clocking up exports of over Rs 323 crore a year (2002–03) which accounts for over 95 per cent of its output (Chart 13.2). These exports meet the highest regulatory standards all over the world.

In GE, when the manufacture of a product is transferred from a high cost to a low cost country, the cost saving has to be 30 per cent or more. Simultaneously, quality has to be equal or better, as defined by the Six Sigma philosophy. And of course, delivery schedules have to be maintained. Says G Manohar, managing director of GE BEL, "Where we really scored over others was the speed with which we absorbed technology, growing beyond the vision set initially." This success in manufacturing was in no small part the result of successful outsourcing. Vendors have been developed who are capable of delivering the highest quality. Hence, GE in India is a source of not just finished equipment but top class components for assembly all over the world.

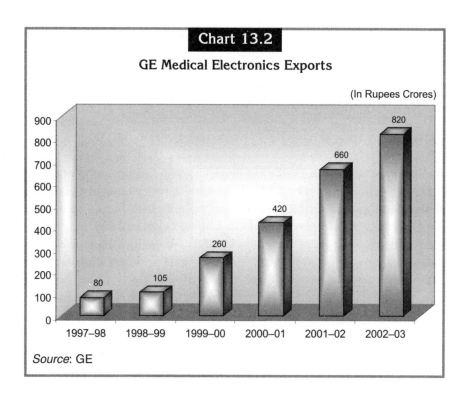

Chart 13.2

GE Medical Electronics Exports

(In Rupees Crores)

Source: GE

The third major arm of GE Medical Systems in India is GE Medical Systems X-ray, which designs and manufactures the complete range of X-ray systems for both the domestic and international markets. It is also a global supplier of surgical C-Arms and components like MRI tables and coils, and generators for CT scanners. The fourth arm is Global Technology Operations which designs and develops products and solutions using the latest computer platforms. Diagnostic software is 80 per cent of electronics and there are 650 people, the largest group, working on medical electronics at the John F Welch Technology Centre which will be discussed later on in the chapter. It works mainly in the areas of medical imaging technology applications, networking and teleradiology. The designing marks the third and technologically the highest level of functioning of GE Medical Systems in India. Ravi Mohan, managing director of GE Medical Systems X-ray, sums up the entire transition thus. "Five years back we started with assembly operations. GE physically did a transfer of the plant to take advantage of lower costs. Once we saw the productivity gains in labour, the next step was locating vendors within India. And once that was done, the next step was designing in India. Now it is 100 per cent designing, 100 per cent manufacturing and 80 per cent sourcing of components in India."

The GE medical electronics team explains that manufacturing high end technology intensive products are their competency. They are good in such manufacturing as it requires high levels of skilled manual intervention for operations like soldering and engineering. Also, the skill sets that are needed to value engineer, to take quality to the next level, and to make a product smaller are all within their domain.

BUSINESS PROCESS OUTSOURCING

The most visible and financially the biggest outsourcing operation of GE in India is in business processes. To lay India it is GE which brought call centres to India and gave IT enabled services out of India their biggest push. The international services operations of GE Capital began in India in 1997 by conducting the simplest of operations like data processing for just one of the dozen businesses of GE worldwide. Then the same work was carried out for other businesses. The next step was to ask what else can be done with that data. This led to applying certain simple rules to the data and taking decisions on their basis. Thereafter, began the job of taking complex decisions based on rules, involving an element of subjective judgement.

The subsequent step marked a qualitative change. With every business it began to be asked, what is it that is done which does not require face to face interaction with the customer? The whole area of finance and accounting was thereby identified. Here also, it began with simple tasks which became more and more complex. After this it began to be asked: Why can't you talk directly to the customer? Again it began with the simplest of tasks, like collecting overdue payment, and moved onto more complex ones like collecting more difficult amounts, equipment finance dues or tracing people who had disappeared without clearing their dues. After calling up customers, the next step was responding to customer calls. The more complex part of this was providing solutions remotely, like trying to solve why a refrigerator is not working.

Today, the work is more or less evenly divided between the following areas—transaction processing (data, images, paper), accounting and finance, collecting different business receivables, handling customer services, providing solutions and data modelling. The last is about the most high end work. A group of mathematics and statistics post graduates and doctorates are conducting cost and price analysis of different product lines to determine which product lines are more profitable and which are not. Pure number crunching also takes place through statistical data modelling and regression analysis, for example identifying which segment of the 65 million credit card customers will react to a Christmas promotion. Now there is a group entrusted with the task of implementing Oracle as a platform in GE businesses. The outsourcing setup also provides the IT help desk for the whole of GE (e.g. responding to a GE employee who has trouble with his computer) and is doing server management for the whole of GE.

The same story can be told in terms of more specific milestones. Recalls N V Tyagarajan, CEO of GE Capital International Services, "The first milestone was when we hit the measurement baseline in the first few processes that we brought in here in the first two months, against the original delivery target of one year. The targets were in terms of how quickly you can give a decision and how low is the defect rate. This created great confidence among the team here as also those who had given the work. The second milestone was when we realised that not only could we deliver better service but were able to completely change the process. We shift a service, run it better and then run it differently. That makes it run better and far more productively—fewer people, lower cost, far more automated processes, all the grunt work gone".

"The best thing for us as a country is that all the people doing the work are capable of making the changes. So we don't have to depend on someone coming in from outside and doing it. That is the beauty of the young, educated workforce. It is they who come up with the ideas and changes. The average age is 26–27, average experience is 4–5 years." They are able to work on global technology platforms sitting around the globe and delivering to global standards to customers worldwide. The third milestone is expanding into new cities. From the beginning in Gurgaon near Delhi in 1997, GE's internationals services operations branched out to Hyderabad in 1992, Bangalore in 2001 and Jaipur in 2003 (Chart 13.3).

How has this become possible? "Our premise always was that in this country we will be able to find a much more educated workforce than in the US doing similar work. That educated workforce would not only be able to work the process better but also improve it over time. The other premise was that not only would the work be done at a lower cost but deliver better quality. So it almost became a slogan with us: Come to us for cost and stay with us for quality. We have 30 different industries in this one company and all the businesses have something happening here. Education plus IT, which this country is good at, plus the process rigour of Six Sigma—that's the value we create for the business and process customers we deal with." When a process is moved, it has to deliver cost savings in the region of 30–80 per cent. After that through scale and improvements 10–15 per cent cost reduction is delivered every year.

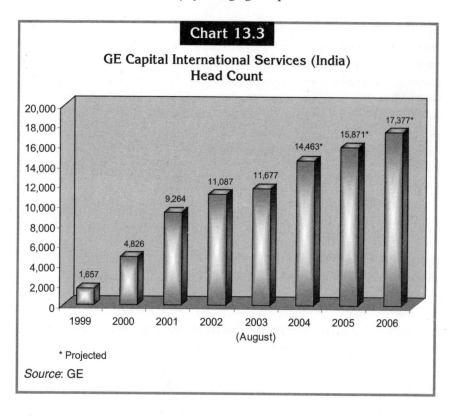

Chart 13.3

GE Capital International Services (India) Head Count

* Projected

Source: GE

ELECTRICAL MOTORS

The Indian success in software and knowledge based areas is contrasted with equal lack of success in manufacturing. The success of GE Medical Systems in producing and supplying to the world top class equipment only marginally alters the pattern. After all, modern day medical equipment is very high tech and, as has been spelt out earlier, requires highly skilled manual intervention, thus setting such operations apart from automated mass manufacturing. But GE in India has scored a major success in conventional manufacturing, too—electrical motors.

GE Motors took over a 33 year old factory in Faridabad near Delhi and put its managers there. Today, the fractional horse power motors that the factory produces are global leaders. How did this change come about? The challenge faced by GE's Indian managers at Faridabad was peculiar. Motor manufacturing in developed countries has the advantage of accessing metal at low global costs but it has to grapple with high labour costs. In India it is the opposite. So the key balance to be struck is between man and machine—which automatic process to convert to semi-automatic or manual, and then use Six Sigma to perfect the manual processes and deliver consistency.

The key decision taken right at the beginning was to opt for evolution instead of revolution. The solution lay not in fully automating an old plant with its given layout and implicit costs. Instead, for every machine, a man versus machine evaluation had to be carried out to strike an optimum balance between capital cost and wage cost. A brainstorming or 'workout' in GE language was carried out with all the stakeholders to identify the hurdles in the way of cost reduction. Global prices being given, the only controllable variable was costs. Aspects studied in detail were process layout, workers' training and motivation. Total cost also depended on some intangibles. Cheaper components which created problems and halted the production line had to be eschewed and costlier components of the right quality procured. And then Six Sigma was used to bring down costs. Along with cost reduction, a battle was waged over quality. In bringing down defects, first reduction targets were set in percentage terms. These were eventually replaced by targets which were set in terms of parts per million.

M K Trisal, president and CEO of GE Motors India, says that the strategy to cut costs used Indian advantages in intellectual capital and labour. "Today we export 60 per cent of our output and exports have gone up from $2 million per year to $20 million in four years' time. The name of the game is to first set yourself global benchmarks. Then, you achieve them by raising productivity process by process and bring about a huge improvement in the motors per person count. Finally, you use GE's reach and size to leverage the productivity and efficiency to overcome the quality perceptions about Indian manufacturing." Initially, getting products accepted globally was a challenge. The Saudis decided to buy the motors for air conditioners only on finding that none of them went bad even after running for two years. These high quality low cost motors are exported to the US and China as they cannot locally source a high enough quality motor for the air conditioners they assemble there.

JOHN WELCH CENTRE

The high point of GE operations in India is the John F Welch Technology Centre where Indian capabilities and global trends converge. When outsourcing began in western economies, it was manufacturing that was first shifted to cheaper locations. Then through the last decade it was initially back office work and eventually entire business processes that have been outsourced to distant locations, made possible by the unfolding telecommunications revolution. Through all this, one area of work which global companies mostly preferred to keep close to their corporate heart is core research and development. But in the last few years, even R&D work has begun to get shifted to distant centres. GE, a leading globaliser and a firm believer in doing everything wherever it can be done best—set up a major research centre in India in Bangalore in 2000. Named the John F Welch Technology Centre, by the end of 2002, it achieved its full staff strength of 1,700, of whom 700 were affiliated with the company's global research centre in the US.

India thus now hosts a part of GE's global research team, with the main research centre in Schenectady, New York, having a staff strength of 1,600 and a much smaller research centre in Shanghai with a strength of 50. Significantly, the Bangalore centre conducts work across the entire range of GE's businesses and is really a backup to the New York facilities. The Bangalore centre's various laboratories work on such diverse areas as advanced mechanical engineering, materials, imaging, micro and nano structures, chemical engineering and modelling, polymers and synthetic materials, e-engineering, information technology and e-commerce.

The mandate for this centre is to do corporate research. When the company needed to raise its research capacity in the later nineties it would have been difficult to find and locate 700 scientists and engineers in one place in the US. That is how the decision to set up the centre in India took place. "This was the natural location for us to go to outside the US. It is very difficult to get this kind of critical mass in any other country," says Bayman. Adds Guillermo Wille, managing director of the Bangalore centre, "We are not in India because of costs, but because of the significant talent pool here, because GE wants to grow with technology." Thus, the centre clearly establishes India as one of the best locations in the world to host R&D, not just in information technology but across a range of disciplines.

The mission for the centre is to team up with the various GE businesses and create leadership products. Adds Wille, "We (the global research centres) are the hub of technology for all of GE. We invent game changers here, products which in the future will change the game for the company. We create growth for the company." How much of the work done at the global research centres is trouble shooting, how much is R&D and how much is fundamental research? Elaborates Wille, "Ten per cent of what we do mostly supports businesses in day-to-day issues. Seventy per cent is driven by the businesses and involves developing their bigger projects that will come to fruition in one or two years, and the remaining 20 per cent is devoted to advanced technology which will bear fruit in 2–5 years or longer."

Altogether, 24 per cent of the scientific staff at the centre are PhDs and 21 per cent have global experience. GE is rather proud of this last statistic. Those that have relocated to India to work at this centre are not from GE facilities elsewhere but people of Indian origin who wanted to come back to India but at the same time, were looking for a world class facility. Thus GE is playing a part in reversing the brain drain. In each of the three GE global research centres, there are prime centres of expertise. There is one in India in numerical modelling to whose experts work will come from all over the world. Shanghai has a centre of excellence in the development of small electronics. In India, the aircraft research work has been growing in complexity. The work done initially was primarily engineering analysis of parts and components that go into new designs. But as such work has gone up the value chain, they have started to design specific components that go into an aircraft engine.

An idea of the specific nature of the work—how high tech it is—can be had from the projects currently being handled by the Bangalore research centre. One is semiconductor based current sensors for the industrial systems business, another is ASICs chips for the medical systems business. In the field of product innovations, the centre has developed an X-ray tube for CT applications that is three times faster than the regular tube and 50 per cent more powerful. Work is also being done on advanced application technologies in areas like plastics—an energy absorbing bumper for the automotive industry that will revolutionise the use of plastics in the industry.

The centre is also developing software for clinical applications, to be used in conjunction with GE's medical equipment. Such software lets the doctor see in a CT scan not only the bones but the vessels of a patient. The scientists have also developed an online application for CT scanners. It shows the doctor on line the progression of the scan. So he can either reposition the patient or stop a scan as he may have seen enough, thus reducing the patient's discomfort and radiation. The global research centres are divided into various technology areas. Each area has centres of excellence with global technology leaders who oversee the work that goes on worldwide in all the three centres. Till now, global technology leaders have all been in the US. In 2002, GE identified its first global technology leader in India, Mukul Saxena, an expert in chemical analysis.

How did it all begin? How was the scientific expertise in India 'discovered'? GE has been collaborating with leading Indian research centres for a long time. Recalls Bayman, substantiating what Mashelkar has said, "It was really the very favourable experiences that we had with some of the labs like the National Chemical Laboratory and some of the IITs that got us thinking about putting up this facility." GE's outsourcing of research, product development, high end medical equipment, software and various business processes validate Indian competitiveness in the sectors that we have examined in the earlier part of the book—software, business process outsourcing, pharmaceuticals and biotechnology. Its ability to produce world beater airconditioner motors validates the global competitiveness of Indian brick and mortar companies like Tata Steel and BHEL.

14

Jhunjhunwala & Co

I ndian competitiveness in anything knowledge based and the cost competitiveness emerging in Indian business from having to live with low Indian buying power have come together in the work of Ashok Jhunjhunwala. The professor of electrical engineering at the Indian Institute of Technology, Madras leads an informal group of 15 faculty members called TeNet (Telecommunications and Computer Network Group) that had less than a decade ago set before itself a simple and critical task—make India a design house in the area of telecom and computer networking and use the technology created to rapidly take the internet to Indian villages. The details of how the first aim is being achieved by entire industries appear elsewhere in the book. In this chapter, we look at the dramatic story of how Jhunjhunwala, fellow academics and engineers charged with the TeNet vision have given India and the world a uniquely low cost technology for rural telecom and internet connectivity. What is more, they have also devised business models which enable this technology to be delivered at the Indian villager's doorstep.

Jhunjhunwala spells out the goals thus: "What we like to see is that if anybody anywhere in the world wants to get something sophisticated designed, to begin with in the telecom and IT areas, they should look at India as the natural destination. Good work in software and IT enabled services is already done. Our second vision is recognising that the internet is power, not just a means of communication. We are focusing on India getting 200 million telephone and internet connections at the earliest possible. It is the second one that sort of got us all involved in all kinds of technologies."

TeNet has by now incubated six product companies, a telecom training company, a rural telecom operations company and a venture fund. Critically, it has developed a number of access products and brought down infrastructure cost per line from $650 to $375. The new technology is being widely deployed not just in India but a dozen other developing countries across the world from Africa (Egypt, Nigeria, Kenya, Angola, Tunisia, Yemen and Madagascar) to

South America (Argentina and Brazil) to Asia (Iran, Fiji and Nepal). One of the companies spawned by TeNet has become the second largest exporter of telecom equipment from India. Within India the new technology is being deployed by both the incumbent state owned and new private telecom service providers as also the service company spawned by TeNet.

We have seen earlier that progress in R&D, as in the case of biotechnology, has not automatically led to business success and a search is still on for a successful business model. In contrast, Indian software has been able to grow and overcome these challenges, keeping way ahead of China, because of its successful business organisations leading the field. TeNet and Jhunjhunwala's quest for affordable technology has been rooted in business. "Though we are hardcore engineers we realised that unless you have a basic understanding of economics and affordability you don't get anywhere." The key hurdle in the way of fulfilling their dream was that at Rs 40,000 per phone line (the cost in the mid-nineties), not more than two per cent of India's population could be connected. Bring this cost down to a quarter, and half of Indians would be connected.

NETWORK COSTS

When the academics first looked at the telephone rollout in the developed countries, they realised that network costs were not going down in India because they reflected network costs in the west. These had remained at $1,000 per phone line for around 15 years. This, as well as the monthly cost of $25–30 was affordable to almost every household in the west. So at $1,000 the western operators were able to saturate the market and provide phones to everyone. The incentive to reduce costs to expand the network and market no longer existed for them thereafter. So their focus became the replacement market where you add features through value addition and mobile telephony. "It became obvious that if India needed to cut down the cost of installing a telephone line, the R&D would have to be driven from within the country, focused on cost reduction rather than additions of features while keeping the cost constant. Indian scientists and industry would have to come together to provide the resources and the drive to design and deploy low cost technology that best caters to Indian conditions." (Chart 14.1)

"So we started focusing on it by doing two things. One, we started speaking about it and two, we started working on it. Then we found there were no takers as DoT was a monopoly which worked on a cost plus basis. We also found that in the first stage when the market opens up, the private providers have zero experience and tieup with the likes of Alcatel, Lucent. These are driven from overseas and are interested in creaming the market. Many of the consultants also didn't understand the paying capability of India's so called middle class. Initially, nobody even thought about this. Nobody really listened

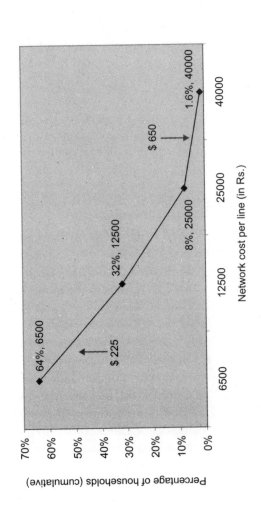

Chart 14.1

Telecom affordability for Indian households at different network infrastructure costs

Source: TeNet

to us. Then they said cost reduction is not possible. But we started analysing the costs and found that the backbone network costs were coming down year after year as in the west they need to expand the backbone network—fibre, large exchanges—to give higher services to each user. Very little work was done on the access part as they had already connected everyone. We found that the access network was costing almost 65–70 per cent of the total cost, the copper wire from the exchange to the home. So that is where we focused. We asked, can we do the same thing by wireless, just basic connectivity, not mobility. So a key feature became wireless in local loop. We also developed a low cost fibre in the loop (DSL or digital subscriber loop) technology. You bring fibre upto the street corner and use copper only in the last 300–500 metres."

Various developments that took place both in India and abroad played into TeNet's hands. Through the period that TeNet worked on lowering access costs, "mobile costs kept falling. To some extent China was doing the same thing, bringing down the cost to expand the network, in a different way. So the focus has shifted from the western companies to the Indian and Chinese companies. In backbone and mobile they (the west) still have the dominance but not in access. Today, the cost of a telephone line is less than Rs 20,000 (rural cost is still high) by our and others' efforts. We still have not reached Rs 10,000 but know it is possible. Many operators believe so. In fibre in the loop Chinese companies have contributed. Operators have also became very cost conscious as the environment has became very competitive. Between 1998 and 1999, the cost focus started arriving. BSNL, TRAI, DoT all adopted the cost focus. This was not there earlier because you believed you could charge huge amounts for long distance. But the long distance collapse brought about the right focus."

DELIVERY STRUCTURE

Technology cannot deliver by itself; it needs structures. So while developing technology "TeNet also started developing new structures to deliver it. How do you do that from a university? We realised we needed very good engineers. So we started getting hold of alumni and incubating companies. We incubated Midas Communications Technologies consisting of nine of our students and asked them to jointly work with IIT to develop this technology." The thrust of this joint effort between IIT Madras and Midas was products that could be deployed effectively throughout India. The major product to be developed was CorDECT wireless in local loop which provides a fixed wireless connection. The connection both delivers voice (telephone) and data (internet) at 35/70 kbps. The radius of this service is 10 km or 25 km with the help of a relay base station. The service is provided by a local service partner who has to invest around Rs 20 lakhs and is able to provide around 100 connections.

In developing an institutional structure, TeNet and Jhunjhunwala took their inspiration from two Indian service innovations—the ubiquitous PCO, the public telephone booths, which run as individual business and contributing almost 25 per cent of the overall telecom revenues, and cable TV which by stringing wires over poles and trees, has connected 50 million Indian households. The two elements behind these successes are private entrepreneurship creating viability and technological innovation creating affordability. The goal set was to bring down costs with technological innovation and then deliver through small businesses. The local service partner was the counterpart of the cable TV operator and the PCO operator was the counterpart of the internet kiosk operator.

"We realised we needed PCO type kiosks for the internet to succeed in villages. These kiosks will be able to provide three services—telephone, internet and stand alone computing. We realised it must be entrepreneurial, they must put in small amounts, maybe with bank loans which we helped them get. Today we have integrated the CorDECT wallset with a personal computer with Pentium processor, colour monitor, speaker, microphone, camera, CD ROM, Indian language software, power backup for four hours, a printer and are able to provide the whole thing as a package for Rs 50,000. If a person gets a loan of Rs 40,000 and invests Rs 10,000, he can earn Rs 3,000 per month to service that loan. We have found that in most villages the person starts to break even in three to four months."

But we have gone a little further ahead of the story. CorDECT was first deployed in February 2000 in a rural area of Andhra Pradesh, where it established its ability to provide connections to 65 villages in a radius of 25 km for both voice (telephone) and data (internet) at 35/70 kbps. But despite this, operators were reluctant to deploy the technology. This was because although operators had an obligation to provide an extent of rural services, their heart was not in it. Neither the volume of traffic nor the density of connection made the rural market attractive for the big operators. Says Jhunjhunwala, "The situation was very similar to that with respect to FMCG goods till the mid-eighties. Before Hindustan Lever made rural areas its rich and prime market, no one believed such goods could be sold in rural areas."

So TeNet decided to create an operating company to operate, according to its charter, exclusively in rural areas, called n-Logue Communications Pvt Ltd. n-Logue's vision is "to significantly enhance the quality of life of every rural Indian by driving the digital revolution." n-Logue divides the country into service areas of about 25 km radius each. To deliver it relies on a key milestone already reached in Indian connectivity—85 per cent of *taluks* are already connected by optic fibre, providing the basic communication backbone. n-Logue sets up access centres with CorDECT exchanges and relay stations which together give an operational range of 25 km radium for the access centre. In the 2000 sq km radius that each access centre covers in the plains, typically there are 300 to 400 villages where 500 connections can be given to individuals, government offices, schools and public health centres.

SUSTAINABLE RURAL INTERNET

The first major test to which n-Logue has been put is the 'Sustainable Rural Internet' (SARI) project launched in Madurai district of Tamil Nadu which it is implementing. It is a private public university partnership to demonstrate that rural internet can be made viable with the use of innovative technologies and business models. Support for the project is coming from a galaxy of important institutions—IIT Madras, Harvard's Centre for International Development, and the MIT Media Laboratory. At the time of writing the World Bank is engaged in a dialogue to also financially participate in the project. Both Tamil Nadu and Madurai have been chosen because of their support for education. n-Logue will set up internet kiosks in every village to create a dense network. The expectation is that a large number of users will lead to a large number of customers for its content and applications, thus allowing the external economies of a network to be reaped.

An important element of SARI is MIN-ARSU (electronic government in Tamil), a government to citizen application jointly developed by the Madurai district administration, National Informatics Centre and n-Logue to boost e-government services. It seeks to leverage the taluk level computerisation initiative of the Tamil Nadu government for the benefit of the people living in villages and small towns in an area. The web site allows e-mails to be sent to the chief minister, the collector and other officials of the district. It provides information on government schemes like those for pension and welfare and how to use them and formats for application forms which can be downloaded. Applications can be submitted online for certificates of birth, death, income and for pensions. It also carries market prices, canal timings and weekly rainfall figures.

A partnership has commenced with the Tamil Nadu Agricultural College and Research Institute to offer agricultural extension services through e-mail and through chat sessions. There is one instance of a disease in a lady finger (bhindi) crop being successfully treated online by scientists by studying transmitted images of the diseased plants. A veterinary service has been started in collaboration with the Tamil Nadu Veterinary Association. This has begun to save farmers unnecessary long trips to get their animals treated. A particular case of illness in poultry was successfully treated, again by doctors studying transmitted images of the diseased birds. Perhaps the most significant treatment is eye care, being dispensed through the net through the well known philanthropic Aravind Eye Hospital. A patient's eyes are examined remotely by seating him before the web camera. When hospital treatment is needed, the hospital e-mails a letter, addressed to its own doctor on duty, asking him to admit the patient. The kiosk owner prints out this letter to the patient who goes to the hospital with it and gets himself treated.

The important thing, as Jhunjhunwala emphasises, is that none of the telecom and internet services which are helping take connectivity and the internet to the villages are subsidised. "Stories of all kinds are now starting to emerge. The empowerment all this creates. Most of the kiosks are being manned by 18 to 19 year olds, mostly women. All have completed their 12th standards, and they pick up the skills needed in no time. One of the recent requests that have come is if the kiosk operators can print pictures and charge Rs 3. The kiosks are being put to all kinds of innovative use—they teach children typing, word processing, even show movies. My own feeling is if we can do this right and get the right support, this particular programme can change the country. We now have 200 kiosks, but our objective is to go to a few thousand by the end of this year (2002). We are in Dhar, Shahpura (Rajasthan), Baramati (Maharashtra), we are doing 10 districts in Tamil Nadu. This will take us to 80–85 per cent of the country's rural areas as there is fibre reaching them."

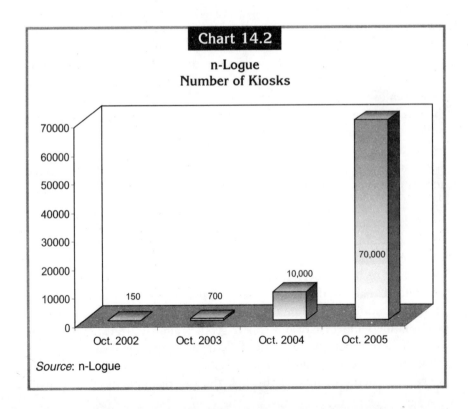

Chart 14.2

n-Logue
Number of Kiosks

Source: n-Logue

Jhunjhunwala exudes the feeling of succeeding. "We have developed a range of technologies, started making a difference. It took us a long time to establish ourselves. We faced all the initial difficulties, just as Sam Pitroda (who took C-DoT to great heights) faced. It is only in the last six to nine months (that is since late 2001 and early 2002) that we have overcome most of the difficulties."

By the end of the year (2002) both Midas Communications and n-Logue had begun to score notable successes. After being put through a lot of due diligence, "Today we are credible partners in the telecom service providers' technology brands," says Shirish Purohit, director of Midas. BSNL, India's incumbent service provider, has raised its order for financial 2002–03 to 550,000 lines from 25,000 lines two years ago. Egypt has placed an order for 200,000 lines. Perhaps the most dramatic of all is in the decision of Reliance Infocom to use CorDECT to connect 1,500 Indian towns. This should result in very large orders. Several Indian companies like the state owned ITI and the privately owned Shyam Telecom and HFCL are manufacturing CorDECT equipment under licence fron Midas, as are BBS Access of Singapore and Omniacom of Tunisia. There are also plans to licence local manufacturing in Brazil to address the needs of the Latin American market. Purohit sees clear signs of orders exceeding the two million mark and expects total orders to add up to 6–8 million lines in three to four years. Midas expects its revenue, which comes significantly from royalty for licensed manufacture, to go up five times in one year—from Rs 65 crore in 2002–03 to $65 million during 2003 to 2004 (Chart 14.3).

As it is with all serious technology businesses, Midas is not sitting idle after developing its first generation technology. Its next switch was slated to be ready by mid-2003 with thrice the present capacity of 1000 lines. A control on costs will be kept in two ways. One, a 15 per cent cost reduction will be achieved by simply using more powerful new generation semiconductors. Two, Midas will do its own bit by achieving another 25 per cent reduction in costs through design improvements. As a result, the new switch will also be able to deliver a quality improvement.

The same kind of exponential growth which results from a technology being accepted, is anticipated by n-Logue, the rural service provider. From connecting 300 villages in late 2002, n-Logue expects to connect 30,000 villages in 15 months' time, that is, by March 2004. P G Ponnapa, CEO of n-Logue, expects turnover to go up by over 20 times in two years from the likely 2002–03 turnover of Rs 2 crore and achieve break even in five years' time, that is by 2007. It is able to look so confidently ahead because the business it is spawning is very viable. A kiosk owner can hope to break even in just a few months' time by earning Rs 3,000 a month. The prospects of growth are enormous as the technology and packages being devised to go with it are so cost effective. For example, n-Logue is considering a proposal to promote the setting up of centres for conducting non-invasive medical tests. The hardware needed by these centres to take your weight, measure your blood pressure and record your ECG will cost no more than Rs 15,000. And to this, if you also add the prospects of conducting e-commerce (the first tractor has already been sold on the n-Logue network) both the viability and potential of the technology goes up many-fold (Chart 14.2).

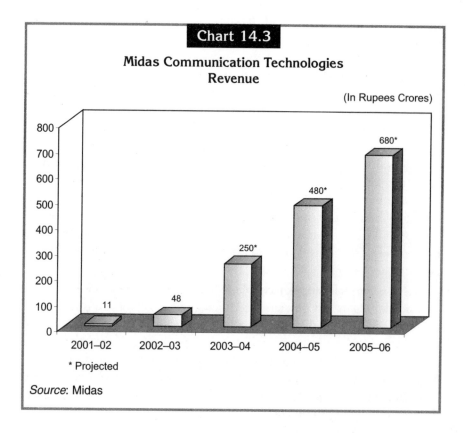

Thus, the nearly decade-long work of Ashok Jhunjhunwala and fellow academics who make up TeNet is succeeding. This establishes the validity of the key proposition that has emerged from our study—India has a competitive advantage in any enterprise which is knowledge based and seeks to tailor its costs to the purchasing power of India's domestic market. The IIT Madras academics and their associates used their knowledge of telecom and computing to deliver a viable package for connectivity and internet access to India's villages at less than a third of the global costs prevailing when they set out to give shape to their dream. The technical and commercial soundness of their proposition has already begun to generate domestic mainstream and international demand for the startups vending the new affordable technology, opening up prospects of exponential growth for them.

15

Why Hardware Failed

After looking at all the examples of competitive sectors and firms in the Indian economy, in this, our penultimate chapter, we will examine what role the government, policy and regulation play in determining competitiveness. We began our study of the most competitive sectors with a close look at software. While researching the software success, a point that kept cropping up was how India failed to make any headway in IT hardware even as it went from strength to strength in software. In this chapter, we will first look at why India failed in hardware and what role policy had to play in this. We will then revisit the software story to see how correct is the conventional wisdom that software grew and thrived as the government kept out of it. Thereafter we will look at the policy setup needed to achieve competitiveness in manufacturing. Next we will turn our attention to the role policy has played in the pharmaceutical sector and what is required to take competitiveness forward in it. The examination of policy will also take us to the role played and required to be played by education. And finally, we will cast an eye on China, to see how policy has played a role in the emergence of Chinese competitiveness and examine if policy in India can take a leaf or two out of the Chinese book.

The enormity of the failure in hardware is driven home by the fact that capability in it predates the capability in software. Since the eighties, companies like Wipro and HCL have addressed the entire spectrum of information technology in the Indian tradition of seeking to develop self-sufficiency. Although hardware contributes a negligible part of Wipro's revenue today, it is not new to hardware design. In fact, it was first in hardware. In the eighties, it had a very integrated domestic business consisting of R&D, development of products, manufacturing, marketing and customer support. Recalls Azim Premji, "We started our computer hardware business in the early eighties under Wipro Infotech Limited, and branched out to computer software development in 1984 under Wipro Systems Limited. The hardware business grew rapidly all through the eighties and was contributing a major part of the topline by the early nineties. Wipro Infotech emerged as the most admired hardware company because of our superior service support. However, by the late eighties software services revenues started rapidly building up. In 1994 we merged Wipro Infotech Ltd and Wipro Systems Ltd into Wipro Ltd."

Why was the headstart in hardware lost? Premji feels that "It is more a case of missed opportunity. India could have become the global manufacturing base for computer hardware with our competitive advantage in hardware design which companies like Wipro had. We have let the advantage pass on to countries like Taiwan, South Korea, Singapore and now China. A large part of the reason is attributable to government policies. We never encouraged development of a component industry in the country. It is difficult to imagine a flourishing hardware industry without a strong component base. The automotive industry is a good example of what one can achieve, given a sound component vendor base."

MANY TYRANNIES

Ashok Soota, who spent decades in Wipro before leaving it to start MindTree Consulting, has a comprehensive view of the Indian hardware-software dichotomy. He feels that the answer to the question—why hardware failed— is a part of the broader issue of "Why manufacturing itself has not been very successful in India, with a few exceptions. Of course, part of the reason lies in the nature of the electronics industry and the fast changing nature of technology. In software we were able to escape the tyrannies of infrastructure like uncertainties of customs, physical infrastructure and high interest rates." Plus there were additional factors in computer manufacturing. There was no understanding that worldwide, computer manufacturing was a very horizontal industry. Manufacturers of items like hard disks and chips have to be very specialised. You have to either bring the manufacturers in, which needs a distinct policy initiative, or facilitate imports. Instead, the import duty structure and clearance hassles made people opt for importing the whole assembled thing and clear it in one go to avoid raking up issues like "what constitutes manufacturing and what does not?"

To illustrate this, Soota recalls a classical instance. There was a rule that "You cannot import populated printed circuit boards. Now, how many PCBs go into a computer? Was the country trying to encourage the sheer process of stuffing a PCB? It was such a low manual job. The whole understanding of people involved in this policy setting was hazy." As a result, India had "an inefficient manufacturing structure in the country as a whole." Added to that was a lack of proper understanding of the imperative of industries which needed a quick inflow and outflow across borders. To make hardware manufacturing succeed, if you did not have massive component manufacturing plants within the country, you needed to do away with customs clearance, have negligible or zero import duties, and also have the facility to pay import duty only when actually consuming the component.

What was needed, says Soota while looking back, was the equivalent of the software technology park for hardware, a full fledged electronic hardware technology park. The suggestion was brought before successive finance ministers who would listen sympathetically but nothing would happen eventually. "Somewhere it would always get bogged down with the revenue department asking, how much of customs duty will we lose? In reality you would not have lost anything. That is the whole sad story." The same lament is echoed by N Vittal. While he dwells at length on the great success he achieved in setting off software services on their winning path (see Chapter 2), he simultaneously admits his one major failure as the head of the government's electronics department at a crucial stage (1990–96) was the inability to get a proper chip making factory going. When the Semiconductor Complex at Chandigarh was burnt down Vittal saw in it an opportunity to build a world class semiconductor plant. But he failed. "We repaired the Semiconductor Complex, but we could not have a state of the art chip making factory that would involve an investment of a billion or a billion and a half dollars." He recalls the poser of Bimal Jalan, the then union finance secretary, if the country ought to spend billions of dollars on setting up a chip factory when providing drinking water to all Indian villages still remained an unfinished task.

SAY GOODBYE TO HARDWARE?

But as the initial advantage had been lost and the world's hardware leaders are light years ahead of India, does the strategy lie in not wasting resources in trying to acquire a capability in hardware at this stage? Premji strongly disagrees. "It is never too late. China is a wonderful example of a late entrant making it big, supported by a large domestic market. India can repeat this success given the right policy environment and a vibrant domestic market."

S Ramadorai, managing director of India's foremost software company TCS, echoes the same sentiment. "Without hardware there is no software. The hardware industry has lagged behind, it is hardly existing. We need to scale it up very very quickly and we need to create all the necessary mechanisms. Software growth does not make sense in certain segments like consumer electronics and embedded systems without the underlying hardware. Today everything is software dependent but the hardware has to be there."

Biswadip Mitra, managing director of Texas Instruments, India, feels India should get into hardware also, "not chip manufacturing, but equipment manufacturing. We can circumvent the fact that we are late by the fact that we are a huge software superpower. If over the next few years we can have a hardware roadmap then that can be a differentiator. For an item like a cellphone or camera, a big part of the differentiator between two competing products is the software, the differentiation done in the hardware with software. We should leverage our software strength and make the differentiating hardware. Using software to differentiate the hardware is an awesome thought for India. The value of the intellectual input is getting bigger and that of the physical input smaller. I don't think it is very important to have manufacturing, but from a knowledge and control point of view, the control point lies in software."

Himangshu Singh of Cadence India has yet another compelling reason for India to get into hardware. The absence of manufacturing activity in India creates a hurdle for the further development of hardware designing in which India has an initial advantage. A lot of electronic design activity is taking place in China as a result of chip and other electronic manufacturing activity shifting there. "When manufacturing shifts in such a big way, design has to follow suit." So to retain the advantage in electronic designing, you need to have hardware manufacturing next to you.

POLICY AND SOFTWARE

If it is the government's economic philosophy and policies followed till now that has led to the failure in hardware, what has been the role of policy in the software success? N R Narayana Murthy recalls that "between 1981 and 1992 the friction to business was enormous. Data communication facilities were not available. It took us a year to get a telephone in Bangalore. The cost of data communication—one 64 kbps line at that time was $300,000 a year, as against $20,000 a year today. So upto 1992, it was primarily one of onsite services where cost was a primary issue." Nandan Nilekani also does not attribute much of a positive role to the government in the development of the software sector. "As the regulatory setup was focused more on the manufacturing side, this enabled software to escape the baleful eye of the government. Plus the nature of the stuff we did was difficult for the government to understand. There is no excise inspector, factory inspector or labour inspector. So we got a much more free market on the services side than we ever had in this country."

However, some see the government having played a positive role before 1991 and more so later. Srini Rajam, chairman of Ittiam, points out that initial scientific capability was built by the IISc and IITs, all state funded institutions. Thereafter, starting with Texas Instruments (1984), somehow the decision making process came together to place a priority on this industry. The independent use of data communication facilities, which till that time was considered very difficult to license, was allowed, as was duty free imports. "All these things created, if not a competitive advantage, a competitive platform. That meant if you decided to do R&D in India, it was as good as doing it in Europe."

To N Vittal, the electronics industry and particularly software, grew from 1990 because there was a strategic alliance between the department of electronics (DoE) which he headed and the industry. "Within a week of my becoming secretary of DoE, I met all the industry representatives and asked them, what is it that comes in the way of your progress. The software industry asked for all the concessions like import of computers under the capital goods scheme, income tax holiday, high speed data communication at 64 kbps. So I prepared a paper and took it to the committee of secretaries. Between 1990 and 1991 there were three governments. So it was only during Narasimha Rao's government with Manmohan Singh's budget that income tax concession, 80 HHE, came."

The high speed data communication facility came in a unique way, with Vittal playing his classical non-conformist role. When DoE refused to provide the connections before 18 months, Vittal diverted Rs 12 crore with his department to set up six earth stations. That was the beginning of the software technology parks which account for 70 per cent of software exports today. "The STPs became a success because they made economic sense. But I had to fight DoE and VSNL. They at times adopted a dog in a manger attitude." He sums it all up by recalling that "this strategic alliance, of government policy with industry, functioned very well in those five years I was secretary of DoE." This is how the government and its policies also played a vital role in enabling the software success.

FUTURE OF IT

Interestingly, the 'no government is good government' school of thought does not find many takers even among multinational IT companies. Ranjan Chak of Oracle recalls that the "traditional answer used to be: keep out of the way. But I think it has to go beyond that. It is a whole infrastructure issue. We all have our own power. There isn't a software company out there that does not have its own generator and UPS to have continuous power, otherwise they are dead. The telecom system is already high on the agenda of not just the development companies like ours but also the IT enabled services. It is a huge issue with them. Why does it still take a couple of months to get a new satellite connection? Then come basic amenities like roads. Fundamentally, you will invest where you can grow. And there is the issue of quality of life. Your raw material, the people you are dealing with, have options worldwide. So not only do you have to create more skilled people, you will have to keep them (retain them here)." Customs procedures, though not a burning issue, remain. Why cannot hardware be imported through the green channel?

If there is unanimity among IT players over one way in which the government must play a major role in promoting both software and hardware, then it is its own use of IT. Mohan Reddy, chairman and managing director of Infotech Enterprises, points to the fact that across the world "the biggest spender in IT is government, be it the US or the Soviet Union. But in India, the least spending is still from the government. It is the domestic industry that creates the global marketplace. We can train our engineers at very low cost if they can get domestic experience. Otherwise, training itself will be very costly."

Arun Jain, founder of Polaris, is even more forthright: "We need to get government to embrace IT. Once it does so the private sector is bound to follow." This will create a domestic market which will both enable Indian companies to grow and provide a springboard for venturing out into the international market. To promote the domestic market, to create a buzz over IT which will lead to its widespread use, success stories are needed. "One of the greatest IT successes in government was the railway passenger reservation system done by CMC. You need two or three successes like that in the public domain." To promote the use of IT within the government, key drivers are needed. "Chandrababu Naidu, former chief minister of Andhra Pradesh, tried to do this in Andhra. If they somehow succeed then we will have a big story to tell to the people."

One of the most sophisticated areas of IT activity in India is chip designing and fabless manufacturing, that is, doing everything to manufacture a chip right upto the stage where the readied and tested design is passed on to a hardware manufacture or fabricator. Hyderabad based MosChip is one of the frontrunner startups in this area and in early 2003 was looking to globally market its products. Companies in this unique space, which lies between the worlds of software and hardware, are heavily dependent on policy. The government will have to evolve policies to ensure that these businesses are provided the same level field of tax breaks that are available to software companies and export oriented units. The government's role will be extremely critical in building this industry and taking it to the highest end of the value chain. The operating business model of these companies is completely different from the other businesses and will have to gain acceptance from various regulatory bodies like Customs, RBI, etc. "As it appears, product companies are ineligible for tax benefits, even though they are going to be substantial foreign exchange earners. Suitable changes in the Income Tax Act are necessary to ensure that this benefit is not denied just because of a few technical points."

If fabless manufacture is at one (top) end of IT, business process outsourcing or IT enabled services is at the other (volume) end. Raman Roy, founder of Spectramind (now part of Wipro), is one of the strongest advocates of the right kind of regulation. "This industry has the potential to create a million direct and indirect jobs. There is a need to have a roadmap and remove roadblocks." A million jobs means half a million seats on a two shift basis. At $5,000–8,000 a seat, it will require $25 billion investment. To attract such investment continuity of tax policy is vital. "My competition is not another Indian company but China and Philippines," notes Roy, referring to the far higher level of state incentives that the ITES sector enjoys in those countries.

Raman Roy points to regulations which are common to other sections of the IT sector as also those that are peculiar to ITES. The common ones are customs. "HP has a godown right across the street but I can't buy from them. As an EOU, I have to place the order overseas and have the new equipment shipped in. It takes me eight weeks to get operational on a new order but in the Philippines it takes two weeks." The regulations that affect only ITES go to the heart of the regulatory regime affecting Indian domestic business. An ITES operation has to work round the clock and the year. "But I can work only 362 days in a year and not 365 as 26 January, 15 August and 2 October are national holidays. Hotels are allowed to remain open on these days, so why not we? Are we under the Factories Act or Shops and Establishments Act? Factories Act means different requirements. To start up you need 30 plus approvals from 8–10 agencies, why can't there be a single window? My battle is with the Philippines, Mexico and Ireland but I am forced to fight the battle internally."

EDUCATION STRATEGY

Indian competitiveness in software and other knowledge based areas is crucially dependent on an adequate supply of skilled people, both in terms of quality and quantity. This makes education a key concern of policy. Two of the questions most commonly asked in public discussion are:

- Will India be able to maintain an adequate supply of skilled people to enable its software and other knowledge-based sectors to grow at a rapid pace?
- Will the quality of skills improve sufficiently fast for Indian knowledge based sectors to keep going up the value chain at a satisfactory pace?

What is the policy framework needed to impart the right type of education to produce the right type of skills? Are India's engineering and science colleges geared to producing the right skills for the future? Srini Rajam feels that "More than building new institutions, improving the quality of education, especially the quality of teaching staff in the existing institutions, may create a bigger impact." The challenge of numbers is being met but "quality is the issue."

"The best thing in my view the industry can do is to strengthen the existing educational system. In the engineering colleges, the physical infrastructure is excellent. There are labs, machines, great connectivity. But the professor who is supposed to be teaching the latest in VLSI and GSM technology is not as good as the professional in the same area in a company. There is a gap in the quality of the faculty and their uptodateness on particular industries. A bigger impact can be made by creating chairs, collaborative projects that incentivise the teaching staff to stay in the profession but still do good research."

A new system of rewards and institutional arrangements will have to be created so that the best brains do not migrate entirely to industry and there is a constant interplay and exchange of ideas between industry and academia so that at higher levels, teachers do not teach outdated material. In this context, what is happening in IISc with the Simputer is encouraging. It is giving a channel to the professors to use their ideas to create useful products for industry. "Now if those professors were to be teaching about internet appliances, I am sure that the quality of teaching would be as good or even better than the best. We need to get innovative, do a benchmarking with Stanford University because they are able to keep some good people there."

Himangshu Singh of Cadence, a global producer of electronic design tools and a important user of high end skills, sees both India's major asset and challenge ahead to be human capital. The whole electronic design activity has become possible because skills are available "at the highest level of quality and at medium cost." Correspondingly, the major hurdle in the way of sustainable rapid growth is supply of such skills. It is difficult to find in sufficient numbers people with both design and domain (industry) expertise. If sufficient design and domain expertise can be imparted at the graduate and post graduate levels, then "a lot of the job will be done." The right sort of initiative is the special manpower development project for VLSI of the ministry of communications and information technology covering 19 educational institutions. Cadence was one of the corporates which participated in it.

To another user of high end design skills, MosChip, it is the kind of work that Indian companies are able to get that partially determines the skills being developed. "While talent is available, it is raw and low in productivity. It is a chicken and egg situation. High-end experienced talent can come in only when there are opportunities for such talent. Opportunities will find themselves in if there is adequate high-end design talent."

PHARMACEUTICALS

We have seen that there are two contradicting opinions on the role played by policy in India's software development. Some felt policy played a positive role, while others held the opinion that a regime of no policy was the best policy that could have governed the sector. But there are no two views on the role policy has played in the development of India's pharmaceutical sector. Most see it as having been both important and on the balance positive.

Satish Reddy of Dr Reddy's Laboratories sees two major influences on India's pharmaceutical industry. The Indian Patents Act was passed in 1970, recognising the process patent but not the product patent. There was also the drug price control order which controlled the prices of essential medicines. "These two regulations were what really shaped the industry in the seventies and eighties. Prior to that, it was all multinationals importing into the country at a very high cost which made affordability of medicines an issue. The two regulations were meant to stimulate the production of drugs in the country and make them available at affordable prices to large numbers of people. This spawned entrepreneurs like Dr Reddy who went on to start their own ventures."

The proactive role of policy did not end thereafter. From 1991 onwards India liberalised, was a signatory to the Uruguay round and, as part of TRIPS, decided to amend its patent law. Recalls Satish Reddy, "Dr (Anji) Reddy had this vision of what was going to happen in the future, that India would also accept patent laws and started construction of a basic research facility, the first company in the private sector to do that. Dr Reddy's Foundation, the discovery arm of the company, started operations in 1993." The same process took place in Ranbaxy. Recalls J M Khanna, head of research, "When the government announced we would honour patents, we also announced our mission statement. That we want to be an international research based pharmaceutical company."

If we cut right to the present, the major lament is not of excessive regulation (there is of course disapproval of continuing price control, despite the reduction in its scope) but absence of proper regulation. Habib Khorakiwala feels that "Unfortunately, our drug administration is not ready to deal with new drug discoveries, nor are they ready to implement high standards of quality in clinical trials. Competency, organisation, the right kind of people—all are lacking. So we have a big gap there. The other big gap is the patent regime. Our patent office does not know how to process patent applications. It is a huge queue and you can't wait for years to get your patent."

Chaitanya Dutt of Torrent Pharmaceuticals echoes similar sentiments. "In industry we do feel that the process of getting regulatory approvals is very slow but some progress is there and we are happy about it. It would help if we can have some timeframes attached. We don't mind if the regulators refer an application to a group of experts, but the experts have to find the time to go through it and come back in a specific period. Today the industry is worried when it does not have a yes or no answer. If it is told within a reasonable period that we need this much more data, then it's fine. But that shouldn't happen at the end of two years."

Dr N K Ganguly, director general of the Indian Council of Medical Research, has a veritable compendium of what the government needs to do to promote research and growth in the pharmaceutical industry:

- An appropriate drug testing and regulatory structure: This will make possible quick evaluation and acceptance.
- Adequate centres for clinical and toxicology trials. The government can play a facilitating role in setting them up.
- Good ethics bodies for conducting research: Regulatory compulsion needed to have an ethics setup has to come from the government.
- A quality control system, totally different from what prevails now: This will ensure proper standards in matters like packaging and shelf life, areas in which Indian drugs tend to get beaten in global competition.
- An adverse drug monitoring system along with an intelligence system to gather information: This information should be readily available to players, possibly through a website.
- Population based epidemiological and genetic data: This is needed to build up databanks on disease patterns.
- A good patenting regime.
- Drug prices: They are a key concern of public policy and the price control regime that the Indian pharmaceutical industry has known has been a most contentious issue. Through the period of liberalisation the price control mechanism has been considerably diluted and there has been a substantial rise in prices. Despite this, Indian drug prices are still among the lowest in the world and the regulatory system has to try and keep it at that, while also recognising the industry's need to earn enough resources for research.
- Taxation policy: The government, through its taxation policy, has to encourage research into new molecules and novel delivery systems.
- Public–private partnerships to promote research: These have to be encouraged so that people can simultaneously work in both the domains. This will ensure that capable people get the right incentives and the public teaching establishments get the best teachers.

■ An authority and policy to make possible compulsory licensing: It does not exist.

The government of India is currently in the process of formulating a new drug policy as also one that will overhaul the system of approval of new drugs. The need for the latter is critical as a far more rigorous system of approval will be needed once the patent law changes to come into conformity with WTO requirements and the Indian patenting regime falls in line with global practices. A globally competitive pharmaceutical industry can be built only in an environment governed by a suitably rigorous and efficient regulatory regime. Also, a research based industry like the pharmaceutical one needs an adequate regime of fiscal incentives to grow and prosper. Thus, the Indian pharmaceutical industry has grown from infancy through adolescence and maturity through key changes in the regulatory regime. In the process it has serendipitously become one of the most competitive in the world. Whether it will be able to grow into full adulthood and continue to compete and thrive in a universal regime of tight patent control will depend to a large extent on the quality of regulation that is put in place.

MANUFACTURING

The lack of Indian competitiveness in manufacturing is widely attributed to the economic and industrial policies adopted by the government of India from the fifties to the eighties and the bureaucratic regime that it gave rise to. The instances of success in manufacturing, or in the brick and mortar industries, that we have focused on, are the few exceptions which have defied the system. They are the ones who have taken the lead in looking outward when they need not have. They have sought to sharply raise exports where feasible or rational and go global. They have sought to benchmark themselves against international cost and quality standards when they could have continued to take shelter behind the high Indian tariff walls and run their businesses as they have been doing for some more time.

The Indian failure in manufacturing has to be set against the Chinese success in the field which has been as policy driven as the Indian experience. The Chinese success in manufacturing, making it the world's factory for simpler manufactures, is not the result of pursuing *laissez faire* or the Washington consensus. It is as much a result of policy as was the case with Japan's developmental state and the Asian tigers. So we briefly examine below, through the eyes of the main players whose roles we have so far been pursuing, why Indian manufacturing failed and if the Chinese experience has any insights to offer. The Chinese experience is relevant for India because the two are similar in terms of diversity and continental size. The policy options available to

China and India on the one hand are not available to say Britain, The Netherlands and Sri Lanka.

To N Vittal, the reason why Indian manufacturing failed is "very clear. I will say one reason is corruption. Competition in India is limited by the licence permit raj, inspector raj, customs, excise, income tax, sales tax. In all these departments to which the manufacturer is constantly exposed, the procedures cause a lot of delay. Today, in competing with the world, time is the most expensive thing. The Indian bureaucracy, particularly its departments concerned with manufacturing, and the element of corruption in them are the main reasons why manufacturing is not competitive. We succeeded in software because, basically, it is a service and the authorities did not know how to assess it. And because of the exemptions, there was no possibility of our authorities and inspectors creating mischief. Today, the government talks about export processing zones or special economic zones. This is what I wanted to create, a mini Hong Kong or Singapore. But customs, excise and finance never agreed. So the project never took off. Second is our labour laws. Third is our preference for small size under the licence permit raj culture. Electronic components, and chips need huge investments."

LONG-TERM STRATEGY

So how can the manufacturing initiative be retrieved? Says Tarun Das, director general of Confederation of Indian Industry, "To have hardware manufacturing in the country you need a longer term strategy and more investment. Tax policies and external environment policies have to be supportive to promote value addition in the country. We have to do a few things to support the hardware industry while not trying to duplicate Taiwan. Take up a few niche products, focus on them, build investments and then upscale. The government has to correct the inverted duty structure. Duty anomalies is a key issue which has affected Indian manufacturing. The most damaging thing that they did in the nineties to the capital goods industry was allowing zero import duty, first with fertilisers and then extended to refineries."

To get back into the battle for hardware and manufacturing (success in one, it seems, goes with success in the other), Soota feels, the country must selectively decide which areas it wishes to focus on—two wheelers, internet appliances or peripherals. Computers have very low value addition potential but there are a lot of devices and appliances which have high value addition and are worth manufacturing. "But for that we have to create a manufacturing infrastructure. Whether it is a computer, peripherial, car or two wheeler, it does not matter. Let that naturally evolve. But at least create the infrastructure and supporting policies."

Das adds: "The policy environment has not supported domestic manufacturing. There is almost a feeling that domestic manufacturing is not important. This has a huge implication for our future economic security." He feels we have several policy lessons to learn from China. The first is China's absence of labour laws, everyone on contract, no right to permanent employment. The second, and perhaps more important, is investment in infrastructure. China now has world class infrastructure, whether or not there is demand, and that fuels growth. But to Das, "Before everything the Indian government has to understand the value of manufacturing and value addition in India. Nobody in the government is paying attention to this. I sincerely believe there is a danger in terms of our long term economic security. If we lose our manufacturing capability in a continental economy, we will be in great danger. It is alright for the UK which has decided to be a service economy. We can't be dependent on China or the US for our manufacturing. So we have to have some degree of self-reliance, have to have the BHELs of the world."

The Chinese policy towards foreign auto companies illustrates Das's point further. "The Chinese know how to open up so that you conserve the existing assets in your country. In India we created chaos so that everybody, new and old, are suffering. (Most auto companies are losing money.) The new people cannot use their capacity fully. They were all given to understand that the market was much larger. They (GoI) should have limited the number of entrants. Have international competitive bidding, allowing three entrants, and get a good deal in export obligation, indigenisation." Das attributes the Indian performance in this regard to a cultural factor. "Our negotiating ability, vis-à-vis government of China is, if they are 9/10, we are 1/10. The Chinese have got everything they wanted out of multinationals. They got the investments by leveraging their market strength. This is basically because the IAS does not understand all this. You cannot have a regulator, controller, deputy commissioner understanding all these commercial issues. The Chinese understood commercial issues."

The above sentiments are shared by Suresh Krishna of Sundram Fasteners who has announced his decision to set up manufacturing capacity in China. "There is a sort of relaxation by the Indian government in terms of setting up manufacturing units. They used to put a lot of emphasis on localising. They don't do that anymore. That's left to the discretion of the manufacturer. Whereas China still does that, sometimes in a very subtle way and sometimes in a very overt way. It requires the Chinese automobile companies to locally procure as much as possible. When we try to export to China the first question they ask is—even to Cummins and GM—fine, we will buy from you but what are your plans for manufacturing here? Because, eventually, if you don't set up a plant in China, you lose the business. In India that kind of subtle pressure to make people buy in India is losing steam. I think the government should do something, not explicitly tell people to buy in India but make it known that it will be better for you to buy in India. I think it can be done in many ways. Second, FDI in this country used to have some riders attached like—you must export so much, you must locally buy so much. I think that has all been diluted to the extent where it has not always been beneficial to India. Now how much you must export and how much you must buy in India you can quibble over. But as long as the perception that you must buy locally is accepted then at least you have made a tremendous amount of progress."

CHINA

The appreciation of China's policy initiatives goes beyond brick and mortar industries. Villoo Patell, who leads the biotechnology startup, Avesthagen, finds that China is doing a lot of international lobbying at the government level. "China is way ahead of India in biotech. They have not only sorted out their patent problems, they are manufacturing. They have made very fast alliances with the west. We do not have any lobbyist in Washington lobbying for us with the biotech industry. Not political lobbyist, but someone who has business and science at heart. They have full teams and you won't believe the connections they have made. They are into it. There were discussions on GMOs in the European parliament and they called in representatives. There was Brazil, there was China, but no India."

Patell recalls that state funded research in biotechnology began earlier in India than in China. "But they moved very rapidly into products and put products in the market. They raised so much money through collaborations from EU, US and in particular the National Institute of Health. China could progress faster also because it put very young people at the helm of affairs in government research institutions. Here it is the same people with the old ways of thought who may read about it but have no idea how competitive it is. China cleaned up its act. They retired everybody and brought in 35-year-olds as directors of institutions. That was a key change."

There is near unanimity that during the era of planning, Indian manufacturing was crippled by the licence-permit raj. There is similar unanimity that the Chinese attention to infrastructure laid the foundations for its manufacturing capability. But there is no such unanimity that India can take a leaf out of China's book in insisting upon local purchase and value addition. The foundations of this policy were already laid when China carefully opened up prior to its joining of the WTO. Just as the earlier East Asian policy of restricting access to the domestic market may not be permissible under the current WTO norms, a policy of regulating market access as a quid pro quo for local manufacture and purchase may not be feasible today.

But despite these differences in perception, what is undeniable is that a policy is needed to pursue global competitiveness in manufacturing. Only a comprehensive policy can simultaneously address such diverse areas as cost of capital, energy and logistics, not to speak of systemic issues such as bureaucratic procedures, the need to obtain clearances from multiple layers of government and corruption. Our conclusion is that a nation needs the aid of policy to pursue competitiveness. Policies which are feasible, practicable and effective change drastically over time. Sometimes the role of policy can be restricted to merely ensuring proper market conditions so as to allow free play to competition. But whatever be its scope, policy is not dead.

16

Knowledge Based and Low Cost—
An Emerging Model
of Competitiveness

We began this study by examining what gave India a competitive advantage in software. History equipped its educated sections with a knowledge of English, the language of software. Culture played a role by imparting a natural proficiency in mathematics, the ability to be innovative on a daily basis, thrive in the fluid environment of software development (as opposed to the repetitive discipline of process manufacturing) and intellectual adaptive skills that are among the best in the world. State policy laid a solid foundation by creating institutions which produced a cheap scientific talent pool. The outlook for Indian software companies, which made small beginnings till the late eighties as almost wholly body shopping outfits supplying knowledge workers at clients' sites, changed with the introduction of new economic policies in the early nineties. These led to the setting up of half a dozen earth stations and software technology parks. The Indian offshore model was born.

Through the mid-nineties, as companies in developed economies sought to IT enable themselves and transform their productivities, Indian software grew rapidly. Even happenstance chipped in. The Y2K opportunity appeared, enabling Indian software companies to gain an entry into Fortune 500 companies. The Y2K opportunity also overlapped with the dotcom boom which reinforced the offshore model. By being able to meet the skyrocketing demand, Indian software established its scalability. Through all this, software companies relentlessly pursued quality.

But in the new century the dotcom and technology bubbles burst, subjecting the Indian software model to its first big test. The downturn created large benches, falling billing rates, a severe shakeout and raised questions about the viability of the Indian software model. But Indian software fought back.

The pursuit of quality remained undiminished. The journey up the value chain continued with securing more and more systems integration and end-to-end solutions work. A concerted attempt was made by the leading companies to acquire domain expertise and offer consulting services. High-end expertise really became manifest with India becoming a global centre for electronic design for complex chips like VLSI, ASICS and SOC (system on chips). A range of startups also sought to plough the lonely furrow of product development. The big software companies got bigger by securing larger orders that took outsourcing to a new level, even though margins remained under pressure. As serious IT offshoring became a must for companies in the mature economies needing to cut costs to fight the economic downturn, India emerged as the preferred destination. The continued competitiveness of Indian software was thus established.

SOFTWARE TO BPO

The same reasons—knowledge of English and cheap skills, that gave India a competitive advantage in software, have also given it an advantage in IT enabled services or business process outsourcing (BPO). Additionally, the middle class Indian's preference for an office job has made a career in BPO attractive in a way it has never been for people with similar skills in the developed countries. While software drew on India's store of scientific skills, BPO has cast its net wider to draw on a range of talents which deliver an almost endless range of services like data entry, transaction processing, voice based customer service, technical support and tele selling. As the growth of software slowed down during 2002, BPO became the engine of growth for the software and services sector. The same compulsion in the mature economies that has led to more and more offshoring in software has now raised the momentum of offshoring of entire business processes, involving both front and back office work. The desire of companies in the developed economies to rely on proven, large companies for outsourcing has prompted software companies to either acquire or start BPO operations to be able to act as one stop shops. And as India as a BPO destination has grown in importance, since early 2003, protests have surfaced in the US and Europe against job losses to India.

The low cost high quality scientific skills that gave India a competitive edge in software and services set India off much earlier, in the seventies, on the road to building a globally competitive pharmaceutical industry. The difference is that while in the seventies, Indian electrical engineers were leaving India because of the absence of opportunities (the government severely controlled the import of computers and frowned upon 'automation'), chemical engineers were replicating the designs of drugs and formulations and manufacturing them in India. The latter was in response to changes in patent laws and the government's policy of encouraging local manufacture to bring down drug prices. Through the seventies and eighties, Indian drug companies demonstrated remarkable skills in process chemistry to first manufacture drug intermediates, then bulk drugs and finally formulations, both at a low cost and also ensuring quality. The initial low cost advantage (cheap scientific skills) was a historical boon for both Indian software and pharmaceuticals but in the case of the latter, market conditions—the low buying power of the Indian consumer who formed the bulk of the drug companies' market—provided a compulsion to keep costs low. Consequently, Indian pharmaceutical companies today have a clear global cost advantage in the manufacture of generic products, where price is the main differentiator. And the leading companies have kept quality firmly in sight by seeking US FDA certification of their facilities.

ECONOMIC LIBERALISATION

A major change occurred in the early nineties when large Indian drug companies, seeing an end ahead to the loose Indian patent regime because of India becoming a signatory to WTO's TRIPS agreement, decided to actively pursue original drug discovery, development of non-infringing processes and novel delivery systems. These companies are today emerging as significant players in the US and European generics markets as a result of their cost advantage, ability to speedily file for the approval of their generic substitutes for drugs going off patent and possession of some IP based on non-infringing processes and novel delivery systems. The top companies have also started out licensing a few of their novel drug discoveries. Other areas in which new companies are coming up are contract research (for clinical trials), custom design of molecules and drug development through the prototype and pilot stages.

The Indian knowledge base and cheap skills have most recently given rise to a nascent biotechnology industry. Its emergence has been aided by a long period of public sector research. Biotechnology firms are developing new competencies in traditional areas like fermentation. Plus there is extensive activity in the development of recombinant products. The pattern here is partly similar to pharmaceuticals—replicating products by taking advantage of Indian patent laws, preparing genetic substitutes for the first batch of products that are to go off patent in the regulated markets, and in-licensing molecules mainly in the field of vaccines. Indian competitiveness in biotechnology is still mostly a promise as, unlike software, it requires substantial funding and long nurturing. The regulatory requirements for biotechnology are also stringent. The emerging or nascent nature of Indian competitiveness is best highlighted by its biotechnology industry which till the time of writing can mainly talk of a promising future.

Therefore, to sum up what we have discussed so far—cheap skills made available by an extensive knowledge base created by publicly funded educational institutions, cost compulsions created by the Indian domestic market and the successful pursuit of high quality have been the basis of Indian competitiveness in software, BPO, pharmaceuticals and nascently, biotechnology.

Now we turn to a fascinating dimension of Indian competitiveness—in the dairying sector, so different from what we have examined till now. It is the result of institutional innovation rooted in history and therefore, uniquely Indian. Farmers' revolt against an exploitative private milk procurer led to the establishment of a milk producers' co-operative in Anand, Gujarat. This gathering together at the grassroots was born out of the experience of the freedom movement. The cost competitiveness came from another innovation. Farmers who mostly owned one or two animals were able to feed them straw, a waste byproduct from cultivation, and thus produce milk very cheaply. The logistical and management feat of collecting small amounts of milk which goes bad quickly from thousands of farmers spread over hundreds of villages, processing it and then distributing it over equally large areas—sometimes transporting it to other parts of the country—with minimal overheads was made possible by a modern management reporting to the farmers' representatives running the co-operatives. This model, once perfected at Anand, was replicated all over the country by a government decision through the National Dairy Development Board. NDDB made many technological innovations along the way from refrigerated tankers to carry milk to manufacturing animal vaccines at a very low cost. As a result, Indian milk and dairy products, mostly produced by Anand type co-operatives, are among the most globally cost competitive today.

COMPETITIVE COMPANIES

After looking at competitive sectors, we have examined individual competitive companies in sectors that are not competitive in their entirety. Tata Steel's competitiveness rests first on its access to low cost iron ore and coal through its captive mines. But this is not the whole story. Tata Steel was not globally cost competitive earlier, despite having the same raw material advantage and the similar advantages have not made the public sector Steel Authority of India a competitive producer. Tata Steel began its journey down the road to competitiveness when the Indian government removed controls on the steel industry in the early nineties and the need to be competitive became clear. It first determined its cost structure and benchmarked them against those of globally competitive firms. It then improved yields, fuel rates, material consumption rates and waste utilisation and reduced the length of the supply chain. As a result it has for years now been cutting costs by a few percentage points every year. Technological modernisation, shop level innovation, changes in product mix to go up the value chain and adoption of modern customer relationship management practices have all gone hand in hand. A virtual halving of the workforce and also, a simultaneous rise in output have raised worker productivity three fold in a decade. Today, Tata Steel is the global least cost producer of hot metal and one of the two least cost producers of steel. It is low raw material and wage costs plus the transformation of the whole company that have produced the competitiveness.

One of the most unusual competitive companies we have looked at is Larsen and Toubro, the diversified company that traverses engineering, construction, cement till 2002 and software. It has been a technology leader in India as a supplier of various manufacturing technologies and has in recent years become a global leader in high tech fabrication. Run by its engineer managers, it has pursued technological excellence as a matter of course. But three years ago, when it was hit by a slowdown of investment in new plants both at home and abroad, it took a corporate decision to become more bottom-line oriented and look for growth outside its home base. This has launched it on a process of benchmarking itself to global costs in its individual businesses. In its bread and butter businesses like low tension electrical switchgear and civil construction it is only marginally competitive. Cost and technology wise, it was competitive in cement manufacturing. It is the most competitive in heavy engineering construction like reactors and is developing a new competitiveness in software and e-engineering services. The company has sought to remain domestically competitive in the last three decades by keeping itself abreast technologically. The quality and cost of Indian engineering skills has made this possible. It has developed a particular competency in high tech fabrication on the basis of the cheap skills of both its engineers and workers.

NASCENT, NOT ARRIVED

The only public sector concern that has been included in our study is Bharat Heavy Electricals Ltd (BHEL). Its basic competitiveness derives from the advantage Indian manufacturing has in the heavy metal fabricating business. Also, BHEL enjoys certain historical advantages. One, it has integrated facilities which make it a one stop shop, a power plant supermarket. Two, its plants and facilities are heavily depreciated but have been kept useful by being continuously technologically upgraded. Three, over the last few years it has drastically reduced its manpower, thus controlling the wage bill. All these translate into an overall cost advantage which proved critical when the new economic policies of 1991 opened up the Indian economy to global competition and its survival depended on the ability to compete with global leaders in power plant equipment. BHEL has successfully tackled this challenge and regularly wins a lion's share of the orders for multilaterally funded power plants in India which have to be placed through global tenders.

The company has additionally improved its overall operational efficiency by reducing the time it takes to deliver equipment. This has also helped reduce costs. The cost advantage has been leveraged by its quality record—BHEL plants, which are largely operated in India by the National Thermal Power Corporation, have maintained a consistent track record of high capacity utilisation, indicating low breakdown and stoppages. The major challenge that now faces BHEL is to keep abreast of the latest technological developments by either being able to buy it or develop it in house. The challenge that the company is yet to face up to and which will eventually determine whether it is a global player is to become a technology leader like GE and Siemens.

Reliance Industries, the youngest of the brick and mortar companies we have studied, is a phenomenon. For over three decades, it has maintained an incredible pace of growth and consistently proved sceptics wrong. It has been accused of manipulating public policy to suit its ends but has grown the fastest in the nineties when government control over industry has dwindled. Reliance began as a synthetic textiles manufacturer, developed respected brands for its fabrics, went into the manufacture of synthetic fibre and the petrochemicals from which they are made, and set up one of the largest and most efficient grassroots refineries in the world. More recently, it undertook to connect the country through a broadband network, turned overnight into a major telecom service provider, entered the life sciences and established a foothold in power generation and distribution by being the largest captive power producer in the country and acquiring control over a leading utility Bombay Suburban Electric Supply.

ASIAN LEADER

Reliance's claim to be globally competitive rests mainly on the size and cost of its petrochemicals and refining operations. It is a leading Asian player in both. It is a cost competitive petrochemicals player but particularly remarkable is its ability to set up its grassroots refinery at a lower capital cost than international benchmarks. This has allowed it to become a highly price competitive refiner. In mobile telephony it is seeking new standards in service charges. If its telecom venture succeeds, it will set new benchmarks as a telecom service provider, taking connectivity to income levels hitherto not attempted. This will reinforce the low cost basis of Indian competitiveness.

The last of the Indian companies we have studied is not one but three—Sundram Fasteners, Sundaram Brake Linings and TVS Motor—which have won the highest Japanese awards for manufacturing excellence. They form a unique cluster that goes beyond a particular industry (automotives) and geography (all are located in Tamil Nadu). They all belong to the same family and are a part of the TVS group. These three independently run companies share a common ethos that anticipated the values underlining the Japanese pursuit of manufacturing excellence. These values which the group practised in the thirties and forties, went into a sort of hibernation during the planning era marked by controls and lack of concern for excellence. Then, through the eighties and nineties when opening up brought back competition, quality and cost competitiveness were pursued by adopting Japanese manufacturing practices. It was a kind of going back to the old TVS values. These are concern for employees, quality and customers. Another common characteristic of the three companies is a fierce sense of independence which has led to accessing technology only on one's own terms and without giving up management control. This has prompted TVS Motor to terminate its relationship with Suzuki and emerge as an independent R&D and designing force in its field—manufacture of motorcycles. The company's successful product development underlines the Indian advantage gained from low cost knowledge skills and the pursuit of quality.

It is now time for another summary. Emerging Indian competitiveness in several *sectors* stands on three legs—a low-cost knowledge base, a low-cost business model and strong quality consciousness. Our study of individual successful *firms* gives us the fourth leg—firm level competitiveness achieved by a management's desire to excel and equal or better global benchmarks. Once this is present, competitiveness can be achieved in almost any field, aided no doubt by Indian advantages, but importantly, despite the hurdles created by the Indian environment. Very importantly, this competitiveness is emerging—biotechnology, BHEL and L&T are more travellers on the road than those who have already arrived.

TESTING THE HYPOTHESIS

To test this hypothesis we have argued—if there are competitive advantages in doing business out of India then they should be bringing operations of global companies to India. To find an answer we have studied the operations of GE in India. GE finds that India offers a good combination of capacity, intellect and quality. In the late eighties, it identified the following positive attributes—an educated workforce, entrepreneurial capability, knowledge of English, accounting practices similar to those followed in the US and Europe and some legal sanctity to contracts. All this, in GE's eyes, created an outsourcing opportunity in India. It also looked ahead and concluded that the competitive advantages won't go away. After the initiation of India's new economic policies GE entered into joint ventures and went extensively into medical electronics. Today, some of the most high end medical equipment like CT scanners and x-ray tubes are not only being manufactured but also extensively designed in India. This is because the high level of skills needed for operations like soldering and engineering and also the skills to value engineer are available at the right cost in India.

The most high profile part of GE's outsourcing to India is in BPO. It began in the late nineties as call centre operations but has quickly graduated to conducting more and more complex tasks and finally entire business processes. Indian operations have not just delivered better service but changed process so that from running it better, things are now being run differently. GE has also validated the competitiveness of a few Indian brick and mortar companies by being able to manufacture motors for refrigerators which are now being exported to the US and China. This it has been able to do by studying costs and processes and determining exactly how much of automation to go in for so as to strike a balance between the cost of man and machine. Quality in semi automated operations is ensured through the rigours of Six Sigma. So it is skills plus use of IT plus Six Sigma that have delivered global competitiveness in conventional industrial operations for GE in India.

The showpiece of GE's operations in India is the John F Welch Research Centre in Bangalore at which research is conducted across the range of GE's businesses, not just software in which Indian expertise is well known. The Bangalore centre is a large support base for GE's main research centre in Schenectady, US. GE decided to build this centre in India in the late nineties because nowhere else in the world could it find scientific talent of acceptable quality in the volumes it required. The centre underlines Indian capabilities in emerging as a global R&D platform, a location where companies will find it cost effective to conduct their research, thus underlining the Indian competitive advantage in anything knowledge based.

The structure of Indian competitiveness that we have built up is validated by another proof of concept, the fulfilment of the vision of Ashok Jhunjhunwala. The Madras IIT professor of electrical engineering and his fellow academics who make up the informal group called TeNet had set out less than ten years ago to make connectivity and the internet affordable and available to 200 million Indians. This they wanted to do by leveraging Indian skills in IT and telecom networking and finding innovative business solutions, based on the Indian experience, for delivery. A driving force behind their mission was to meet the cost challenges that Indian affordability posed.

When TeNet started off in the mid-nineties, a telephone line cost Rs 40,000; at the time of writing, this cost has come down to not quite the aim of Rs 10,000 but around Rs 13,000-14,000. The local village internet kiosk operator who stands at the base of the pyramid that the TeNet group of companies is building can buy a wallset for connectivity, a Pentium processor based computer, printer, speaker, camera, microphone and four-hour power backup equipment for all of Rs 50,000. This he can do with Rs 10,000 of his own and Rs 40,000 by way of a bank loan. In three months he can be earning Rs 3,000 per month and be on the road to viability. The content is being delivered through pilot rural internet and e-governance projects. Also, the mainstream business, large incumbent and new private telecom service providers, are increasingly coming forward to buy TeNet's CorDECT technology. Thus, technological capability, developed with Indian scientific skills and an eye on affordability, is leading to mass empowerment that can be a powerful weapon against poverty. In doing so, the TeNet group is also giving a practical demo of the model of emerging Indian competitiveness.

THE WAY AHEAD

We have both identified the attributes of Indian competitiveness and validated our overall hypothesis. We have also looked at the role of policy in all the sectors we have studied and concluded that policy is not dead but must keep changing to deliver what it alone can do. The main deliverer of current Indian competitiveness, its knowledge base and scientific skills, has been built up through public investment in science education. (Conversely, policy neglect of literacy and primary education has arguably led to continuing overall economic backwardness and high levels of poverty.) The competitiveness in pharmaceuticals has resulted directly from policy initiatives implemented through statutory action. Clearly the biggest push to Indian competitiveness was given by the new economic policies that introduced competition, priced the rupee realistically, offered fiscal incentives for exports, lowered tariff barriers and vastly improved connectivity. All this created a new environment that encouraged entrepreneurial initiative and striving for competitiveness. So, a larger policy initiative is needed to make large parts of the Indian economy globally competitive.

But waiting for policy to change in order for competitiveness to arrive is received wisdom. As stated in the introduction, this study does not seek to go down the well trodden path of identifying what is wrong at the public policy level, leading to the lack of competitiveness of large sections of the economy. Instead it seeks to restrict itself to a few micro lessons borne out of the study of competitive sectors and firms to gain insights into what business must and can do on its own in order to become competitive. The special insight we have gained from our study is that a lot can be done by individual initiative without waiting for policy to change.

MANUFACTURING

For larger areas of the economy to become competitive, manufacturing will have to set itself right. How? By waiting for policy to change and remove the impediments? No. K Mahesh of Sundaram Brake Linings recalls, "The Deming inspector said, Mahesh don't try to change India, the problem is just too big. Build a wall around your company and make it excellent. And that's what we have tried to do. I know the quality if our roads is bad, quality of power is bad, ports are a problem, but those are irritants. Despite all this you can become world class. And when those improve, then you will really take off. The problem is inside, your company; don't blame the government, or the world or the politicians. You can't change all that. Eightyfive per cent of the problem is internal. The manufacturing opportunity can still be retrieved provided the management changes its thinking and acknowledges that all is not hunky dory, the future does not lie in licences or keeping the competition away. The future lies in realising that you have to go global."

The same sentiment is echoed by Suresh Krishna of Sundram Fasteners. "People complain all the time that the brick and mortar industry is going down the drain. We are not getting the kind of support from the government, etc. While it may be true of specific sectors—in many of these sectors export/ globalisation also depends on the government initiative—the government cannot export it for you. You have to make your company viable in terms of quality, price, etc. Then you'll find yourself a market. What the government can do should not be detrimental to your quest. Like not putting undue levies on you—an export levy or making your raw materials so uncompetitive that you cannot export in the international market. But the initiative for exporting, making a product globally competitive, depends on individual companies. It does not depend on the government. If a company is determined enough to export, then you can definitely export."

In the true spirit of a global corporate mindset he has an ultimate solution, should it come to such a pass, beyond Indian shores. "Even if for some reason government policies do not allow you to export, nothing stops you from going and putting up a plant outside this country where government policies are more supportive and exporting from there. Today, the government allows you to take money out and invest in any country." And he has walked the talk by being the first Indian automotive company to set up a plant in China in 2004.

LOW COST MODEL

Mahesh and Krishna have outlined their recipe for achieving global class in conventional manufacturing. What is the view from the emerging esoteric world of new age manufacturing—virtual or fabless manufacturing? How does our low cost model fit into this world and what lesson does new age manufacturing have for achieving and retaining global competitiveness? Tejas Networks, one of the boldest and most innovative of Indian startups, designs and develops optical telecom hardware. Kumar N Sivarajan, its chief technology officer, outlines, first, the model that has emerged and then the opportunity it holds. "We have learnt that you have to make the system as low cost as possible because in India it is very difficult to get a premium for features. What people want is the same cost but better stuff." The idea of having to cut costs is almost forced on any company trying to sell in the Indian market (Chart 16.1).

"The challenge we face is to use all the innovations to make a low cost system that still meets all the specifications. In fact, significant time is spent by the design team in lowering the cost of the basic system. Of course, we do more with the system but rarely at the expense of adding a lot of cost to the basic system. We have spent a lot of time coming up with a no frills, basic system that still meets all the specifications and works very well. That's the only way we can be healthy in this business. This is forced on us because of the prices prevailing in the Indian market. If you are selling in Europe, prices are very healthy, in the US they are equally healthy or healthier. In fact, there you can get a premium for software features."

Sivarajan's recipe for being competitive in both the domestic and overseas markets is to "have all the premium features to be able to compete in the advance markets, but also deliver at the lowest costs possible by removing the premium features to be able to compete in the Indian market. With such costs, in the advanced markets we are either able to improve margins or market share. We are seeing this in our telecom equipment market. We find that cost is the topmost thing on our minds. In every design decision the issue is, what is the implication on the basic cost of the box."

KNOWLEDGE PLATFORM

These three examples give us a clear idea of how to achieve competitiveness in conventional manufacturing as well as new, high technology manufacturing. But perhaps the greatest future lies in leveraging India's existing advantages in the field of knowledge and scientific skills and the person who has had a vision all along on how to make it happen is R A Mashelkar, director general of the Council of Scientific and Industrial Research. His idea is to make knowledge-based activity itself exportable. "I started speaking about India as a research, design and development platform in 1989 when I took over as director of National Chemical Laboratory, two years before we had even liberalised and woken up. At that point in time, I had said National Chemical Laboratory should become International Chemical Laboratory. We should be able to export the knowledge we generate. At that time it was a startling concept as we were supposed to be always doing reverse engineering, copying."

So how do you make a business out of just transferring knowledge instead of going on to actually making the products that people can buy? "My simple hypothesis was, ideas can be born anywhere. If you are able to think ahead of any competitor, you can create knowledge itself as a product. There is a sharp difference between knowledge as a product and creating a real product in the market. The second requires a lot of capital equipment, endurance, infrastructure, marketing as well as markets. But the generation of knowledge itself is fundamental on which you base the rest of the real pyramid. So I said, we can operate at that level." He was, in fact, anticipating the current situation when India has begun to sprout high end fabless chip manufacturers who design an electronic product and then pass it onto the fabricators and manufacturers to do the actual manufacturing at their billion dollar facilities.

To achieve this vision, Mashelkar changed the entire focus of CSIR by the time the new economic policies came around. He switched the credo from "publish or perish" to "patent, publish and prosper." In a decade, the results had started coming in. In 2002, CSIR secured 100 US patents, the highest in a calendar year till then. "In order that we export knowledge, I had to make certain fundamental strategic changes in the way we operate and international patenting was one of them. Supposing I generate a new idea, concept and say I am selling it to you, the first thing they are scared of is infringement on some other patent and it can become a multi-million dollar suit. So if I am selling to the US then I have to make sure that prior patent search is done to determine that I am not infringing on anyone. But more importantly, patent my innovation there so that nobody can infringe."

As a result of Mashelkar's new approach a whole range of global companies joined up with CSIR laboratories—GE, Du Pont, Ciba Gigey. Boeing became partners with NAL; Amoco, Mobil with Indian Institute of Petroleum, SKB with Indian Institute of Chemical Technology. "A paradigm shift took place in the way we were running the laboratories. They added value to what we did and vice versa. For example, GE trained our people in Six Sigma. So I could create new soldiers who could fight these wars in the knowledge market by delivering at a substantially higher level than our Indian trained scientists. Thirdly, a lot of things got opened up. The GE partnership was such that they wanted us also to be as strong as them. So our scientists went there and saw how technology management is done, how technology gets integrated into business. Those skills became very crucial to us which for love or money we would not have got."

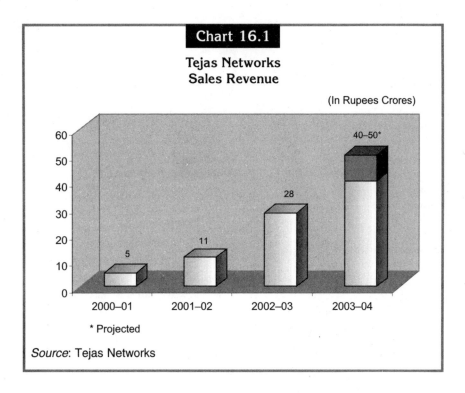

Chart 16.1

Tejas Networks Sales Revenue

(In Rupees Crores)

* Projected

Source: Tejas Networks

In 1995, Mashelkar told his audience, "I wish to share with you an exciting vision…see India emerge as a major global R&D platform. (This involves) wealth creation in India, not only through international trade and business but export of knowledge-based products and technologies …. Today competitive advantage lies in the power and effectiveness of the allied network, which a business team is able to assemble and manage in a short time, rather than in the in-house capability." So Mashelkar had given CSIR and India a vision and a strategy, by defining a new product and a new process in CSIR. The new product is "research as a business". The new process is—"doing research in a business-like manner".

In the process he outlined a strategy for India to build its competitiveness around its knowledge capability. Eight years down the road a lot of the vision had already become a reality. Moreover, the model had proved durable enough, to remain the engine for progress, for a much longer period of time.

Index